THE FIRST OFFICIAL REDNECK FOR US SENATE

My True Story

D A V I D   X U

ISBN 978-1-63784-181-5 (paperback)
ISBN 978-1-63784-182-2 (digital)

Hawes & Jenkins Publishing
16427 N Scottsdale Road Suite 410
Scottsdale, AZ 85254
www.hawesjenkins.com

On the cover:
The author with his campaign banner and American made 2013 Harley-Davidson Breakout with the Easy Rider paint job from the 1969 movie.

This work is largely opinion, reflects the author's recollections, and some events may be compressed. Facts and opinions are portrayed on every page for maximum entertainment and some dialogue has been recreated from a faulty memory and/or other people.

Printed in the United States of America

The Lord's Prayer

Our Father who art in heaven,
hallowed be thy name.
Thy kingdom come.
Thy will be done
on earth as it is in heaven.
Give us this day our daily bread,
and forgive us our trespasses,
as we forgive those who trespass against us,
and lead us not into temptation,
but deliver us from evil.
For thine is the kingdom and the power, and the glory,
forever and ever. Amen.

This book is dedicated to the rednecks of America and the world. They work hard and play hard. I am a proud redneck from Virginia, North Carolina, and Florida. Rednecks stand and salute the beautiful United States of America flag. I thank God and Jesus for all rednecks. Rednecks ride Harley-Davidsons and not rice burners unless money is tight. If money is tight, we work harder and improvise.

Rednecks know that freedom is not free, and fossil fuel is one of the greatest inventions of our time in delivering great power. Drill, baby, drill. Rednecks despise long-term and full-time corrupt politicians trying to impose socialism or communism on great Americans. We love the limited government mandated by the original thirty-page constitution. The politicians are parasites on the back of hardworking taxpayers. God bless the awesome, capitalistic, strong, free, conservative, and Christian United States of America!

CONTENTS

INTRODUCTION

They call Washington, DC, the Hollywood for ugly people. That is where I want to go. I would fit right in with these folks. Have you seen Pocahontas or Bernie in bright light? It is scary stuff for sure and enough to chase a bear up a tree.

Well, well, it is just not the same. I liked the United States the way it used to be with limited government and no or very few corrupt politicians running around buying votes with free stuff paid for by hardworking taxpayers. Most politicians back in the day swore their life to the sacred constitution before getting elected to anything. That was a good thing. Creeps like Joe Biden or Kamala Harris could never make it through basic training. Kamala's former boyfriend Willie Brown should be punished for helping her get elected for the first time many years ago.

Our problems today were caused by worse and worse folks getting elected. Where is the holy man in a cave when you need him? All we have now in government are foolish, myopic children buying votes with other people's money. The wise men have left the District of Columbia and our state capitol, Harrisburg, Pennsylvania. Biden, Harris, and so many others must be dumped.

Let us go back to the 1950s when most politicians obeyed the constitution. During the 1960s, corrupt Democrats and RINOs such as Lyndon Johnson and Samuel Rayburn taxed, borrowed, and wasted trillions on the fight against poverty. It was really a Democrat and RINO voter support bill to get elected and reelected time and time again. All they had to do is stick with limited government and promote hard work.

Some of the civil rights laws were good, but the politicians exaggerated racism day and night to buy votes. We looked around as kids in Virginia and did not see many racists. It was a small group then and smaller now. Most Americans just want to work hard and have the government idiots leave them alone.

Let us remember that the poverty rate for blacks went down over 38 percent from 1940 until 1960. This is long before the corrupt politicians exaggerated racism to pass the civil rights laws and the long-term welfare programs that paid women more if their man did not live with them.

They spent so much money that they had to take the United States off the gold standard by 1971. Before this time, you could exchange a US dollar for a piece of gold. After this stupidity, the US dollar has been backed up by nothing. Many voters joined the religion of huge corrupt government in order to get massive welfare day in and day out. Many lazy folks ride welfare for decades and vote for only Democrats.

"If you stop lying about us, we will stop telling the truth about you," said the corrupt Republican to the corrupt Democrat back in the 1960s. This group is known as the establishment or uniparty now. They are very bad for the American meritocracy.

This election process is like some odd, ill-conceived high school prom king/queen contest with many insults and lies flying around. I have learned that the voters are angry...and brutal. Some guy informed me that I have a big head the other day. I think he said my nose was crooked too. I have not heard these insults since the tenth grade.

Nancy, the wife, gave me a pep talk last week after several Dems and RINOs said some bad things about me. She said, "You know all the candidates for US Senate are pieces of crap, including you. But you are my piece of crap." She is so sweet and inspiring.

She said we had a breakthrough polling at 1 percent during December 2021. Not showing off, not falling behind. Harris (Willie Brown's girlfriend) only had 2 percent in the Democrat primary when she dropped out. We had nine candidates, and I was the best qualified. One guy is criticizing General Michael Flynn. Good luck with that. Another guy used to be a Democrat. He has no chance. One guy was gleeful when the tattooed guy had a bad divorce. He showed his true colors shall we say. That is bad for him but good for me. The other guy lives in Connecticut and loves the World Economic Forum and globalism. The Muslim guy lives in New Jersey, hangs with Oprah, and is a citizen of Turkey. The MAGA crowd will love that guy.

We have lived in Pennsylvania for fourteen years. We live in Ashland. It is known as coal country and has so many kind and Christian folks. These good people work hard and play hard. The people are tough, yet kind. This RINO shook my hand the other day in Clifford but did not look at my face. I should have told them that if he did that in coal country, someone would punch him in the face. He is running for governor or lieutenant governor. The time for RINOs is over. We call them fake Republicans.

I met Bill McSwain, candidate for governor, at this long luncheon for voters and candidates. He is the lawyer Trump hired for US Attorney for Eastern Pennsylvania and loves to mention that Trump nominated him. Many folks say that McSwain would not investigate election cheating in the 2020 election and that Attorney General Barr told him not to investigate electoral fraud, but others say he is lying to get Trump's endorsement. Barr denied this claim. There are many opinions on this.

"One person in Pennsylvania who I will not be endorsing is Bill McSwain for governor. He was the US attorney who did absolutely nothing on the massive election fraud that took place in Philadelphia and throughout the commonwealth," President Trump said during April 2022.

So many government employees are not doing their jobs and should be fired. Many voting machines were connected to Wi-Fi or the internet. This is very illegal and allows massive cheating. Check out www.frankspeech.com sometime for a lot of evidence.

There is a mountain of evidence of many government people violating our Pennsylvania and US constitutions in order to install creepy Joe. If half of this evidence is true, many people must go to prison. The folks who refused to investigate should be punished. Many in the Biden gang are anti-American criminals and/or traitors.

The socialist Democrats say Biden won Pennsylvania by 81,000 ballots, but we had 21,000 dead people vote. Trump had over one million patriots at his rallies nationwide. Biden had about 3,000. Also, the government idiots mailed out 1.8 million mail-in ballots, and 2.5 million were somehow counted just in Pennsylvania. See www.auditthevotepa.com and frankspeech.com.

What about my Democrat competition? Fetterman is my favorite. He is a very disturbing person. A very individual person. I told this kid the other day that if two limousines pull up, one with Fetterman and another with a stranger, get in the car with the stranger. That is from a bit by Wanda Sykes about Dick Cheney. Perhaps it will be a good stranger. That would be the safer, smarter option. The stranger has to be safer than Fetterman. Let us go with that.

Fetterman appears to love criminals, drugs, unnecessary union government jobs, and the Kardashians. What is not to like? He reminds me of the guy in tenth grade who sniffed glue at the back of the class at George Washington High School in Danville, Virginia. Perhaps he can represent conservative and Christian hard workers who hate big and corrupt government in the US Senate. Do their values align? He wants to have open-air safe injection sites for drug dealers and addicts. He will pay for this nonsense with our tax money, of course. It is reported that he lived off his parents' money until he was forty-nine years old.

It is just not the same. I loved America with limited government. We worked hard and played hard in Florida and Southern Virginia as children. We must have accountability and honesty from our folks in government. Too many of them are not doing their jobs. Many roads are crumbling, but they find plenty of money for welfare.

At least seven million work for the US government now. This is absurd. Over 20 million work for the local, state, and federal government. We must drain the swamp of the over 4,000 terrible government employees who are nominated by the president and confirmed by the Senate. Our founding fathers would be very angry. Thomas

Jefferson would shoot down a drone if it flew over Monticello. My platform is based on the values in the Bible and constitution. Isn't that enough? That was good enough for decades and decades until the socialists and communists cheated and got elected. We must remove them now.

You must be a nut to talk about politics and religion with total strangers. I met a veteran the other day. I said, "Dave Xu, first-time candidate, I want to cut back government by at least 10 percent," and handed the guy my campaign flyer.

He glanced at it and gave it back and said, "We must destroy the whole government." He then walked away.

"How about 20 percent? Come back, sign this stupid form to get on the ballot, you piece of crap!" I yelled at him. Being an Army veteran of thirty years, enlisted, OCS, Artillery, Airborne, LTC, MBA, Pentagon and combat duty, IT business owner, real estate investor, volunteer, and Christian helps in dealing with other veterans. But they are a grumpy bunch sometimes.

Veterans will say anything. We do not care what politicians or anyone in power says. I only care what normal, common people say. I am very irreverent. Most soldiers in artillery are like this and will cut off generals if they are being unsafe or just plain dumb. In the military we are both blue collar and white collar at the same time. Everyone chips in to accomplish the mission.

I have gotten kind of cranky. There are different kinds of cranky. Good cranky, saying the next generation is lazy. Bad cranky, criticizing someone's looks and intelligence to their face. I do not condone it. My administration does not condone it.

It is just not the same. We used to have two distinct parties in DC. What happened? The RINOs and Democrats are like one party now. I end my talks with "Let's go, Brandon." It always gets a laugh. This RINO running for Lieutenant Governor Coleman gets up after I gave a short speech in Clifford in March 2022 to one hundred Republicans. He said something like he was so upset when he had to explain to his young daughter who Brandon is. He said that we should not insult folks like this and be bipartisan. Is that a joke? It just means that, in our opinion, Biden is a failed, corrupt, and long-term politician. Is this guy super RINO Mitt Romney's protege? This is opinion.

It also means that Biden and supporters lie all the time, just like that reporter who lied about what the NASCAR fans were chanting after the race. The weak RINOs are beta males and should just hang it up and become long-term baristas at Starbucks. He can have his safe zone there talking about race as the CEO suggested a while back. Coleman talks about kindness. Good luck with that in dealing with communists in the Democrat Party who will throw noncommunists in jail or exterminate them after they seize power. This is opinion.

Trump was right; RINOs suck and must be removed now. They are worse than Democrats because they infect our party and are enabling socialism and communism to flourish here in the land of the free and the brave the United States of America.

People will say anything these days. We saw two road-rage incidents driving to Clifford in March. The Democrats and RINOs will say anything. They know their time is coming to an end. Most Americans have seen all the corrupt and immoral folks exposed by Trump. Most polls show that most Americans are awake now and want to cleanse government of myopic fools lying every day.

January 6 was not an insurrection. Those folks were just very angry about all the election cheating and government fools not doing their jobs. I will tell you another thing. The government idiot who killed Ashli Babbitt should face a grand jury. What were the rules of engagement? Did he give a warning? Could he have retreated? Was she armed? I do not think so.

For example, the RINO local politicians say to me, "You do not have billions and millions." And they say it like that is a *bad* thing. I have two words for these people who think I have no chance of winning the primary. Edward Durr. He defeated the horrible union-supporting Democrat guy in New Jersey for state senate with only about $8,000. The Democrat wasted over $300,000 mostly from union workers. Ed is my hero. My opponents have wasted over $30 million already on this senate seat. Most of them are pretending to be something they are not.

I speak the truth and do not care very much how you feel. I want to know what you think. Just give me the facts and opinions, and I will make a decision. I commanded three artillery units in the military, and my staff gave me facts, opinions, and two to three courses of action, and I chose one. We planned, executed the plan, and then evaluated the plan. That is the US military way. The 545 in DC do everything based on polls, emotions, money, power, fame, and moving us toward socialism and communism.

I worked at the Pentagon from 2006 until 2009 and saw many bad things. I worked on the Joint Staff. This the highest-level staff in America with about one thousand people. Do not let my Southern accent fool you. They do not invite fools to be on the Joint Staff. Well, perhaps a few fools slip through the cracks. I was a heartbeat away (just kidding). We prepared General Pace for meetings at the White House, National Security Council, and other places. We prepared two pages of facts, opinions, and two to three courses of action on many different issues.

I saw Democrats and RINOs support soldiers in public and then try to cut pay and benefits in private. Paul Ryan was the worst. They look at the federal government as a jobs program for voters. They only love ballots filled out for themselves. We have many unnecessary, high-paying union jobs in the Pentagon and throughout our bloated government. At least 7 million people work for our government. I saw partisans leak top secret information to promote different and false narratives. I saw goal displacement where you push your own goals over the goals of your supervisor or the president or secretary of defense.

General Pace got fired for supporting marriage only between a man and woman on TV and other things in 2007 while I worked on his staff at the Pentagon. He should have served four years as chairman of the Joint Staff. This is the normal situation. Bush, Obama, Biden, etc. ran him off after two years. He was the first Marine to be chairman. He was good to us, and we had some fun times. One day we had to run him down on the golf course at Fort Meade to sign something.

At the Pentagon, certain documents and orders must be signed by a one-, two-, three-, or four-star and no less. Sometimes a senior civilian can sign it. One day we needed a four-star and only had two on the Joint Staff. Admiral Giambastiani was out of the country, and Pace was nowhere to be found. An aide told me that those two did not get along very well. Pace would never agree to let Giambastiani live in the chairman's house on Fort Myers even though he would not use it himself. We finally found Pace on the ninth tee on the Fort Meade golf course and sent a runner for the signature. This is opinion, and my memory is less than optimal.

When the Obama-Biden gang came in, their priorities were not ours. They began talking about systemic racism and woke issues and neglecting national defense. Remember crooked Hilary flew to Russia with the red reset button from Staples. They allowed our folks to be slaughtered in Benghazi and then lied about it. They allowed weapons to sold to drug gangs in Mexico, which were then used to kill and hurt American border agents. These people are ideologues and not very bright. We observed these terrible people in leadership positions from the basement of the Pentagon. It was an ugly sight.

I saw lazy union people at the State or Peace Department refuse to deploy to Iraq and Afghanistan. We had to send more soldiers in their place. I met deep-state actors who bragged about going out for lunch and dinner with corrupt people in the House and Senate. I met Democrat and Republican generals who put their relationship with politicians above their oath of office to support and defend our constitution. Think Milley and Austin. I saw their schedules every day. I saw backstabbing generals trying to get that next star by telling their boss that their dumb ideas were great. Many generals are, yes, men and women.

I answered some letters from Democrats just trying to make Bush and the Republicans look bad. I answered one from Hillary Clinton just wasting my time. They say statistics do not lie, but statisticians do. We used to proofread White House speeches. Many speech writers are young and inexperienced. I caught an error in one of Bush's speeches. The politician can look good or bad depending on the time frame of the statistic or question. Are we talking about the last year or eighteen months? You get the picture.

I saw generals and senior civilians lie about lowering military standards for enlisting or reenlisting. It got so bad during the Afghanistan buildup that they lowered the standard for real teeth. You have to have a certain number of real teeth to join the Army. They lied about lowering moral standards regarding criminal convictions. They are still doing this stuff today and weakening our military. The good news is that about 80 percent of our troops will still fight and die for our constitution and would reject any illegal order. I talk with active soldiers all the time.

I saw the Chinese military shoot down an aging weather satellite, and Xi and the group dictators did not even know about it. I saw Putin and the Russians pretending to be a world power by sailing several ships in the Mediterranean Sea. The main ship broke down and had to be towed in to port. We had a good laugh at the Pentagon over that one.

I worked on the budget at the Pentagon. All the departments submit budget requests to the White House. They consolidate and adjust and send a phone book budget to Congress. We asked for thirty airplanes. The corrupt politicians gave us fifty. Why would they do that? The plane is made in twenty different states and fifty congressional districts. My numbers are off some, but you get the point.

Three teams monitor worldwide events in two hundred countries. I was on one of those teams within the Joint Staff. I was on duty when the Air Force folks flew live nuclear bombs from North Dakota to Louisiana. Many got fired for that stupidity. The general said, "You know this is the generation that was told they were so smart and given medals just for competing and not based on merit. It sucks to be them." The folks on the ground mixed the live rounds and dummy rounds. The flight crew did not check the bombs under the wings. The ground crew in Louisiana caught the huge mistake and called us.

I saw many attempted and successful coups while working at the Pentagon. They happen all the time in poor and tribal nations.

They had one thing in common. Many folks believed their government was illegitimate. I believe the Biden regime is illegitimate. We need an audit and vote on decertification now. If half the evidence is correct on frankspeech.com or peternavarro.com, the election was stolen. Many people violated our state and federal constitution and must be punished. Bill Barr just said many rules were not followed, but it was not his job to enforce our sweet constitution. This RINO and other immoral fools must be punished. The Supreme Court members should have stepped in to enforce our constitution, which says that the state legislators control elections and not corrupt people in the executive branch or Dems on the Pennsylvania Supreme Court who just approved a Democrat redistricting plan for our seventeen congressional seats.

The Democrats in our big cities have already made them tribal lands by buying votes with tax money. Many cities look like Somalia or Iraq or some corrupt, poor country in Africa or the Middle East. The roads have huge potholes, but they have plenty of money for welfare for free apartments and taxis. We must stop these Democrat fools now before America becomes a tribal and horrible place to live.

The thing is, countries with professional institutions can borrow money. Countries with corrupt institutions run by fools cannot borrow money. Who would loan money to Cuba and Pakistan?

Most Democrats in a recent poll said they would not fight or die for America if we are invaded. These people are weak and ignorant. We need a draft. You cannot have strong and patriotic Americans defending lazy and ignorant Americans. That does not work for long. Another draft would not have to be every young person. Perhaps one in four would serve to protect us and our freedom. Freedom is not free, and we must preserve our meritocracy.

Only 30 percent of people who try to join the US military qualify due to obesity, crimes, drugs, alcohol, and other stupidity. We must teach our youth good values. I suggest the values in the Bible and constitution. We need strong alpha males and awesome women in uniform now. These union teachers grooming beta males must be fired and now. This is a national security threat. We only have

2.2 million in uniform out of 330 million Americans. We will be invaded tomorrow if we become weak.

"An uneducated people would not long remain a sovereign one," said Samuel Adams. He was a great leader in Boston and our revolution against the corrupt British monarchy and knew that we must properly educate our youth and inform our peers with the truth.

Putin and his gang thought that the Ukrainians would be weak and give up. They were wrong, and we should support them fighting for their freedom. Perhaps the corrupt government folks should have bought weapons instead of paying Hunter and Joe millions of dollars for nothing. The creepy Bidens should be brought before a grand jury asap. Hunter's laptop is real. Most media folks hid it before the election and are communists for sure. We should deport them to China or Cuba. The boat to Cuba would save us tax money. More than fifty immoral and lying former Democrat government idiots said the laptop was Russian disinformation, and the media and big tech folks covered it up to get creepy Joe elected. Somehow we must get back a tough and independent media.

I am the only US Senate candidate who worked at the strategic level at the Pentagon…for three years. We, as the most powerful, successful nation ever, have four ways to influence other nations. Diplomacy, information (speeches, true propaganda), military (show of force, kinetic operations, military equipment sales and training), and economics (trade, sanctions). That is the way DC is supposed to work. These foolish Dems and RINOs do everything now based on polls and getting elected. They are myopic or shortsighted and very dangerous. They will say or do anything for power.

The Democrats and RINOs are like one party. They made a corrupt bargain about sixty years ago. The Rep said, "We will stop telling the truth about you if you stop lying about us." We will get rich by giving out massive welfare, and you get rich from waste, fraud, and abuse at the Pentagon and endless wars. By 1971, they had spent and borrowed so much that they took us off the gold standard.

The uniparty fools have wasted over $24 trillion since 1964 on welfare buying votes from many folks who refuse to work. We must cut this crap and pave the roads. Many Americans are ignorant of this childish behavior by politicians like Biden, McConnell, Ryan, and Harris. They think it is still 1984 with Reagan in the White House.

Biden and other fools surrendered in Afghanistan. That was not a withdrawal. The Taliban did not kill one American in eighteen months during the Trump administration. They killed thirteen of our troops and injured many more due to the weak and corrupt Biden team. They should be impeached or worse now. About half the Democrats are really dumb and corrupt and want socialism or communism and must be removed from government. I used to count every single rifle and pistol once a month as a unit commander and would be fired and thrown in Fort Leavenworth if one was missing. Why is Biden not held accountable for leaving $84 billion of great US military equipment in Afghanistan? It is just not the same. Many generals were fired during WWII. Did anyone get fired over this? Did anyone quit? The so-called leaders we have now are the worst. I would not follow them to the bathroom. Austin, Milley, McKenzie, etc. should be fired and punished.

The current-day Democrats are just like the weak and dumb Truman gang in 1951. They refused to destroy the Korean and Chinese armies to achieve total victory that year. There would be no North Korea threatening the South Koreans and Japanese if Truman had completed the task at hand. I guess he was too busy getting drunk in Key West, Florida, to notice. He had a huge advantage on the battlefield and with the US economy and war machine at that time. The Chinese commies were weak from pulling off the civil war in 1949. Biden should be incarcerated for killing thirteen Americans and wounding many more in Afghanistan during 2021 with his stupid surrender.

We must cut back the power of the Federal Reserve. This iteration was started in 1913 and enables huge, corrupt government. Andrew Jackson, my redneck hero, got rid of it in 1832. Nancy and I just toured his home in Nashville a couple months ago. These Dems and RINOs are supposed to enable steady growth in GDP with low inflation and unemployment. They cannot do that or forecast anything correctly, so now they are pushing fake climate change and fake racism. They raised rates to hurt Trump and lowered rates to help Obama, Biden, Clinton, etc. They print or create USD like drunken sailors. They do this through twenty-four big banks on Wall Street, and many people get rich off this crap. They are driving America toward bankruptcy. Printing so many US dollars hurts all of us because most of our pay and retirement is in US dollars. They fly to Jackson Hole on tax money and tell us how smart they are or how dumb most Americans are. The Fed is supposed to independent. It is not. These people go to the same parties. Dems, RINOs, deep-state actors.

Powell, Yellen, and other arrogant fools are cheering on more wasteful spending and borrowing to buy votes with free everything. Yellen had many security guards and vehicles paid for by us pick her up and drop her off at her house near DC. The neighbors complained that she thinks she is a queen. How about creepy Joe cruising around in an eighty-five-vehicle convoy in Rome last year? This is getting embarrassing. Is it just me or does Janet Yellen look like an older Pekingese dog?

The Fed has 780 economists. We need to cut back to twenty or no more than one hundred. The economists are ten to one Democrat to Republican. The economists working for the BOD are forty-eight to one Democrat. Perhaps it is time for layoffs? The NY Fed "stands with those who oppose racism, hate, and violence." That sounds like the violent, immoral BLM or antifa fools. Created in 1913 and has seven on BOD and twelve regional banks, the Federal open market committee has twelve members (seven from BOD and five bank presidents). They control open-market operations or monetary policy. Balances available for banks and foreign exchange operations are also under their control. The people in Congress should cut back their power.

The Federal Reserve employees assess the economy and policy options best for Dems and RINOs to be all they can be. That was the old Army slogan. Some of these folks just quit or were fired for insider trading. Many folks in and around our corrupt government engage in insider trading. Many federal judges just got busted for this too. It appears that Pelosi and her husband were insider trading. Hilary made a lot of money on pork-belly futures. It is very hard to prove, and many in DOJ will not even investigate it to keep their easy, great-paying union jobs.

The folks running around promoting socialism in order to deal with climate change should read history. They will find that about thirteen thousand years ago, the last ice age ended, and the oceans rose. Cars and fossil fuels have only been around for about one hundred years. The coast of China used to be about six hundred miles east of where it is now because the water was locked up in ice. The climate changes over millions and billions of years. Nobody can change or predict that.

Americans have been excellent stewards of the environment. The CCP folks have devastated their environment with communism, socialism, and other stupid laws and policies. We should ignore them regarding so many topics including the environment. I think most of the Chinese people are okay, but they should get rid of their foolish government folks. The British are cranking up coal plants again because they did not plan ahead on energy sources.

The Dutch, Germans, and other Europeans are now burning more coal because they shut down too many nuclear, gas, and oil power plants. They foolishly pushed wind and solar power too fast. Their power grids are unstable now with blackouts. The Democrats in California did the same thing.

Trump did a fantastic job. The economy was great before the Chinese Communist Party (CCP) sent their virus. They need to be punished. We need to bring back our jobs and factories. Capitalism is the best economic system for the last three hundred years. The younger provide the labor, and the middle- and upper-income groups provide the capital, and everyone lives in harmony. We saw this in 2019.

The Dems are attacking the workers and their work ethic. They are promoting laziness and ignorance. Labor is critical for capitalism. The workers cannot dictate to the owners of business. The stockholders own the business and not lazy community organizers such as Obama. It does not work. That will never work. That is communism. Look at Cuba, Venezuela, North Korea. The Chinese tried it.

Many places tried it. Israel tried it. You cannot pay the skilled and unskilled the same. It ruins the incentive to learn and work hard.

We need to cut welfare. There are able-bodied folks in Pennsylvania making $40,000 year doing nothing. We believe in welfare, but it must be short-term and very targeted.

I grew up in Florida and Southern Virginia, and had a great time. The summer nights were magical on my hog with the ladies. The parents were not around, and we ran wild. My parents did not even know our names. We did not wear seat belts or helmets in cars, on dirt bikes, and on go-karts. Thank goodness there was no politician saying, "Here you go, free apartment, Internet, phone, beer and drug money, TikTok." Do you want to change your gender? We had long hair too.

We are Christian and love everyone, but you cannot push the woke crap on our kids. This is not the role of government. We must stop the CRT madness and fire bad teachers and other government employees.

Have you called the government lately?

Employee: "Yeah what do you want? Can you hurry it up? It is almost time for my two-hour lunch break."

Me: "Can you help me with this or that? Is the tax really that much?"

Employee: "We can call you back. I bet you voted for Trump. You know I voted for Biden and Harris, and you cannot get me in trouble or fired ever. It's a union thing. Have a nice day, sucker."

We have almost a total breakdown in government. They cannot do anything right. Remember that the IRS targeted conservatives and Christians, and nobody was fired. Why did Lois Lerner walk free? Obama and his friends harassed the Tea Party folks at least from 2004 until 2013, and nobody went to jail. Should they be waterboarded or at least behind bars? They should put Lois in the box as shown in *Cool Hand Luke*. Good job, Department of Justice and FBI, in destroying your own reputation.

The Trump administration paid a lot of tax money to over four hundred conservative nonprofit groups to settle discrimination lawsuits in 2017. We should take Lois Lerner's pension as a refund.

We need accountability and honesty from our folks in leadership positions. We have dumb children running our government now. We love smart ones but not the dumb ones. Children do not prioritize anything. All they want is candy. Unethical people in government lie on TV every day. This cannot stand. Many people must be removed from government and investigated for crimes. The DHS people like Mayorkas should be brought before a grand jury for not protecting us and the border.

We need to continue the Trump agenda and bring back jobs to America. Let us lower spending, taxes, and regulation. The uniparty folks in government and big business shipped many good manufacturing jobs to communists in China and Vietnam and other places in the 1990s and 2000s. This was so stupid and devastated millions of hardworking families. Many politicians and business folks got rich off this stupidity. Unions were partly to blame for demanding high salaries and benefits. I remember the Delphi union folks were making $60 per hour. The business owners and managers offered $40 per hour to keep the car part factories in America. The union folks refused to take a pay cut. The business filed for bankruptcy and shipped the jobs to Mexico and China. The union folks had no jobs and went on welfare and unemployment.

We helped them in North Carolina at my community college. I was a program head of the business department, and we taught them about business. Many did not want to go to college and just wanted to work hard and play hard and live the American dream. These sick politicians got rich on this.

I am from the South. We tolerate unions in private businesses but want them out for all government employees. A good union worker once told me of the havoc unions wreak on businesses. His union got a contract at the Harley-Davidson factory in York, Pennsylvania. The problem was another union had the same contract. What happened was Harley paid both unions for the same job, and many workers just stood around all day doing nothing.

This aggravates me as a conservative and also as a devoted Harley rider. The business owners just pass the cost on to consumers like us for this stupidity. All workers should be thankful for their jobs and not be able to go on strike or be lazy, greedy, or incompetent.

Many of these immoral pols are still in DC. They call it Hollywood for ugly people. That is where I want to go. I would fit right in. The Dems and RINOs make a huge mistake to think Trump and Republicans are dumb. Trump is many things, but he is not dumb. We are not dumb. Nobody worships Trump as they say on TV. We loved his policies, and he stood up for the normal, common, hardworking American. We love the American meritocracy, where is everything is based on merit. Hiring, college admission, promotion. Nothing here should be based on race. Did you notice many colleges are doing away with standardized tests? They are discriminating against Asian Americans who study hard. Everything should be based on merit. That is America!

It is sad that many folks go through their entire life being dumb or ugly, and nobody ever tells them. So sad. This is your opportunity to tell the candidates this bad news. Seinfeld said something like that.

It is a good time for a Joan Rivers bit. We loved her acid tongue. She did something dumb in high school, and her mother kept saying, "Why can't you be more like your cousin Sheila? She was the best."

"But, Mom, she died when she was two," Joan reminded her stern mother.

We must remove the bad politicians now through voting. We can expel them with 290 in the House and/or sixty-seven in the Senate. That is in the constitution. AOC, Pelosi, Omar, Bernie, Pocahontas never talk about that rule. I loved when Trump spoke of her. She told people she was an American Indian to get jobs. I wrote *Redneck Dystopia* about Pocahontas in the White House after stealing the 2020 election. She was leading in the polls when I wrote the book. I could not believe that so many people liked her. I guess welfare is popular.

I think we should force AOC, Bernie, and other folks who seem so enamored with communism to the new Victims of Communism Museum in Washington, DC. The $40 million project illustrates the evil ideology and those behind it. Over 100 million people have been killed by socialists and communists since 1917. Many union teachers across America are ignorant of the horrors of socialism and communism. The Biden regime is moving America toward this murderous ideology now. We must destroy it in the United States before it is too late.

I wonder if AOC knows that over one thousand pounds of minerals were dug up and processed for her silly Tesla. How much pollution did that cause? What will she do with that huge battery assembly when it goes bad? How much coal, oil, or natural gas will she burn charging that thing all the time? The California politicians have restricted power so much that you cannot even charge electric vehicles when you need to. They have caused brownouts and blackouts with their climate change lies.

Over 78 percent of energy in a US home is generated from fossil fuels. She should really wear her college degree on her sleeve to warn others to avoid attending Boston University. I would guess that the professors and students at that school have gone through their entire lives being dumb and lazy, and nobody ever told them. That is so sad.

John Adams said, "Only moral Christians should run the government and enforce our sacred original constitution." It is only thirty pages and worth its weight in gold. They say it was written by geniuses so our government could be run by fools.

When you get elected in China, they say the whole family goes to heaven. Only 8 percent are members of the CCP, and they are evil, brutal folks who will do anything for gain or maintain power. The Dems and RINOs want that here. They want some kind of weird socialist group dictatorship. Someone asked the corrupt fool Biden about the Republican Party last year. He said that they might not be around very long.

We must break up big tech, media, and business. The good news is that we only have about five hundred huge corporations in America (the S&P 500). We have over 30 million smaller businesses run by outstanding, hardworking people. All organizations go through peaks and valleys regarding leadership and performance. Many weak, woke, and foolish people run the big corporations now. The boards pick idiots like themselves as senior managers. James

Mattis was on the board of Theranos where Elizabeth Holmes and others lied about blood testing devices.

Sam Walton served in the Army, taught Bible study at his church, and started Walmart. He had Made in USA signs everywhere in Walmart. He died in 1992, and his stupid greedy kids took down the signs and shipped millions of jobs to the communists in other countries. We need moral people back in charge. Many American businesspeople and pols have sold their souls for the Chinese yuan.

Many in our media are socialists or communists. They protect corrupt and dumb politicians and would make the CCP media proud. I was watching golf during October 2020, and they started hammering Trump. I said, "What is going on? Can I please just enjoy some great golf shots? Oh, I see Comcast owns, NBCUniversal, Sky News, and the Golf Channel. Oh, I see the Roberts family in Philadelphia is mostly Democrat.

Socialists/commies spread lies and propaganda across our society. They cover up the truth and try to elevate horrible and immoral people. Forty percent of Americans do not read anything now and believe anything on TV. Most Democrats say they would not even fight or kill if we were invaded. Let us have the draft, please. This is opinion and fact.

Let us get rid of unions for all government employees. Even the socialist hero FDR was for this at one point. Many union people work hard but give money to union bosses who give millions to socialists and commies to get elected. The government has become too big and expensive because of this.

We need to get back to energy independence. Trump had us there. The Biden gang stopped the Keystone pipeline and drilling, and we must drill, baby, drill. Americans have been great with our environment. Ride across America and see beautiful spaces. America and Canada produce about 16 million barrels of oil per day and could easily go to 20 million if many Democrats were removed and/or prosecuted for violating our constitution.

We need to cut welfare and Pennsylvania legislators' salaries and pave the roads. These parasites make $92,000 per year plus per diem. Give me a break. Our folks in the Pennsylvania house and senate Twardzik and Argall are very worried about the Chinese lantern fly but will not answer my question. How many illegal ballots were counted during the 2020 election? Are they lazy, corrupt, and/or dumb? We are tired of people not doing their jobs. If you make coffee, make the best. If you run the government, keep us safe, arrest the criminals, pave the streets, and shut up. Stop begging for campaign contributions and obey our state and federal constitutions. When did politicians start ignoring our constitution and laws?

Fetterman is a very disturbing individual. I could not remember what he reminded me of. He reminds me of biology class in ninth grade. We studied these turtles that could stay under ice and snow for weeks at a time. They did it by reducing their brain activity down to nothing. They were just barely maintaining consciousness. Fetterman is just like those turtles. He has taken a lot of money from the union workers to fund his lifestyle and nice trips.

Conor Lamb lied to get elected to the House. Trump said he sounded like a Republican on the campaign trail. He has voted with Pelosi 99 percent of the time since getting elected. He reminds me of that bumper sticker, "No human being is worthless. They can always serve as a bad example."

Who do we have on the Republican side? Iz? Ooz? No, Oz. Let me see. He was in the Turkish army. I was in the American army for thirty years. That is not good for him. That is good for me. He hung out with socialist, communist Democrats. He said he went to war for blah, blah. I do not think so. The only war he was in was when he helped Oprah try to lose twenty pounds…but she gained it back. They went down in flames. She is big as a tent. We need Abdul the tent maker to make some dresses for her and Hillary. I think Oz looks like a con man on TV. He would be a good used car salesman.

The good news is that America is still very strong. About 75 percent of business transactions around the globe share two aspects. They are in the English language and US dollar (USD). US GDP is $24 trillion (number one nation). China and India should have passed us long ago with triple the population each. Their socialism and communism and corruption hold them back.

We have the three equal branches, and most Americans still work hard. We have the most valuable and efficient stock and bond markets. We can turn this ship around by electing normal, common, moral outsiders like me. People around the world still love America and are dying to come here for the equal opportunity and the American dream. Many do not want the socialism, communism, or group dictatorship they are escaping from. Limited government rules!

"No power on earth can stop an idea whose time has come," said Victor Hugo, a French poet and writer in 1880.

We must fire anyone trying to corrupt our youth. TikTok is controlled by the CCP, and they ban it in China and laugh at our ignorant and lazy youth. They learn how to cook chicken in Nyquil on TikTok. Is that bad for your health? Are union teachers good for America?

Most of our young folks are good, but many are too lazy and support corrupt politicians for free stuff all the time. Let us cut back government and get the politicians off TV and out of our lives. Obama was the worst about getting on TV and bragging about taking money from hard workers and giving it to lazy folks.

I love rock and roll and loved Lynyrd Skynyrd from the land where I grew up, Florida. That is my favorite band of all time. People want to be free. That is the meaning of the song "Free Bird." We need strong leaders like Ronnie Van Zant to enforce our sweet constitution. We love the South, and the good people there have more limited government, lower taxes, and less welfare than the folks in the north. I loved growing up in the south.

I need two thousand signatures. How hard can that be? I told everyone that I do not want your money but do need your signature to get on the ballot to push the conversation to the right. Let us stand up for our thirty-page golden original constitution and the limited government and capitalism it mandates and reject socialism and communism together.

A Democrat is a Republican that has not been robbed yet. Many Democrats are switching to the Republican Party, and we helped some of them on the campaign trail. Many Hispanic folks will not support immoral Democrats anymore.

Editors, publisher, and many folks want to know the purpose of your book. The purpose of this book is to tell the story of a normal, common man from the South trying to get into the United States senate in order to severely cut back government and obey our sacred constitution. Hard work must be respected and laziness rejected. That is one reason that America is the most successful nation ever.

Could it be that I am not as smart as I think I am? No way. Thank you for reading my book, and we thank God and Jesus for kind, conservative, Christian folks! God and Jesus always win. It is exhausting being with you. Let's go, Brandon!

CHAPTER 1

THE UPSET REDNECK

The American Communist Censors, 2019 through 2020

> To me there's nothing freer than a bird. And
> that's what this country is all about. I think
> everybody wants to be free like a bird.
> —Ronnie Van Zant of Lynyrd Skynyrd

I am rolling down Highway 29 at 110 mph on my 1971 Harley-Davidson Super Glide. It is the summer of 1984, and my 1979 Harley Super Glide is in pieces over at Tommy Keck's house. We are painting it blue and putting a stroker kit in the engine for more speed.

I bought the 1971 Hog to ride while the 1979 Hog was down. I am addicted to Harley-Davidsons. Joe Moore, my twin brother Tommy, Tommy Keck, Jim Gerry, Charles Winstead, Troy Welch, and I are riding from Danville to Greensboro to go out to eat and visit the Hog shop.

Life is good, working and playing hard. The ladies love Hog riders. We do not even know the names of our politicians, and that is the way America is supposed to be. There is no government idiot promising us welfare, a sex change, and free stuff if we vote for him.

Limited government is awesome in the land of milk and honey. We are free as birds with small government and low taxes.

A candidate for US Senate was driving around in rural Pennsylvania somewhere near Ashland, Pennsylvania, getting signatures to get on the ballot. All of a sudden, a three-legged chicken passed his car. It was the fastest chicken he had ever seen. He followed it to a farm and spoke with the farmer.

"Is that a three-legged chicken? I have never seen one before," the candidate said.

"Yes, we breed them because Ma likes the drumstick, Pa loves the drumstick, and now baby Junior goes crazy for the drumstick," the farmer explained.

"Wow, that is amazing. How do they taste?" the politician asked.

"Well, we do not know yet. We have not been able to catch one," the frustrated farmer explained. This is a joke from Ronald Reagan adapted to our current situation for this redneck candidate for US senate. You will notice that I do not capitalize the word *senate* because most of the senators are childish Dems and RINOs and must be removed now.

The Democrats and RINOs in America have conspired to impose an informal communist regime. The CCP folks in China are brutal, but at least they are open and formal about their ridiculous communist regime. Our corrupt politicians outsource their censorship to fools in big business, such as Twitter, Comcast (NBCUniversal), Google, and Facebook.

The socialists in America sneak around subverting our sacred constitution in the dark on courts, in government office buildings, and in legislatures. They know that most Americans reject socialism and communism and will never vote for that crap.

Thank goodness the workers at Facebook are not geniuses while trying to implement the Chinese model of the surveillance state. Facebook's artificial intelligence (AI) system mistranslated a post saying "Good morning" from Arabic to Hebrew. The poor Palestinian author of the post was arrested in 2022 by the Israeli police until the misunderstanding could be cleared up. The dimwitted Facebook employees are experimenting with AI surveillance state hardware and software abroad and would love to bring it to the United States in my opinion.

It is amazing that our politicians allow the Facebook folks to apply dumb banners to our posts. They do it with my posts about exaggerated climate change, fake racism, massive election cheating, and other topics. We will not have a great country if we do not destroy these folks soon through politics. Our sweet constitution will be enforced coast to coast by politics or by force soon.

Why are the liberals so obsessed about gun control? The states with the most guns have lower crime rates. Over 60 million people have died from gun control by the German Nazis, Chinese commies, etc. The corrupt media people never report the many self-defense killings in America and indeed around the world. Florida has a fine and broad self-defense law. I believe that Ron DeSantis would be a great president by the way.

"Affirming truth and denying falsehood are the same act. Aristotle teaches that every positive claim negates another claim," Crispin Sartwell explained in the *Wall Street Journal*. Our communists in the media are helping lead America to communism by lying and covering up for immoral communist Democrats. They tell weak-minded people that Republicans are deniers because we speak the truth and enforce our constitution.

The CCP folks in the Forbidden City are laughing at us. They love useful idiots such as Biden and Harris. It is reported that the Chinese donated over $50 million to Biden's dark operation at the University of Pennsylvania. I would guess that the number of Americans who want socialism or communism is under 15 million. We must destroy this ideology in America for our children.

The law-abiding good Americans will not let Biden and other idiots take our guns as the CCP did seventy-two years ago in China. We use guns over two million times per year to prevent crimes. Many times even flashing a gun can deter criminals. Why are most Democrats opposed to arming teachers and administrators in our schools? They create soft targets in these no-gun zones. We must ignore these fools and enforce our sacred constitution.

I identify as American. That should be and used to be enough for everyone here. E pluribus unum or out of many one is what this nation is all about. This is our outstanding American motto on the Great Seal and awesome for rednecks and the lesser beings too. We love God, Jesus, the US meritocracy, "work hard and play hard" lifestyle, personal responsibility, and limited government.

Fools who want free stuff to sit around and do nothing should move to Venezuela and sit around the slums with nothing and worship Maduro. Idiots who worship politicians for welfare, free apartments, and free health care can move to Cuba and worship the communists who kill and imprison innocent folks every day of the week.

Let us destroy socialism and communism here in the capitalistic and wonderful America. Make the lazy folks work and improve themselves. That is the American way. Nothing is free, snowflakes.

I am a proud member of the National Rifle Association (NRA). We love and obey the constitution and freedom. Many Democrats want to undo our great American experiment in freedom. We will destroy them at the polls and avoid the need to destroy them with guns. The liars calling for gun control should be deported to socialist or communist places such as China or Cuba. They can live their best life in these places and stop bothering us.

"Life is short...but not short enough," Gary Shandling explained to Tom Petty who had a good laugh about the quip. They were together in Petty's house for a funny interview. We love dark humor as much as Jerry Seinfeld. A short life would be better than a long life under Democrat communists for sure.

The ultimate dark humor would be to look down from heaven (if we are lucky enough to make it) and see the fools voting for communist Democrats now for free stuff in another twenty years. They will be poor, in bad health, toothless, with worthless high school and college degrees, and ignorant in tiny apartments or hovels like you see in Venezuela, Cuba, San Francisco, Philadelphia, Africa, China, and Brazil.

They are voting year after year for the destruction of the greatest capitalistic society and nation on earth. I guess they cannot see their path ahead with the Fettermans of the world. They are blinded by envy and laziness. They want the good life but will not work hard to earn it. Many people see that you can make more money on welfare than working hard at a normal job in many American cities and states. Dumb people walk right down this stupid road paved by crooked politicians like Obama and Wolf. Fetterman and his dumb friends will be living like kings while the ignorant masses are living in hovels within twenty years if we do not save America from Democrat and RINO fools.

When Fetterman walks into a room, it looks like an ugly old man in a hoodie riding a chicken. Can we please get this guy into the gym to work on those calves? This must be embarrassing for his wife. He has flamingo or chicken legs. Why is life so hard for this imbecile? Fortunately, he does not look a day over seventy years old. Us rednecks love the ad hominem attack.

The lazy folks watch a lot of television instead of working hard. The media folks exaggerate everything. The truth is that only seven people per year have been killed in mass shootings at schools according to Charles Cooke in *America's 1st Freedom* magazine. The liberals act as though mass shootings happen all the time. The real problem is that most Democrats are too soft on criminals. Can we please arrest all criminals and cut the welfare and get back to the awesome American dream?

The corrupt politicians pretend that America is racist to get votes, power, and money. Their 1619 project is a lie. We got rid of slavery in eighty-nine years (in 1865). It has existed for thousands of years in many different countries. It still exists in several places such as Sudan and Nigeria. "More African slaves were sent to the Islamic world than were ever sent to the Americas. The Republican Party and many whites helped create the NAACP," says Jason Riley.

Our focus should be on arresting all criminals and supporting our police. Most Democrats support criminals more than they support our police. There were 492 homicides in Chicago during 2019, and only three involved the police. Systemic racism is a lie.

My first real and personal taste of communist censorship in America was during the fall of 2019 when I published my book *Redneck Dystopia*. It is a dark tale about Pocahontas in the White

House after she beat Trump in 2020. Elizabeth Warren was in the lead in the Democrat primary when I started writing this fiction. I could not believe that this fool who lied about being an American Indian was leading in the polls.

The folks at Amazon rejected the pistol and bullets on the cover of *Redneck Dystopia*. I was shocked at their ignorance and illegal activity of spitting on our sacred, original constitution. Our corrupt politicians and judges allow the big tech idiots to censor conservatives and Christians. To a normal, common American, this is illegal and sick.

The socialists running Google did not like the word *redneck*. They censored me also. Communists, socialists, and/or Democrats control many platforms, and conservatives and Christians are at risk from these fools.

I stopped trying to advertise the *Redneck Dystopia* book because of their censorship and deciding that I did not want to give my hard-earned money to fools. This experience made me really think about running for office. Many Americans are still asleep to the threat from the communists and socialists on American soil and in our government.

Writing and selling books is hard work for sure. I remember looking at a book in the Wright Brothers museum and gift shop in Kitty Hawk, North Carolina, one day. It is a fantastic place celebrating their first powered flight on December 17, 1903, in Kitty Hawk. A guy walked up behind me and asked if the book looked okay.

"It looks pretty good. I am trying to decide whether to buy this one or the other one," I told the stranger.

"I wrote that book," Tom Crouch explained to me. He was excited to have his book in the store. I bought his great book *The Bishop's Boys: A Life of Wilbur and Orville Wright*, and he signed it. I never thought of just hanging out in bookstores to encourage people to by my books.

Tom Crouch worked at the Smithsonian National Air and Space Museum in Washington, DC, from 1974 until 2018. It was great to chat with this aviation expert and skillful author. He helped plan and conduct the one-hundred-year anniversary of the first flight. I took my nephews there to watch the air parade and other events.

We should have removed the socialists and commies many years ago but did not in the name of free speech. My grandmother used to say, "Sometimes I think we have too much freedom in America." I understand what she was saying all those years ago.

The fools at Facebook, Google, YouTube, and Amazon censored me and my work of fiction. This made me very angry because I had put my life on the line for the constitution for thirty years in the Army and take it seriously. The "Charlie bit my finger" video was cute in 2007 on YouTube, but the Google commies must be punished for violating our constitution daily by censoring us. The politicians must stop the big tech folks from discriminating now. Most Americans are conservative and/or Christian.

Speaking of the fools at Facebook, Zuckerberg and friends burned over $400 million to steal or rig the election for creepy Joe. They paid and embedded Democrats into government offices that ran the election in 2020. This is illegal, unconstitutional, or immoral, and many folks should go to jail. Biden is an illegitimate president and should be under the jail with Harris.

The Zuckerberg gang said that the money was to keep everyone safe from the CCP virus. The American Democrats love the way the CCP rule normal Chinese folks with only 8 percent of the population being members of the corrupt party. In America in reality under 5 percent of the money went toward virus mitigation. The rest was a huge get-out-the-vote operation for Democrats.

Many government employees in Wisconsin and other states were working for Biden and not the taxpayers from all political parties. Treason comes to mind as well as the gallows. Where were the Republicans? Why did they allow the immoral Democrats to cheat so much? Are they weak or stupid or both? Trump won that election.

"Live free or die. Death is not the greatest of evils," General John Stark said in 1809. Let us rise up now to avoid being slaves in a socialist or communist hellhole. Many in our government have sold out America and its good citizens. God bless America!

Why did the commies at Google's YouTube recommend ISIS videos to users, according to a lawsuit? Nohemi Gonzalez was killed in the ISIS attack in Paris during 2015. Her family sued the Google fools for recommending harmful conduct, and the case is headed to the US Supreme Court now.

I hope their sweet liability shield with Section 230 of the Communications Decency Act of 1996 is pierced once and for all. The fools running our public squares online must be forced to obey our sacred constitution. The Democrats have spit on our constitutional rights for too long. They are being protected by corrupt politicians in the District of Columbia who want one-party rule, just like the Chinese.

The Democrats led by Governor Wolf and Lieutenant Governor Fetterman violated the federal and state constitutions with drop boxes, mail-in ballots, and other election processes. The state legislatures control the elections and not the executive or judicial branch folks. Even the Pennsylvania Supreme Court members violated our sacred state and federal constitutions to help idiot Biden win. They will be lucky if they are not found in orange jumpsuits holding long sticks with nails on the end beside the highway collecting trash. The US Supreme Court people should have demanded that all state employees obey the sweet US Constitution *before* the November 2020 election.

Never forget Elizabeth Linscott from Kentucky. She tested hot for the CCP virus in 2020, and local government idiots tried to get her to sign a form to get permission to leave her house. She refused, and the Nazi sheriff came to her house with ankle bracelets for her and her husband. Perhaps these government folks earned a little jail time.

Perhaps we can even have justice with Zuckerberg and gang behind bars. They have been censoring conservative Christians like myself for years and years. Why have the politicians allowed this stupidity? Even today when I explain that the climate change fools only want socialism or communism, Facebook places a propaganda notice on my posts. The CCP folks have taught the American useful idiots well. They must be destroyed now through politics before war breaks out.

Never forget that True the Vote has hard evidence that Trump won in Pennsylvania in 2020 as follows. There are 500,000 ballots in dispute. Joe says he won by about 82,000 votes. A full and independent audit was begun but shut down by idiots in the Pennsylvania government. Senators Corman and Argall did not follow through. Why did they back down? We had illegal security controls for mail-in ballots.

This Argall fellow is like a weed in Hitler's bunker. They are hard to get rid of. How has he been allowed to serve in the Pennsylvania house and senate for the last thirty-seven years? Perhaps we should primary this old RINO and make him get a real job. The taxpayers are going to have to pay this guy a pension for passing dumb laws and expanding government almost every year. What would Benjamin Franklin say about so much waste and burden on the taxpayer? Can we please have term limits to reduce the size of government and run off many fools? Six years is long enough for any government idiot. This is opinion.

There were 170,000 more votes counted than people recorded as voting. We had unobserved ballot counting in many places. A large batch of over 580,000 ballots went 99 percent for creepy Joe. Some counties did not have chain of custody documentation. A tractor trailer containing over 144,000 completed ballots disappeared. We had significant statistical anomalies. Many dumb or corrupt judges blocked the presentation of election cheating evidence. Other than that, it was a free and fair election in Pennsylvania. Somebody must go to jail. Zuckerberg is a good candidate for a grand jury.

> Facebook is a great company, but it's no
> longer a company. It's a country. That's how
> powerful it is. And its behavior lately has kind
> of been getting into the foothills of creepy.
> —Senator John Kennedy

I am reminded of the cliché, "I was born at night but not last night." Most Americans do not want socialism and communism by Democrats and will help destroy it.

We have many fake Republicans too. I tried to run ads for *Redneck Dystopia* during December 2020 in AMAC magazine. The woman was interested at first and then ignored me and my money. I even tried to get the AMAC people to cover the censorship at Amazon and Facebook, to no avail. One email is below.

December 18, 2020

Hello!

I love your magazine and have a scoop for you. The online censors rejected advertisements for my fictional book *Redneck Dystopia*. Can you believe that they censor fiction now if it describes a brutal and socialistic America in 2021?

Please check out my book entitled *Redneck Dystopia* selling on Barnes and Noble, Amazon, etc. It is a fictional tale about a brutal socialist America beginning after the 2020 election if Trump and other Republicans lose to Beth Warner (a Pocahontas-type character). The Christian composite characters roam from Pottsville, Pennsylvania to Hamburg to Washington, DC and try to cope with the horrible socialist system.

The Supreme Court is the weak link to enabling one-party rule after 245 years of free enterprise and immense success. Send questions to me at dave224422@yahoo.com. The Amazon and Facebook censors keep my books down by rejecting my advertisements. Can you help? I guess Bezos and friends support socialism, Biden, and big government. I have other books too. I am an Army veteran with thirty years of service defending our constitution which mandates capitalism and limited government. I have some health issues. My wife Nancy and I embrace a capitalistic, Christian America and think socialism and communism suck! Nancy grew up in China. Thank you for your time!

"Whenever the people are well-informed, they can be trusted with their own government," said Thomas Jefferson. TJ spent time with the corrupt and immoral kings and queens of Europe and knew that America would suffer under that ridiculous form of government. Does it appear that the Obamas would love to be a king and queen of a corrupt communist nation?

Even many in the local media in Pennsylvania are corrupt or very biased. They did not even mention the great elections in Virginia, where the parents fought back against big, abusive, corrupt, and immoral government idiots. The local media would not even return my emails and calls to cover my senate campaign. They love the uniparty of Dems and RINOs. But the good news is that most Americans are conservative and have finally awakened. The sacred, original constitution will be restored and enforced soon.

The Republican Herald, WNEP, WNET, Fox 29, and many more media folks would not return my emails and calls about me and my campaign. I think they are hurting the voters by not informing them on the issues and candidates for office. Most Americans do not like long-term welfare.

The *New York Times*, Fox News, *Military Times*, Newsmax, USA, Gab News, Pulse News, and many more national reporters would not return my emails and calls about the campaign. They should cover more candidates to educate the voters.

President Trump rails about the communist media folks all the time. He is spot on with that criticism. Our corrupt and biased media are promoting communism in America, and we must destroy them. Perhaps we should deport them to China to be in those communist propaganda organizations. China has increased spending on military over 70 percent in the last ten years. They are not joking around with their childish ambitions to bully other nations.

I believe that we will replace many dumb people in government soon with people who obey the constitution and their oath of office. They should do the right thing but now will not because they are immoral, and the media people help hide their scandals and illegal activity. We need more God, Jesus, and the Bible!

I believe now that Trump won the election back in 2020. I have seen mountains of evidence to back up this opinion. Pennsylvania had 121,000 more votes than voters. If I am right, many folks must go to jail. I just want some grand juries stood up to look into this possible criminal activity. Is that asking too much?

Most Americans think the election was stolen. They want accountability and honesty from everyone in government. We are a long way from that now.

The US government is illegitimate and does not represent most Americans. About 296 fools in the US House and 92 in the US Senate voted to certify a corrupt election in 2020. We trust in God, and this, too, shall pass.

The swamp is huge in DC. I remember being at the Pentagon from 2006 until 2009. It is mostly democratic there. This surprises most people when I inform them of this. Most of the offices do not work for the other offices.

The services (Army, Navy, Air Force, Coast Guard, and Marines) man, train, and equip the forces as per the constitution. The combatant commands plan and execute training and operations from orders from the president and secretary of defense. These two huge groups exist with tremendous tension and waste a ton of tax money annually. The politicians love huge DOD budgets and wars. They get rich and famous from so much waste, fraud, and abuse at the Pentagon.

We need to remove so many myopic fools in our government. They ganged up on Trump and ran him out of town because he threatened their high salaries, health care, and retirements. We need outsiders like Trump now to clean house.

I met a woman in a restaurant. She is a great server and good with customers. A drunk guy was chatting with her at the bar and gave her a roll of stickers and told her to place them on gas pumps and everywhere. The sticker has Joe Biden's old and ugly face with the caption, "I did that."

She said that customers say and do crazy things all day every day. This woman said that she scratched her leg while bathing her two young kids at home and used profanity. The kids were outraged and told her not to use bad language. The mother told them that people with jobs can say whatever they want. Whoever pays the bills makes the rules.

I like this rule and the following. The hard workers, taxpayers, and business owners should always run the government, businesses, and everything. Idiot politicians who never had a real job should not be charge of anything. Clinton, Obama, Biden, Harris, Schumer, Fetterman, Lamb, and Pelosi are bad for our capitalistic America. Also, the workers and especially union workers should not be able to dictate to managers and business owners. The owners put their money at risk and must have absolute control of their investment. This union crap is a recipe for communism, and we must stop it.

The Democrats have a monopoly on bad ideas these days. This idiot named Lauren Book in the Florida senate proposed a law to ban dogs from hanging out car windows. Is it not enough to harass humans with stupid laws? Now they are going after pets. She actually wants to require man's best friend to ride in a cage rolling down the road. This is an insult to the dog and also to the biker who loves to feel the breeze on his face. Perhaps we should require all politicians ride in cages. This would prevent Biden from touching anyone.

Dog-eat-dog American capitalism is awesome. It needs workers and managers, and they have different jobs. People who do not pay tax should never be allowed to write laws for those who actually pay tax. Many good people rent apartments, but they do not pay one cent of real estate tax and should not be involved in making laws for hard workers who pay a ton of real estate tax. Democrats love these people and shower them with welfare in exchange for ballots. This is terrible for America.

A man next to me mentions how awesome the cheese-covered fries are. He then goes off on a coworker of his who is a health food nut.

"This guy I work with is a germaphobe and health nut. He would never have the cheese fries. He works out at a gym all the time and is vegetarian mostly, and yet he is sick all the time. He uses hand sanitizer constantly and is very thin. He bites his fingernails all the time. His name is Jeremy, but we call him Germany," the coworker explains.

Germany's coworkers harass him because his girlfriend just broke up with him and moved in with a guy in California. They tell the loser that she sure wanted to get the maximum distance from Germany. A move from Pennsylvania to anywhere this side of California was just too close for comfort. She had to be sure that she never saw Germany again.

We see the protesters on TV all the time defacing and destroying statues. They should be arrested for sure. This has been going on a long time. Do you remember Samuel Worthington Dewey who took a rowboat out in the rain in 1834 to cut off the bust of President Andrew Jackson off the USS Constitution? Some jail time would have been great for this guy.

Dewey was a dumb Whig party member who hated the Democrats led by the awesome war hero Jackson. He tried to present the severed wooden head to Jackson at the White House but failed and met with Vice President Van Buren, who refused to take it. Unfortunately, Dewey and many of our current-day leftists never did any jail time for their childish stunts. We still have time.

It only took Lenin and friends three years to kill tens of millions of Soviets under corrupt, evil, incompetent, socialist, communist rule. Biden and many other fools want one-party rule here in the great USA. The CCP learned how to kill to gain and maintain power from the Soviets. Thousands of Russian advisors flooded China to help them dominate normal folks with sick communism. Many hard workers died because they knew that communism is stupid. We must stop them now in America.

We need more attractive people in government. Have you seen Pramila Jayapal in the US House from Washington state? I hope you have been spared of this dead snake in the road. She is ugly for sure, but her face is like a frying pan too.

She could make Godzilla or King Kong run up a pole in a dark alley. She is fifty-seven and does not look a day over seventy-seven. This fool lost her US green card while pumping out a baby in India one time. The Indians should have kept her and protected us. She loves mandatory vaccines, masks, and anything forced on private citizens. How on earth do these ugly and dumb people get elected? This is opinion.

We should arrange a steel-cage death match between Jayapal and Yoda-look-alike Janet Yellen. The bill would be Frying Pan versus Yoda. We could set it up like the first one in Atlanta in 1937 with steel fencing and chicken wire. That would be awesome, and it would prevent them from passing dumb laws all the time. We could sell tickets and pay down the $30 trillion national debt.

We can withstand a while with the socialist Biden gang in charge, but not very long. They are corrupting all parts of the government with immoral and ignorant Democrats. The worst thing is that the regime is totally illegitimate. Trump and Pence won that 2020 election for sure. Even the Democrat Party fools running the Federal Aviation Administration (FAA) trumpet corporate welfare for airlines and lazy labor union folks and their love of lockdowns that punished tens of millions of freedom-loving, conservative, and Christian Americans.

"Joe Biden went from stealing someone's wife to stealing speeches to stealing money to stealing an election. He has really grown as a politician," Michael Moore said.

The Pennsylvania secretary of state Boockvar and other fools let many liberal groups access our voter registration system during 2020. The secretary of state should be prevented from creating or perverting laws to win elections for Democrats. Governor Wolf and many others should face grand juries now. Very few right-wing or conservative groups were included in this illegal and/or immoral scheme to rig our elections. They used the catalyst system for this.

Many people need to go to jail for being partisan within the government. We used to say in the military that there are no Republican or Democrat soldiers. We only should have American soldiers and government employees. Heather Honey of Verity Vote has a lot of evidence about our unfair elections. She is very knowledgeable and professional and testified in Arizona about election cheaters and incompetent folks.

The RINOs and RNC were asleep while the Democrats were surveilling voters years before the 2020 election in order to predict, manipulate, and control them. Zuckerberg and friends gave over $420 million to people working inside and outside the government to collect as many ballots as possible without much verification.

CTCL is one of the Zuckerberg groups that train county election workers. We must ensure that government employees are not overtly partisan. We must remove anyone promoting socialism, communism, or dictatorship. Many people support this crap. George Soros should be in or under the jail for working against capitalism and limited government.

Many corrupt people access the Electronic Registration Information Center (ERIC). Thirty-three states are trying to register everyone to vote. You can fill out mail-in ballots all day long if you have plenty of names and addresses from the bloated registration databases. This is how the Democrats cheat with fifty days of voting instead of the one day required in our Pennsylvania and federal constitutions. Many judges are asleep or corrupt and will not stop this illegal activity.

Many people should be prevented from voting for crimes, etc. The Democrats are trying to register many criminals and welfare folks. Rock the Vote and Hillary Clinton's group register many suspect people to vote for bad Democrats. Republicans must get better at legally collecting ballots to win elections if we cannot get rid of the mail-in ballots, cheating, and long voting periods.

It is sad that a bunch of shadowy government uniparty employees obsess about collecting ballots from drunks, alcoholics, and other ignorant people. We love the American idea that elections should be about educating and persuading voters to support intelligent and moral candidates. Most uniparty people in office used to hide the fact that they do not care what the voters want.

More and more of the uniparty fools are open about moving to socialism and communism regardless that most Americans reject those systems. Most of these immoral politicians ignore our laws to gain and maintain power.

If they do not peacefully agree to abide by our constitution and laws, force may be necessary to enforce our original constitution. We have so many immoral people in government trying to brutally rule a mostly conservative and Christian population. I doubt that AOC and gang have ever read our constitution.

I think this is what President John Adams was thinking when he said, "Our constitution was made only for a moral and religious people." Are Bill and Hillary Clinton moral? Are Bidens honest, religious, or accountable to the voters? Did the Obamas get rich off politics? How did Liz Cheney and Nancy Pelosi get rich *after* getting elected to the US House?

We have tolerated criminal judges and politicians for decades and now at a breaking point. I pray to God that we can solve this problem peacefully. America is being operated outside the constitution. This never should have been allowed. FDR should have been removed and put in jail for many policies and laws that violated our constitution, values, and laws.

Do the emails you get from politicians address the concerns of conservatives and Christians? Do they promote more and more government programs and antibiblical values? The uniparty must be defeated once and for all to save our capitalistic and great America. The time is short, my friends.

Here is the question. Why are the Democrats and RINOs paying lazy families over $80,000 per year not to work? Here is the answer. They are buying the votes of lazy and ignorant folks to move to socialism and communism. The fools in Venezuela did exactly the same thing when they had some extra oil money. The voters better wake up before it is too late to save the American meritocracy.

The uniparty folks have enabled over 3 million Americans to leave the work force since 2000. New Jersey, Washington, and Massachusetts pay over $100,000 for imbecile families not to work. Are most Democrats paying attention? Why are independents voting for the communist Democrats? It may be too late to maintain a great and successful United States of America peacefully. Analyze Venezuela if you think I am exaggerating.

The Democrats gave over $54 billion to the airlines because of the unnecessary pandemic shutdowns, vaccine, mandates, and mask requirements all the while Fauci and other union idiots ignored the natural immunity of actually getting the CCP virus instead of the ineffective vaccines. Many experts say that the Fauci gang funded gain-of-function research in Wuhan that led to the pandemic that killed millions of people.

> Man is not free unless government is limited.
> —President Ronald Reagan

How much money have the drug companies given corrupt RINOs and Democrats? We do know that over 66 percent of the politicians in DC receive drug company money annually.

Speaking of unions, it is an outrage that Biden and Congress wasted about $90 billion in tax money in 2021 to bail out bankrupt pension plans that pay employees much more than nonunion workers. It would be much better to balance the budget and remove all unions from government and other workers.

Nonunion taxpayers should not be forced to bail out pensions that are too generous. This is pure vote buyers at its worst. Unions have caused many businesses to fail by driving up the cost of doing business. The benefits should be cut for unrealistic pensions. The fools who ran the pension plans with overly optimistic earnings forecasts should be punished by chipping in their money to pay for these outlandish pensions for over ten million mostly union folks.

The California unions and politicians are putting a dumb initiative on the ballot for the third election in a row in November 2022. Proposition 29 would require dialysis clinics to have a doctor, nurse practitioner, or physician's assistant on site during all patient hours. Many ship owners are sailing to ports on the East Coast to avoid the poorly run union ports in California.

The union boss fools love Proposition 29, but it would cost each clinic more than $376,000 per year. Many clinics would shut down or raise prices. Why are the Democrats so dumb? Have they ever had a real job? Are they aware that many highly paid employees are moving to Texas?

We are not trying to grow flowers in the desert, but can we please elect someone like me to the US Senate who will stand up for America first and try to abide by the Bible? Do you remember when Obama, Biden, and Kerry were so arrogant and condescending in dealing with our allies? They did this for eight long years before Trump put America and common sense first.

"The only thing that will save Israel is for John Kerry to win his Nobel Prize and go home," Moshe Ya'alon, defense minister, said in frustration during 2016.

I had many foreign officers tell me things like this while I worked at the Pentagon in 2008 and in the combat zone during 2003. They respected American success and strength but abhorred the dumb and immoral woke crap spouted by fools in leadership positions.

These good allies would share with me how offensive the Americans could be in promoting sick stuff like transgender surgery, gay conversion, and criminal rights. They knew that the Obama gang did not speak for most Americans. Our allies will just ignore the dumb statements and take the US tax money every time.

"We need more men with chests and not breasts," the preacher proclaimed on TV. He is right on the money about destroying the transsexual promotion industry and promoting God, Jesus, and the Bible. We need strong and Christian men to protect our great nation and women and children. God help us to follow the Bible and be fine. The sick American communists must be defeated. This, too, shall pass.

Obama and Biden had Al Sharpton to the White House over seventy times to exaggerate racism, get on TV, and/or make money. The moron Obama said that racism is part of our DNA. Speaking of DNA, it appears that he has the dumb gene. It appears that his brain is smaller than a gnat. Obama and the gnat share the trait of blood sucking, only he sucks the money out of hardworking tax- payers instead of their blood. Many folks wonder whether or not

Michelle is a man. I can see that. It would not surprise me. Check her/his DNA. They call him Michael. This is opinion.

These socialist Democrats really hurt many uneducated black folks by telling them they were victims when they should have been encouraging them to work harder and shun welfare. Welfare creates divisions, and hard workers reject it when lazy folks are paid for nothing. Paying someone for nothing is stupid, but Democrats love the ballots.

France outlawed mail-in ballots and drop boxes in 1975. They require an ID at the polling station and do not allow computerized tabulation. The paper ballot is the only ballot in France. They laugh at the Americans for allowing so much election cheating and dysfunction. Most French people are socialist, but they are smarter than the American socialists.

The 2020 election cheating by the Democrats is the biggest scandal since Toiletgate. There were strong words during the 2006 World Championship of Chess. Veselin Topalov's team accused Vladimir Kramnik of taking too many bathroom breaks in order to cheat. Perhaps we should give the Democrat cheaters and Kramnik a swirly.

The swirly is a high school procedure of holding someone upside down with their head in the toilet and flushing. Shall we start with Mark Zuckerberg? I remember a bully trying to give a kid a swirly in high school. He told the kid if he told one more lie, the punishment would be a swirly. The kid barely wiggled free above the rim after ignoring the warning to speak the truth. That was close and hilarious after many beers.

Perhaps it is time for a brief history lesson on the US Senate. James Madison and others wanted the Senate representation based on population just like the US House. They argued about this during the Constitutional Convention until the end on September 17, 1787. The small-state founders could not believe their good luck in getting the big-state folks to agree on each state having two senators. This just seemed then and still seems to me now to be unfair and very odd. The small-state people said they feared the big states colluding to harm the small states.

Most of the framers were tired of long debates and wanted to wrap things up and get back home, so they approved the two senator-per-state plan. It only took twelve long years to finish writing and approving the constitution (from 1776 until 1787). George Mason slipped in the convention of states procedures in article five when most people were sick of sitting around debating and arguing about setting up the new nation and constitution.

Article 5 allows for amending the constitution if thirty-eight states agree on almost anything. I think this would work today to take power from the federal government idiots. It took the founders and others fifteen years to ratify the Bill of Rights or the first ten amendments to the constitution (1776 until 1791). I wonder if they were nasty with one another and told the verbose folks to sit down and shut up during those fifteen years.

Pat Toomey is a RINO from hell. He and his type are responsible for allowing the socialist Democrats to move America toward socialism and communism. He voted to impeach President Trump for no good reason.

Toomey and other establishment Republicans are responsible for Pennsylvania's failings as follows. People work until April 22 each year just to pay for all the dumb federal, state, and local government programs. Pennsylvania has 203 full-time (most of them idiots) in the state house sucking up $92,000 each in salary. Over 11,000 state workers make over $100,000. This is opinion.

We have too many politicians in Pennsylvania and America. The same can be said about real estate agents. There were more agents in 2020 than houses for sale. That sucks for them. Many folks started selling houses because of the pandemic and all the unnecessary lockdowns by really stupid politicians. Wolf imposed really dumb and illegal lockdowns. Judges should have ruled against them quickly.

All the Democrats running for this US Senate seat remind me of Frank Kellogg (former US senator and secretary of state) and Aristide Briand (former prime minister of France). These geniuses negotiated a pact in 1928 that outlawed war forever. Kellogg even received the Nobel Peace Prize for this stupidity. A smart person realizes that war is never pleasant but sometimes necessary to kill very bad folks.

The Kellogg-Briand Pact is still in force as many wars rage on. The climate change Democrats are the same and will waste untold amounts of our money for meaningless treaties that China, India, and many nations ignore.

"Neck Has Gross Politician Growing Out of It" was the headline from the Babylon Bee. These writers nail the headline every time. "The hoodie makes sense now. It was there so the neck lump could hide from view," said one TMZ journalist. "I'd hide my face too if I had a politician growing out of me like that." Fetterman is a disgusting leftist failure for sure for letting violent criminals out of prison early. The press said that he drew an allowance from his parents until he was forty-nine years old. This is opinion.

The uniparty folks, such as Obama and Bush, have enabled millions of young Americans to become fools on social media claiming to be some sort of victims. These youngsters are the weakest American generation ever and threaten our strong and capitalistic nation. These fools vote for whomever will give the most welfare or free college. We need more conservative and Christian young folks and not big babies like Fetterman. Ignorant adults raise ignorant children, and America is paying a big price for this today.

Now here is some good news out of California for Fetterman. Scientists at Stanford transplanted neural tissue from humans into the brains of baby rats. The human cells grew and made functional connections within the rat brains, according to the *Wall Street Journal*. That would be awesome to try on Fetterman to make him smarter. The rats could smoke Fetterman in a race for the cheese in that confusing maze.

They should transplant rat cells into this guy's tiny brain to make him smarter. Perhaps this would reduce the number of dumb statements from my man. The scientists could inject a lot of rat cells into the neck lump and then connect that piece of fat to his tiny brain. There must be some way to help this dimwitted, union-financed senate candidate named Fetterman. He must agree to lay off the pot before we pay for the operation.

There are two hunters seated next to us in the restaurant. They complain about how complicated the Pennsylvania hunting laws are.

The topic turns from our corrupt and incompetent government to hunting.

"We flew to Montana to hunt last week. I got an eighteen-point buck mounted on my wall right now. You must come to see it," one hunter said to the other.

"Man, what is wrong with you? You hunt for the wrong reasons. I hunt only for the meat. My wife would never allow a dead animal head on our wall," the other hunter explained.

Some people never learn. The Democrats under Carter raised taxes on energy producers in the 1970s, and production went down. The Biden gang is doing the same thing now with more regulation and taxes on US energy producers. It is worse now because of Russians invading Ukraine and getting hit by sanctions from the Western countries.

The Chinese and Indians are laughing all the way to the bank by getting discounted oil and natural gas from the Russians. Biden and other climate change imbeciles are shooting themselves in the foot. The CCP folks are actually buying oil from the Biden gang and reselling it on world markets for a profit. Most voters will vote GOP down the line to stop the stupidity from the Democrats in 2022! Another red wave is coming.

Did you say you want more government? Shapiro and Fetterman surely do. You better take a closer look at Illinois and all those union government employees sitting around doing nothing. Over 132,000 employees in state government make over $100,000 per year taking it easy. Do you think most vote for corrupt Democrats?

The Biden gang and Congress gave the state a $200 billion COVID bailout to avoid bankruptcy and junk bond ratings. The schools in the state fail on every student metric, but the teachers in Chicago make $108,000 on average and live very well. I see why so many hard workers are leaving Illinois.

That big fat governor Pritzker who inherited tons of money from the Hilton hotel empire should cut back on his meat intake and pay for some of the union idiots. We could cut him up and feed a family of four in south-side Chicago for a month. His huge carcass could feed a family of four in Ethiopia for a year.

Do you remember when Michelle Obama had a no-show job at the hospital just because her stupid husband was in some kind of government office doing nothing? The corruption runs deep where the Democrats rule. How is the crime rate in Illinois? What is the inflation rate? How many folks were shot this year in Illinois? Do the lazy welfare people really get more money and benefits than the uneducated hard workers? That does not seem right. This is opinion.

I want lower spending and lower taxes. The good news is that eleven states lowered income taxes in 2021. Most politicians would continuously raise spending and taxes if allowed to. Let us cut back government now.

I saw a good video the other day. A lady with a British accent was trying to educate a fool at a swim meet where a man was competing against women.

"Do you have ovaries?" she asked the woke idiot.

"Everybody is different. Are you a biologist?" the idiot asked.

"I am not a vet, but I know what a dog is," the smart woman explained to the fool.

Here is some good research out of Sweden. The grades of attractive female college students went down after the dumb lockdowns, but the grades of attractive male students remained the same.

Why is this? Are dumb professors blinded by beauty? I used to cover the name on tests while I was grading to prevent bias while working for community colleges. We need to treat everyone the same and base everything on performance. How about that?

The Trump Department of Education discovered over $6.5 billion in foreign funding to American universities. The colleges are supposed to report this, but many hide the money. Weak politicians are allowing foreigners from China, Russia, Saudi Arabia, and other nations to influence our college students. This must stop. Why do so many dumb college students love socialism, dictatorship, and communism?

The Chinese communists have given over $60 million to the University of Pennsylvania and the Biden Center. Who profited from this money? How much did creepy Joe get paid? Was Hunter soaking up this money? There were stolen classified documents there courtesy of Joe Biden. Where is the grand jury for all this?

Europe is not the answer. Biden, Kerry, Obama, and other fools love the EU. They love socialism and communism. Let us destroy this crap in America now. Several EU nations are bankrupt, but they increased the number government jobs by 4 percent in the last two years. These fools want government to own or control everything. American Democrats are the same.

Spending by the EU governments is 51 percent of GDP and only 45 percent in the United States, according to the *Wall Street Journal*. We need to lower this crap because government is always more wasteful and corrupt than small to midsized businesses. Many big businesses are woke, corrupt, and wasteful. The motivation to work hard or invest in business goes down when government gets big.

The Democrats and controlled, weak Republicans are about to destroy American prosperity by ignoring the good citizens. They are borrowing and spending like fools while Rome burns. The market for US Treasury securities or debt froze up during March 2020 when the CCP virus came on strong. This could happen again at any time with a system built on so much debt.

"US government bonds are the bedrock of the global financial system," explains Andrew Ackerman in the *Wall Street Journal*. The stupid politicians are playing with the destruction of the American dream by giving away so much free stuff for votes from other fools. We must stop these dumb people such as Shapiro and Fetterman. This is opinion.

Anyone creating doubt with elections or cheating should remember Ceausescu and his wife in Romania in 1989. Good folks with guns get tired of communists after a while. I am not suggesting this.

I pray for a peaceful solution to all the election cheaters ignoring US law and our state and federal constitutions. This is a nation of laws. This is not a socialist or communist country. It was awesome when the Romanians destroyed the communists in their land.

"We found thousands of mail-in ballots in Pennsylvania that were received back by the government before they'd been mailed out," Dan Gelernter explained. He and many others examined the 2020 election and found massive cheating. "Election fraud is not about ideology. It's about money," Dan said.

So many people are angry these days. I do not like profanity much, but I have to tell you about this one. One nut on Highway 61 in Hamburg has a big professionally made sign in his yard that reads, "Slow the Fuck Down."

I have seen the "Slow Down!" signs my entire life but not the profane version. Some blame Trump and others blame leftists. It is just not the same. I bet is this guy has road rage every day.

Some things just do not make sense. Fetterman running for US Senate does not make sense. He is too dumb and lazy. You can drink unlimited amounts of beer or wine for one hour in Las Vegas for $20 at the Pampas. That does not make sense either. Please keep Nancy Pelosi out of that place.

The Bible and US Constitution are the primary documents and references for myself and my campaign. We need more God, Jesus, the Bible, and limited government to keep America great. Of course, good insults are involved also in any successful political campaign.

I visited Theresa and Mike McDonald one day in Ashland. These conservatives always have some good thoughts and support my campaign. They keep the local government idiots on their toes. One county employee complained that they were feeding and taking care of wild cats. You would have to be a jerk to do this in a rural setting such as Ashland. This couple just loves the animals, and most of the houses are spread out in this area.

This couple put another county employee in his place when he complained about their old truck not having license plates. They hired a lawyer and had the dumb complaint thrown out. If the voters were smart, they would hire Theresa and Mike and others like them to help run the government. They are good people and love the job Trump did. For the record, any government idiot who harasses citizens for no good reason should be fired. All government employees work for the taxpayers.

CHAPTER 2

THE COMMITTED REDNECK

> Our constitution was made only for a
> moral and religious people. It is wholly
> inadequate to the government of any other.
> —John Adams, president from 1797 to 1801

I decided to run for US Senate on February 10, 2021, after we returned from Savannah the previous week. I was shocked that immoral, corrupt, and ignorant Democrats were running our government and doing sick things daily. We had fun in the warm weather in Georgia and then got stuck in our backup driveway in one foot of snow and ice. I managed to drive the truck to the house but had to leave the enclosed trailer and Harley in the woods and snow and ice. The neighbor Jim lets us use his driveway in bad weather, but this time the trail connecting to his driveway was jammed with snow and ice.

The first step was to write my platform based on the values in the Bible and constitution. I love those documents because they give boundaries for our behavior. Children and adults need boundaries. "The buffet is a bad idea. Nobody would go into the restaurant and order one of everything. That is why we need a menu. Humans need portion control," said Jerry Seinfeld.

The next step was requesting an Employer Identification Number (EIN) for the redneck campaign from the Internal Revenue Service (IRS). I filed as "David Xu, redneck for US Senate" as a joke to get free media attention. Boy, that strategy failed.

Most media folks ignored my emails and phone calls to cover the campaign and platform. Over 90 percent of journalists are Democrats and horrible for America. If they loved America, they would want several honest and successful candidates per race. In actuality, the local, state, and national journalists censor and lie for the communist or socialist Democrats every day.

I thought the redneck noun was funny as we used to call one another rednecks all the time in Florida and Virginia as kids. The word used to refer to farmers with sunburn in the 1830s. Did you know that it is in the top three most researched words with the online *Merriam-Webster* dictionary?

I started the campaign out as an exploratory committee. My interpretation of the confusing and dumb Federal Election Commission (FEC) rules led me down this path. I later changed to a full-blown candidate after reading that if I referred to myself as an actual candidate that I must stop with the exploratory stuff to avoid a fine from the government idiots.

I called the FEC one day with a question. The employee asked if redneck was really a part of my given name. I wondered if she was joking or serious. I think she was serious. She sounded like an older woman. She seemed to lack common sense from being in government too long. She said she has lived and worked in the federal government in DC her entire life.

Most of the swamp rats are dedicated union Democrats who make a lot of money off the taxpayer. We should lay off many of these folks tonight. Over 21 million people work for our local, state, and federal governments now.

"I bet you have never had an official redneck candidate file with the FEC," I asked the employee.

"No, we surely have not. This is a first for sure," she affirmed. I felt like I was really getting somewhere. I was really just trying to keep the campaign light and put smiles on some faces.

The Democrats have perverted most parts of the government and seemingly begging for a civil war. I pray to God against one and will do everything in my power to avoid one. The FEC employees ruled that it is fine for Google to send 67 percent of GOP candidate emails to spam and only send 8 percent of Democrat emails to spam. This happened in the 2019 and 2020 election cycles. The FEC is supposed to be nonpartisan.

"War is a mere continuation of policy by other means," Carl von Clausewitz wisely observed back in 1820. Nations and people can settle differences through politics or war. I pray to God for peace because I do not want to go to war again. Once is enough for this redneck from the South.

I rented a post-office box for the first time in my life. I kept reading about idiot protesters harassing candidates for all kinds of things and knew they would go after me and my family if they knew I wanted to cut back welfare and most parts of the government. Many Democrats view government as a religion with so much free stuff. We worship God, Jesus, and the Bible and reject big government.

I ordered campaign business cards. There was the redneck version with "Redneck for US Senate" at the top. It had some of my platforms such as enforcing the constitution, cut spending, term limits, balanced budget, and border wall. I would give these to anyone I met. I would leave them in stores and restaurants trying to get allies.

I received a nasty email below from a restaurant employee in Hazleton. They were triggered by this very conservative platform and threatened legal action. I wondered, "What exactly is he/she so upset about?" I did not see the no soliciting sign at the place.

Hello,

Many of your cards were found all over our restaurant. We have a strict no solicitation policy and do not appreciate garbage like this being spread all over our facility. The type of information being spread is not welcome in our facility.

Any further incidents involving this type of behavior will be handled legally.

—Grill

Hazleton, Pennsylvania

I was shocked that they would get so mad about these basic American values and positions. I wondered if they had read any history books about what happens when you get one-party rule by socialists, communists, and liars as presented by the Democrats in government. This is opinion. Shouldn't they just throw them in the trash?

I had a nonredneck business card too. I would give this one to people in Levi's and the other one to people wearing Wranglers. Everyone knows that most Democrats and RINOs prefer Levi's, and most Republicans prefer Wranglers. This strategy was to avoid rejection and anger when approaching strangers to speak of politics.

I guess the angry restaurant employee does not realize that many of the government idiots who imposed lockdowns for the CCP virus that punished tens of millions of American hard workers were done by the same folks who were in government back in the 1990s. They worked together with greedy business owners and managers to shut down many factories in the USA and ship the jobs to communists in China and Vietnam.

These people are sick and do not care about hard workers and taxpayers. Shutting down businesses for the CCP virus or to give our good jobs to communists proves beyond a shadow of a doubt that we need term limits for all politicians, government employees, and judges. I would suggest six to eight years in government. That is enough before going back to the private sector and a real job.

One of the worst things in life is to see Americans who want to work but cannot find a job. Many government and business folks do not care as long as they get paid every month. Many in the media love socialist, corrupt government and turn a blind eye to unemployed people getting addicted to drugs and alcohol out of boredom.

I learned that most people do not trust strangers anymore. It is sad that we have so many folks in government with no honesty or accountability, such as creepy Joe. We must kick these fools out of government and take back our great and capitalistic America. The globalists have had their day with open borders, throwing US citizens out of their factory jobs and giving their jobs to foreigners, letting illegal aliens run wild committing crimes, and getting rich.

Democracy depends on the citizens accepting laws, customs, and institutions. Biden and other fools are violating our sweet constitution by allowing millions of illegal aliens to cross our borders. Many of these people do not share much of anything with the American taxpayers. Most of the illegal aliens will cost hard workers money to support. Many do not even speak English and cannot or will not support themselves and their children. This is illegal and immoral behavior from the Democrats to force Americans to pay for these criminals. It is also playing with fire to treat good American taxpayers like fools.

"In 2012, I looked at support for Obama. And among all noncitizens, about 80 percent supported Obama. Among noncitizens who cast validated votes, it was about 90 percent who said that they supported Obama," Dr. Jesse Richman said. He teaches at ODU.

Biden and other traitors tried to include $105 billion in their budget in 2022 for illegal aliens. They are trying to federalize our elections to prevent voter ID and allow cheating so illegal aliens and noncitizens can vote. The traitors must be stopped and punished. The American taxpayer is paying over $130 billion each year for welfare for illegal aliens.

I was surprised when a RINO said that my nonredneck business card would offend Christians. This genius thought "Socialism and communism suck!" would upset the Christians. I let him know that I thought that was a dumb thing to say. He and so many voters are thinking it is 1982 when most politicians embraced and obeyed the constitution. Those days are long gone, and he should know that.

We have almost 100 percent of the Democrats in DC pushing for a socialist, communist group dictatorship. They want the CCP model in America and must be defeated. Gina McCarthy, Biden's climate czar until 2022, is the former president of the Natural Resources Defense Council (NRDC). She is the one uttering dumb things all the time. Why are so many in the Obama-Biden stupid? Perhaps affirmative action and political correctness lead to grossly unqualified people in important positions.

The NRDC folks have worked with the commies in China for decades. They work with the Fred Munster-look-alike John Kerry now. The Israelis were so tired of dealing with Munster as secretary of state that they said, "The best thing for us would be for Kerry to win the Noble Peace Prize and leave us alone."

I believe that about half the Democrats still believe in our sweet constitution and limited government, but their so-called leaders are lazy, dumb, and corrupt. We call DC Hollywood for ugly people. Have you seen Swallwell, Pelosi, and Schiff? They would be ugly even in the dark.

I began calling and emailing most of the sixty-seven GOP county organizations in Pennsylvania. I thought they would help me get in front of the voters to have a good competition in the primary. I was wrong.

Most of these establishment types did not even return my calls or emails. I guess they were set on other folks running for the US Senate seat. Many volunteers do not put in much time for the common, normal voter. It is a shame that we have come to this. This is one reason why so many bad Republicans or RINOs were elected over the last few decades. It is why America is teetering on the brink of a socialist-communist group dictatorship or one-party rule by the Democrats.

Some of the county folks were very nice and helpful to me. They suggested various meetings and Lincoln Day events to speak or get signatures to get on the ballot. We need a system to get as many as possible to compete in the GOP primary.

We need to help good Christian folks get elected without forcing them to burn a lot of their hard-earned money. The GOP county committee people should try to get at least two good conservative Christian candidates per primary to face off for the voters.

Most Americans think it is dumb to waste a lot of your own money to get elected for anything. They would never do that. Nancy and I are surely in that camp and agreed that we would not burn much money for this activity. The wife of Teddy Daniels allegedly said that he said that they would have to sell their house if he lost the election and remained unemployed. That is odd because he told us in Clifford that he had plenty of money and a pretty wife. Is that a dumb thing to say at a long and boring GOP candidate brunch? We are lucky that this fat man went down in flames. It is a win-win because he has more time for Chinese buffets now anyway.

Wives will do and say funny things. Lucas Glover's wife on the PGA tour allegedly told Lucas that he could not see their children if he shot over seventy-two. Now that is a demanding PGA tour wife. I guess it worked because he is finally playing better these days after many years of sucking after the US Open victory. This is opinion.

Daniels reminds me of that marshmallow man on TV or perhaps a male version of Lizzo. I wonder who copied who with the cowboy boots. Perhaps both of them should avoid trying to be an image for body positivity or self-confidence.

At least Teddy does not say he is a vegan as Lizzo does. Most people do not believe her. How can she be that fat and not eat meat? She reminds me of that large woman online who said she is anorexic. How can that be? The most dangerous place to be is between Lizzo and the buffet. Can we please get her some loose-fitting winter clothing and hide the leggings?

Let us take this to a serious place for a moment. I am worried about Lizzo's heart. That organ is working overtime supporting all that meat with blood. She better be careful so as not to be like Slash from Guns and Roses. He says he was declared legally dead for eight minutes one night while doing drugs. Now that was a close call for my boy. He said it is a good thing they did not have the internet back then to document all the wild nights.

Most successful Americans will not run for office, and I do not blame them. But we cannot continue to allow so many fools to run our government. The full-time and long-term dumb politicians must go. They do not care about our kids and will send them to war at the drop of a hat. They will always put their pocketbook and fame above the long-term strength of America and normal, hardworking citizens.

I am reminded of a young and strong woman we met in Bloomsburg. She worked with horses and is sick of big, corrupt government and weak politicians. She said that we need to get back to tough love. We must stop coddling kids and criminals and hold them to high educational and moral standards. We have prisons for a reason. I could not agree more. She was short and had huge biceps and grew up poor and very successful now due to hard work and trusting in God, Jesus, and the Bible. Her cowgirl boots were worn. That is the best way to go through life.

The Northwest Ordinance is great from 1787. "Religion, morality, and knowledge being necessary to good government and the happiness of mankind, schools, and the means of education shall ever be encouraged." Good government is impossible with ignorant citizens. The Democrats have given us too many ignorant citizens coming out of high schools that do not teach civics or much of anything. The union teachers continue to get paid though.

I spoke with a German American lady while pumping gas one day. She moved to the United States as a young woman. She lives in Virginia and is tired of politicians trying to divide Americans to gain or maintain power. She said that if we can agree on the Bible and constitution, that is enough. She pulled the lever for all Democrats for decades and now realizes that it was a huge mistake to go with the establishment folks. I told her that I feel the same way except I pulled the lever for Republicans in Name Only for decades.

She and her husband rode their bicycles from Richmond, Virginia, to Chicago, Illinois, a while back. Now that impressed me. They stayed at campgrounds and met many conservative and Christian people along the way. This renewed her faith that the voters will cleanse the government of corrupt socialists and come back stronger than ever. I agreed with this smart, strong, and very short great American.

We must stretch to be optimistic with Biden in the White House, but the US government could borrow another $29 trillion and still be less indebted than Japan and Italy. We want to cut spending and take power from the Democrats, but the country could withstand more dumb and wasteful welfare programs. Conservative Christian Republicans can reverse a lot of the damage from the Biden years in 2023. I hope and pray that the idiots in Washington are not lying about America's debt burden.

Let us remove fools like Wolf, Fetterman, Shapiro, Davis, and other Democrats who want to legalize more and more drugs. More than 500,000 Americans have died since 1999 from opioids. The Chinese Communist Party (CCP) must be punished too for sending this crap through Mexico to our open border provided by Biden and Harris. This is opinion.

Fentanyl is the number one killer of eighteen-to-forty-five-year-old Americans now. A lot of research has shown that pot is a gateway drug to psychotic and violent behavior and stronger drugs. The Democrats want dumb and lazy voters who are easily controlled.

The GOP should direct our awesome military to help destroy the drug cartels in Mexico and elsewhere when they take over in 2023. Trump and his team considered this in 2017 but did not follow through. The Democrats refuse to do this and put all Americans in danger from drug dealers and addicts. Southern and Northern combatant commands have huge budgets to eradicate all enemies foreign and domestic. It is time we let them loose on the cartels and corrupt government folks here and abroad.

I helped give the four-star generals in charge of Southern and Northern commands (SOUTHCOM and NORTHCOM) money for their operations while at the Pentagon from 2006 until 2009. We are wasting this tax money if they are not protecting us. Many Democrats want legalized drugs to keep the voters ignorant and loyal.

Sweat in training so you do not bleed in war. We trained hard and were brutal in combat during my thirty years in the Army. We must remove the current corrupt politicians who are reducing our combat effectiveness with dumb woke policies before it is too late. The strong will always rule the weak and stupid.

Always remember the Opium Wars in China. The sick British and French imported and sold drugs made in India and Turkey to the weak Chinese during the 1830s until the 1860s. The Europeans easily defeated the Chinese for lower tariffs, favorable trade deals, and even reparations and territory.

The British should have never controlled Hong Kong. They held it as a colony from 1841 until 1997. The Chinese are embarrassed about this domination by the stronger and more successful Europeans. Let this be a lesson for the weak, immoral, and socialist Democrats. If they continue to promote drugs, sloth, and other stupidity, the United States will be invaded and subjugated by stronger nation or nations.

Fetterman, Shapiro, and other fools want to legalize marijuana nationwide. They are so lazy or dumb that they will not even observe what is going on in Canada. They legalized cannabis in 2018, and now four years later over 34 percent of cannabis sales are still in the black market.

The Canadian politicians could not figure out that the illegal drug dealers would have a lower price without paying taxes to anyone. How did commie Trudeau and other idiots miss that one? The drug addicts save money with the illegal drug dealers by not having to pay sales tax. Thirty-five US states have at least partially legalized marijuana. Can we deport these Democrats and their weed to Canada? They could chain Fetterman to the refrigerator and charge tickets.

We should initiate a prisoner swap-type operation by deporting our socialist, communist folks to Canada. Those awesome Canadian truck drivers can then drive down and settle in our great county. They protested the weak little blackface Trudeau and his communist policies for the hard workers of Canada. I worked with some good Canadian military folks while I was in the US Army.

Let us turn toward the principle of personal responsibility. This is a basic element of sound leadership. Biden and company refuse to fire anyone for their many failures. Was anyone fired for the surrender in Afghanistan that killed thirteen American soldiers and injured hundreds more? Was anyone let go for causing massive inflation? Did anyone quit because of the policies that restricted energy production in the United States? The Democrats caused horrible inflation, and it hurts lower- and middle-income Americans the most.

Did any FDA employee get fired for sitting on the application to reopen the baby formula factory? Many mothers could not buy formula and refused to breastfeed. Many of them wanted that free government stuff over feeding their baby with their own milk. Perhaps the entitlement complex is widespread nowadays?

Has anyone been fired for spouting all the lies from the White House podium? Biden and others lie all the time with no consequences. Has Attorney General Garland or anyone been fired for not prosecuting Hunter Biden and all the violent criminals from the riots of 2020? Has anyone been fired for lying about most Americans being racist? We need to clean house at the DOJ and FBI.

Has anyone been fired for allowing the CCP folks at TikTok to harm and harvest the private information of many Americans? At least two children died during 2021 while participating in the blackout challenge on TikTok, where the people choke themselves until they pass out. China-based ByteDance owns TikTok.

"TikTok is China's digital fentanyl," said FCC Commissioner Brendan Carr. They show a very different version of this platform in China to protect their kids from filth and stupidity.

Has any Democrat been fired for obeying their socialist party leaders over our sacred constitution? Did anyone quit for helping the social media owners censor conservative Christians daily? Did anyone get fired for leaking top-secret information about conservatives? Did any IRS employee get fired for hurting Tea Party people? Did anyone at the Supreme Court get fired for leaking the draft decision about returning the abortion issue to the states and the people where it belongs? Most Democrats want abortion up to and after birth. They are the party of destruction, envy, and hate.

Did anyone at the Pentagon face the axe for making soldiers shower with transgender people? Perhaps creepy Joe refuses to fire anyone because he realizes that he should have been fired many years ago, and if he sucks at his job, he has no moral authority to fire others who suck at theirs.

Why did Biden, Fauci, and many others keep their jobs while hurting so many people with their destructive lockdowns? Why did nobody go to jail for pushing faulty vaccines and masks, ignoring natural immunity, and preventing millions from getting elective or preventive surgery? Did anyone get fired for forcing millions of homeowners and apartment owners to allow deadbeats to live in their real estate for free? All this is clearly unconstitutional, and the judges need to wake up and work harder.

Did anyone at the Federal Reserve Bank or the Treasury Department get fired for saying that inflation is transitory, doing nothing, and refusing to raise interest rates until inflation was out of control at a forty-year high? Think Jerome Powell or Janet Yellen. They are part of the problem for printing too much money in 2020. That causes inflation like overspending. We have too many fools at the Federal Reserve Bank. May we have some layoffs to make America great again?

They cheered during 2021 when the Biden gang was borrowing and spending their way to forty-year-high inflation. They said the inflation was temporary over and over for months. They were wrong again. They are wrong most of the time. We could just hit the gong if they were on the *Gong Show*. I loved that TV show in 1976. Chuck Barris and gang would bang the gong if the amateur performer was untalented. Was anyone fired for keeping our Southern border wide open with Mexican/Chinese drugs killing over 100,000 Americans annually? Has anyone been punished for allowing illegal aliens to kill and injure so many Americans? This corrupt and incompetent man named Biden should not be allowed to walk anywhere near the White House. The orange jumpsuit is the perfect outfit for this lazy, immoral, and dumb person.

Speaking of orange jumpsuits, anyone who promotes discrimination in girl-women sports must be punished. The Democrats are waging a war on women by allowing boys and men to compete with females. Conservative and Christians love strong women.

The Persian king Xerxes agreed with us and had an awesome naval commander who just happened to be a woman. The king said, "My men have become women and my women men." He encouraged his men to step up and work harder to be as good as the female commander Artemisia I of Caria. She led the Persians in the destruction of the Greek navy in 480 BC.

We must get back to limited government. Just look at the mission creep and strategic incompetence of the Biden gang in Afghanistan, China, and elsewhere. These folks are obsessed with power, money, and race and are so ignorant about our constitution and actually running a government. Many people inside and outside America are stunned by the stupidity and immorality of the Biden gang and so many state government people such as the Wolf regime in Pennsylvania.

The executive branch led by Wolf and the Pennsylvania Supreme Court members ran an illegal election in 2020 by ignoring the US and Pennsylvania constitutions. The legislature has control over elections and not the other branches as per the constitutions. The founders knew that the people's representatives should rule the elections and not corrupt government employees.

The US Supreme Court will hear a case about ensuring that only the state legislatures control elections. This should prevent immoral state executive and judicial branch folks from changing election laws and stealing elections as they did in 2020. When will these people be punished? Trump won that election.

Here is the 2020 election in approximate numbers: 176 million registered voters, 118 million actually voted. The corrupt government folks say Trump got 73 million votes. That leaves 45 million for idiot Biden. The Democrats say Joe got 81 million votes. That is impossible, except for communists. How many FBI agents worked to elect creepy Joe with illegal tactics? Arrest all the cheaters!

We need a secret weapon to take back our country from socialist fools. The Olympic runners found their secret weapon to double the number of women running the five-thousand-meter race in under fifteen minutes and ten seconds in recent years. They found the awesome racing spike shoe, and the rest is history. Dave Xu is the secret weapon for the conservative Christians in taking back our country. Send that joker to the US Senate, and all will be well with the world. He could wear sandals and still improve the DC swamp.

"Civilizations die from suicide and not murder," Arnold Toynbee explained. Traitors and fools within nations destroy them most of the time. I want to destroy the deep-state and socialist politicians in America and get us back on track for dog-eat-dog capitalism. That made America great and not absurd government programs.

Viktor Orban, Hungary's prime minister, has done a lot of good in this world. He and his team closed their border in 2015 to stop illegal aliens from invading. Creepy Joe should follow his lead here in the USA. Obama and other fools criticized Orban for protecting his people from criminals.

He also stopped the promotion of the gay and trans lifestyle. It is one thing to have equal rights and quite another to promote a high-risk lifestyle that violates the Bible. The Obama gang went berserk on that one. The ultimate slap in the face is to George Soros who funded part of Orban's college tuition. Is that great?

DeSantis reminds me of Orban. He is destroying the woke corporate managers down in Florida every day. He stripped Walt Disney World of its sweetheart tax avoidance scheme and promotes the nuclear Christian family. Florida has some of the least generous welfare and unemployment benefits of the fifty states. We need more God, Jesus, and the Bible. Tough love is the best approach to those in need.

"Give a man a fish and you have fed him once. Teach him how to fish and you have fed him for a lifetime." We could save a lot on welfare if we followed this proverb.

Fetterman, Shapiro, and other Democrats are soft on crime and caused a 48 percent increase in homicides in Pennsylvania in the last two years. Instead of arresting and punishing criminals, they focus on destroying our right to defend ourselves.

These Democrats want reg flag laws to take guns away illegally. They must be destroyed at the polls and arrested if they violate our constitution. Our constitution ensures the right to carry at any time. This applies between states also. Fetterman has earned an F from the NRA for being a socialist commie of the worst kind. Mastriano, DelRosso, and Oz would help us arrest the criminals and keep our guns to keep America safe and great.

"I make $20 per hour and did not miss a day during the dumb lockdowns. I get so mad at so many people soaking up the welfare and doing nothing while I am out working my butt off every day. The younger generation is a lazy joke. They cannot perform the simplest of tasks at work. I am voting Republican from now on," said the garage door installer. I could hear the frustration and anger in his voice. He joined a We the People group after Biden stole the election in 2020.

I would love to represent hard workers in the US Senate. The greedy big businessmen and corrupt socialist politicians forgot about these good Americans decades ago. BlackRock and other huge investors push climate change and Environmental, Social, and Governance (ESG) investing when they should focus on the stockholders. The stockholders own the business, hire managers, employ good workers, and make great goods and services. That is the American capitalist model.

ESG fools want to tax the heck out of business owners and workers and give massive welfare to lazy and ignorant Americans in the Democrat Party. They do not care about the Republicans, conservatives, or Christians. George Washington and John Adams warned us about big business and big government getting in bed together.

Instead of dog-eat-dog capitalism, which made America great, you have fools like Larry Fink at BlackRock in charge of $8.5 trillion of investors' money hanging with socialist Democrats and pushing their stupid communist ideas. This idiot Fink said in 2020 that his asset managers would "place sustainability at the center of our investment approach."

Is this dumb statement from Al Gore or Larry Fink? It is hard to tell the difference. Is he a talking head for lazy community organizers like Obama who covet money made by business owners and workers? What climate models and advice is he pushing? Does he want a corrupt socialist-communist group dictatorship run by his Democrat friends?

You be the judge and invest your money with the socialists or the capitalists such as Vivek Ramaswamy. Vivek started Strive Asset

Management "to represent everyday citizens in the American economy by leading companies to focus on excellence over politics."

The Democrat Party is controlled by sick, rich, socialist communists. We must get normal, common people like me into government before it is too late. They are racing for a group communist dictatorship as we see in China. Join a We The People group and get involved now to settle this peacefully at the polls. Redneck David Xu is your man.

We were waiting in line at a restaurant self-serve window, and a man and three little boys were in line. All of a sudden, the man said, "Why did you do that? Why would you do that? This is my brand-new hoodie!" the man said to one of the little boys.

The boy had ice cream and chocolate syrup all over his face and wiped his mouth on his father's hoodie. The poor little starving man did not have a napkin. The boy shrugged off the criticism and continued devouring the hot fudge Sunday.

There was no thought or time for remorse. The ice cream was melting. It may have been a huge banana split. I remember those on many hot summer nights in Apopka, Florida.

Have you seen politicians act like this boy? The socialists and their media friends just move on and never talk about all their mistakes and scandals. The corrupt politician just moves on with no learning, apology, or remorse for damaging our capitalistic America and hardworking conservatives and Christians. Think Obama, Biden, and Harris. They actually tried to get The Little Sisters of the Poor to pay for contraception for young women who enjoyed having sex all the time.

Do you remember when Trump stopped the absurd eight-thousand-mile fiber optic cable from California to Hong Kong in 2017? The communists at Google and Facebook hooked up to lay this cable so they could collaborate directly with the Chinese communists. We must follow President Trump's lead and destroy this communist cancer before they destroy our capitalistic and free America.

I have thanked God many times for not being addicted to gambling. Casinos are monuments to gambling idiots. The people I have

known who were addicted were all bailed out by their parents and/
or filed for bankruptcy.

We noticed a website with odds for political races one day. They
had me at 150/1 to win the Republican primary for US Senate. I was
thrilled with the odds because I remembered that Louis Oosthuizen
won the British Open at 200/1 odds in 2010. Anything is possible. I
am glad that I did not take the bet on that redneck.

*Odds to win the Republican primary for 2022 US Senate election
in Pennsylvania (www.us-bookies.com) (parentheses indicate odds from
December 6, 2021):*

- Dr. Mehmet Oz: 8/5 (17/10)
- David McCormick: 17/10 (5/4)
- Jeff Bartos: 9/2 (6/1)
- Carla Sands: 19/2 (20/1)
- Kathy Barnette: 50/1
- Everett Stern: 50/1 (100/1)
- John Debellis: 100/1
- Sean Gale: 100/1
- James Edward Hayes: 100/1
- Bobby Jeffries: 100/1
- Ronald Johnson: 100/1
- Richard Mulholland: 100/1
- Max Richardson: 100/1
- Martin Rosenfeld: 100/1
- David Xu: 150/1
- Craig Snyder: 150/1

The Bookie website provides this interesting disclaimer. I wondered if betting on political races is legal in America. The odds posted
in this article are for illustrative purposes only as wagering on such
props is not currently legal in any US state. The data was based on
betting markets offered by UK/European/worldwide operators regulated in jurisdictions where wagering on these props is legal.

My goals for the campaign are the following: get on the primary ballot, win the primary, win the general election, educate vot-

ers, meet nice conservatives and Christians throughout the state, expose Democrats to conservative views, get Democrats to switch to the Republican Party, get new material for another book, move the political conversation to the right, move current politicians to the right, remove Democrats and RINOs from government, learn about the political process and elections, find and help candidates for office, fund political action committees, put smiles on faces, and have fun with Nancy, family, and friends.

What is this obsession with race from the Democrats? The federal government idiots demanded that Hillsdale College count students by race and the college leaders refused and stopped taking federal tax money. Nancy and I love this college and donate money to it. We believe in equal rights and ignore race in dealing with folks. Normal Americans could care less about your race. Racism is a minor problem in the United States.

"Our oldest building was dedicated this Fourth of July with the claim that ignorance was the seed of slavery and that Hillsdale College would work to eliminate ignorance in the name of freedom," Hillsdale College President Larry Arnn said in the *Wall Street Journal*. What a concept. That school believes in the meritocracy. Everything should be based on demonstrated ability. Can we please take race off the census form now? Racism sucks!

I like the funny politicians. I love the funny preachers. There was a hilarious country preacher on a radio station in Danville, Virginia, back in the 1980s. A distraught guy called in one night.

"Preacher, man, I am having a hard time. I lost my job, owe a lot of money for the car, furniture, credit cards, and the house. The wife left with another younger dude, and I am filing for bankruptcy. Can you say a prayer for me?" the sad caller said.

"Of course, we will pray for you and your family, my son. But first let us pray for your creditors," the preacher responded.

We are starved for good news. So here it is. Fewer singles in the USA are mostly interested in looks since the pandemic ended. I guess there is hope for ugly people. Many folks were isolated during the dumb lockdowns and now less picky about how attractive their mate is.

Now that is good news for sure. Let the hookups begin. Can we turn down those lights in the restaurants and bars? My brother Al always said, "All cats are gray in the dark." Some folks just look better in dim lighting. Fetterman comes to mind.

"I wish the climate change folks would calm down with all the soybean stuff. A squirrel chewed through the gas line in my Lexus last week. It was no problem before they started making fuel lines with soybeans. The squirrels love it," the voter complained to me.

This good man keeps his cars outside in rural America, and it was fine when fuel lines were made from petroleum products. The squirrels did not like the taste of that stuff. Did you see the new thermostat that has a scowling face of Greta Thunberg when you turn up your heat? That ugly bitter site will make you want to save some energy.

The imbeciles in Pearl Jam put this unstable child in a music video as a fortune teller. Their songs suck nowadays. Perhaps they should focus on music and not fake climate change and communism.

Riley Gaines was a top swimmer for the University of Kentucky and swam against Lia Thomas. They tied, and the dumb officials gave the trophy to the man competing against women. We must stop this stupidity now. I could have racked up many trophies in high school if I had identified as a girl. My trophy shelf is empty, and that is so sad.

This man was ranked below five hundred when competing against fellow males, and now he has a national title while competing against true and strong women. The trophies should be taken away from this cheater, and the idiots in charge should be punished.

Steve McQueen would never allow this. He was full of sperm and always ready for any possible dating or erotic action. Did you see him in "Le Mans"? He was a pallbearer at Bruce Lee's funeral. Now that is extremely manly. The King of Cool knew that men belonged with women the day he was born (1930) until the day he died in Mexico (1980).

Perhaps we need a genital check before the races. What is going on in this great country? Why are so many people stupid and immoral? Is TikTok that powerful? Does TikTok make smart folks dumb? Are dumb folks somehow made dumber by TikTok? AOC has a weak mind and is a bad role model. This is not a culture war. Rednecks call it a war against stupidity.

I would do everything in my power to cut government spending from the US Senate. Americans enjoy a higher standard of living than most other people due to several factors. We pay less tax. We work harder. We have less regulation and fewer government idiots (employees). We have less welfare. The Democrats are trying to change all that.

The average house in America is over 2,200 square feet and only 1,200 in Germany. Britain's average house is a mere 810 square feet. Do you want these tiny homes and hotel rooms so corrupt politicians can live like kings? Look how Obama and Biden live. We must wake up all Americans to the fact that most Democrats want socialism or communism with massive welfare paid for by hardworking and awesome Americans.

The amount of money the US politicians confiscate from taxpayers equals about 34 percent of GDP here while the European parasites take in from taxes an amount that equals 50 percent of their GDP. The Europeans keep much less of their money after paying for all the welfare and unnecessary government programs and overpaid union employees.

Part of their problem is that the taxpayers also have to pay for the European Union (EU) ridiculous operations also. Have you seen their beautiful and massive headquarters in Brussels, Belgium? Never forget that the Belgians were evil and cruel to the African people during the 1800 and 1900s with their colonies. The greedy Europeans exploited the poor people for resources and money. Many indigenous people were injured or killed making stuff for King Leopold II and the Europeans back in the day.

Leopold had an awesome beard but was a nasty and horny fool. He spent much of his time in France with teenage girlfriends…when he was sixty-five years old. Millions of innocent people in the Congo died harvesting rubber for the stupid king and his subjects. The king's men held many African women and girls hostage until their husbands and fathers produced some rubber. He was the Joe Biden of his time.

Many view the Belgians as the cruelest colonizers. Many of the EU fools talk themselves up with climate change nonsense and fake racism talk now to try to look virtuous. How much damage do they inflict on our planet by flying around acting like royalty? They remind me of John Kerry. He really needs some work done on his ugly face. That is a face only a mother could love.

The EU is a government that is above the other twenty-seven government operations. These bloated operations push socialism and communism 24/7. Most uniparty fools in America have grown our federal government so big that they think they have a shot at socialism or communism here. We must stop them.

The commies in Europe would love a communist USA. There is a big corruption scandal going on now in the EU. Some folks took some bribes. Does that surprise you? The British were smart to leave this crap back in 2020.

CHAPTER 3

THE LEARNING REDNECK

MAY THROUGH JULY 2021

> The big lesson in life, baby, is never
> be scared of anyone or anything.
> —Frank Sinatra

The sixty-year-old chubby Italian man gets out of the brand-new Mercedes 580 sedan outside the sports bar. He wears a dark-blue blazer, tan chinos, and small brown suede shoes. The blazer is expensive and high quality but too small for the man. His turtleneck shirt is purple with several gold chains hanging down in front. Several large rings adorn his manicured and sun-tanned hands.

Enzo has requested a meeting with the county GOP chairman to discuss the upcoming primary. He informs the local party leader that he works with the state leadership, but you will not see his name on any organizational chart or official documents.

"Can you support these candidates?" Enzo asks the local chairman. He hands the chairman a chart with the names of four candidates on it.

"Yes, as a matter of fact, we already do. Those are the best Republicans we have here," the chairman explains. He is relieved that the request is an easy one to accommodate.

"That is great. Let us destroy these Democrats and RINOs. I better hit the road. I work in the family business, and it is tough duty for sure," Enzo says as he is leaving the bar.

What he does not say is that he is a member of a mafia family. They have their favorite candidates and will lobby anyone for support. The chairman knew who he was before the meeting and was very nervous about dealing with the mob. The state GOP folks helped arrange the meeting. He is so thankful that their interests are aligned and hopes that he never sees another mobster as long as he lives.

The band Chicago was struggling to come up with more hits many years ago. A record label guy told them that if they got rid of the horn section, he would sign them for another record deal. The band told him where to go and refused.

The Chicago tale reminds me of the awesome United States of America. An America without limited government run by Christians and conservatives is not America. We must replace the corrupt folks in DC with Christians and conservatives who want to cut back government to enhance our freedom. The atheists and other fools must go.

We have too many quasi-government operations such as the Federal Reserve Bank and the Red Cross. Both are public-private operations and run by people who love huge, corrupt government. They will not bite the hand that feeds them.

I remember going to Red Cross meetings for General Pace when I was on the Joint Staff in 2006. President Bush appointed Pace to the board, and he thought it was a waste of his time and sent flunkies like me to the meetings. The swamp rats in DC love wasteful programs paid for by the hardworking citizens. The rats enjoy many free trips around the world on the taxpayers' dime. The Red Cross folks caused a scandal by being dirty and infecting people with dirty blood. The deep-state and corrupt media folks tried to cover it up. I heard the details in those meetings. It was a waste of this LTC's time to sit through those gabfests in the paperclip building next to the Pentagon.

I think back to college and the story of Pygmalion when I hear about our entitled youth. Even Eric Clapton complains about how entitled our youth are these days. I put the blame on corrupt politicians for teaching kids to accept free stuff in exchange for votes.

Pygmalion was a sculptor who fell in love with a statue he had created. It is a myth, but I bet some drunken fool really did this at some point in history. It sounds like something Vincent van Gogh would do. This idiot drank and smoked heavily, avoided eating meat, and cut off his ear and gave it to a prostitute in 1888. But he was a fantastic painter. What a man.

My comparison is that if we continue to treat our youth as stupid, entitled, and lazy, they will continue to act like that, and that will be the end of our capitalistic and awesome America.

I propose to get back to the 1970s and light a fire under the butt of every American youth. We had to work to earn money to buy music, cars, and meals. If you were lazy, your chance of a date on Saturday night was low. We worked hard to play hard and bought into the American dream. We need to get back to that today.

I wonder what type of statue Pocahontas would create and fall in love with. Elizabeth Warren lied and said she was an American Indian to get jobs, so I bet she would sculpt someone like Chief Sitting Bull for her lover. Perhaps I would suggest that she change the name to Chief Shitting Bull to match this embarrassing senator from Massachusetts. The real Pocahontas lived in Virginia, where I grew up.

You should really stop reading this mediocre book and get a copy of the classic *Redneck Dystopia* by David Xu. That guy is an outstanding writer. He is very manly. It is a fictional tale about a brutal socialist America after Pocahontas cheats and prevails over Trump during the 2020 election. She would have been worse than Biden.

A lady asked me about running for office again if I went down in flames. I informed her that facing so much rejection and hostility from the voters had scared me straight and that this would be my first and only campaign for anything. The voters treated me like a used car salesman or perhaps a corrupt politician. I told her about being in high school and doing dumb and illegal things. Our mother had the bright idea to scare us straight after we were caught stealing gas for our car.

The government folks had a program just for juvenile delinquents such as my brother Tommy and me. The program was entitled Scared Straight. It involved taking a prison van from Danville, Virginia, to a dirty state prison in Richmond, Virginia. A repeat offender started a fight with Tommy on the way, and the driver had to stop on the highway to break it up.

The guards searched us at the prison. I guess it was a simulated booking situation. We walked down the main area in the prison with the prisoners doing their cat calls. They said things like "New meat. Isn't she cute? I want some of that. What is your name, little girl?" I wondered if this was a normal day or they behaved like normal folks usually.

We had long hair, and some of the prisoners seemed to enjoy that look. A guard told us how popular we would be in prison. We straightened up after one day at this horrible prison with the criminals. Thank God we left at four in the afternoon and did not spend the night.

We saw many tattoos and rotten teeth. They really seemed to enjoy yelling at us from their cells. I really hoped that nobody would get parole ever. We were so glad to get the heck out of that sick place and get back to a normal life in free America. I have never spent the night in jail. I think this stunt worked.

Nowadays we have to defeat the socialists and communists in our colleges pushing ignorant students to join antifa and BLM. These professors and students are scheming against our sweet constitution and laws to move the country to socialism.

I remember reading Mark Levin's book *American Marxism* and "how the core elements of Marxist ideology are now pervasive in American society and culture for our schools, the press, and corporations, to Hollywood, the Democrat Party, and the Biden presidency. This movement is often cloaked in deceptive labels such as progressivism, democratic socialism, social activism, or community activism."

Many of the antifa and BLM fools harvested illegal ballots during our 2020 election and helped install Biden and gang. We must stop the brainwashing at our colleges and get back to learning. Anyone pushing socialism or communism must be fired and incarcerated. Our constitution requires that the federal government ensure that all fifty states have a republican form of government. This is opinion.

"The problem in 2020, a domestic totalitarian movement intentionally threw America's elections into chaos, using the COVID crisis as cover. Today, anti-American organizations, activists, attorneys, lawmakers, and bureaucrats are working together to exploit the already weakened state of our elections. This is organized crime," according to True the Vote.

Biden reminded me of Prince Charles in the United Kingdom. During the campaign, Biden stayed in his basement just barely existing. Charles wakes up each day realizing that to get the ultimate prize, all he has to do is stay alive. The Biden gang knew about the elaborate cheating being planned and barely campaigned. Does Charles have horse teeth and elephant ears? It is unbelievable that Diana would overlook both for the big bucks. Diana could have done much better, but she was whiny.

It was obvious during December 2020 and is definitely obvious now that Trump won that election. He said that when a criminal steals diamonds from the jewelry store and is caught, he does not get to keep the diamonds. The Democrats planned and executed the biggest election cheating operation in the history of the world. The cheaters must go to jail now. Their voting machines are in over three thousand counties, and many were connected to the internet, thereby violating many election laws. Thousands of mules in different states stuffed ballot boxes in the middle of the night with illegal ballots. Let us decertify now and get back to the constitution, laws, and capitalism. Some Democrats must go to jail for election cheating.

Fifty-one former government idiots said the evidence of crimes showcased in Hunter's laptop was Russian disinformation during October 2020. They and many others helped a corrupt, lazy, old, and/or stupid man become president. Good job, Democrats.

"One of the reasons we know the 2020 election was illegitimate is that Joe Biden's results had no down-ballot success, a statistical improbability because of what we know about political science, behavior psychology, and down-ballot participation rates. In fact, not one House Republican incumbent lost. House Republicans actually gained fourteen seats in 2020," said Ali Alexander of the Gateway Pundit.

America will get back on track. Most American citizens are Christian and work hard. I like the following prayer in the devotional My Daily Bread: "Almighty Father, thank you for the loving-kindness you have shown me through your Son, Jesus Christ. Please help me to reflect your love in even the smallest things I do today."

I think about my grandfather and what he would think about today's politicians. He was a Democrat, kind of like JFK. Poppy said to me, "The wise man plans for generations. The fool plans for Saturday night." He explained that I must work hard and make a lot of money and then plan for retirement. Idiots do not care about any of that.

He was a millionaire from Southern Virginia and was full of nuggets for this juvenile delinquent. He greeted me at his door late one night while I was staying with him during the summer college break. I was halfway drunk and lost my door key to his huge house. He told me, "Davey, there is a snake in that bottle." Then he turned away and went back to bed in his slippers and one-piece night suit and cap.

I thank God for firm, conservative, and Christian people like him to help the youth learn right from wrong and smart actions from stupidity. Albert and Glenn Cox taught me so much about how to be a successful person. They read the Bible to us and explained the rules and boundaries in that wonderful book. They taught us how Jesus Christ forgives anyone and that nobody is perfect.

His favorite wall hanging in his house was a black-and-white drawing of a bum sitting on the curb reading the *Wall Street Journal*. The character looked very content and intelligent. His clothes were old and worn with holes. Dr Weaver at JMU made us read the *WSJ* every day and gave a quiz on it once per week. Most of the MBA students failed, but not me. I have read it every day since 1990 and love it.

Poppy used to eat the eyeballs out of lobster boiling just to freak us out. He would laugh so hard when we noticed what he was putting into his mouth. MaMa would tell him to stop doing dumb stuff and get out of the kitchen. I remember enjoying that succulent lobster with them and dipping it in melted butter. Those were good times for this broke college student.

MaMa, my grandmother, almost had a stroke the time I put *at* at the end of a sentence. I think I said, "Where do you shop at?"

She said, "Never put *at* at the end of a sentence. It is wrong and sounds horrible." Boy was she right about that one. She was a stickler for proper English and always pushed me to be a better person.

She took me shopping for my first business suit. I needed one for an interview and had no money. She was the sweetest person I have ever known. I remember paying car insurance, food, and rent and having nothing left over and realizing that I must work harder to have a great life and plan for retirement.

We must teach our youth these things and help them be successful. Many union teachers are lazy and ignorant on so many topics. They teach our kids that many Americans are racist, and that is a big lie. Racism is a minor problem in the USA, and most people know that. The socialist Democrats will be thrown out of government soon. Our faith is in God, Jesus, the Bible, and constitution. Life is too short to put up with lazy, union fools soaking up our tax money and doing nothing constructive or good.

Forty-five percent of local government employees are in a union now (about 30 percent of all government workers). Let us reduce that to zero soon as it was back in the 1940s. These folks are ruining the American dream for young and old alike.

The myopic politicians set a terrible example for our youth. They only think about the next election and never about the long-term financial and spiritual health of the United States of America. This Christian society is the most successful of all time. It is based on the values and principles in the Bible and constitution. We must get rid of the corrupt and immoral fools in government and teach our youth right from wrong.

I will end this chapter now due to my ruminations about an old and sweet college professor who advised me, "Sometimes less is more." He corrected me after I submitted a long and boring paper covering a business topic for my MBA. I thought it was great, but he lost interest pretty fast with the mediocre writing. I carry that pain with pride.

I am thinking of starting the American kleptocracy tour based on a current tour offered in London. Tourists ride in buses with a tour guide describing mansions and other property of criminals or alleged criminals from other lands who raided their nation's treasury to live their best life.

It is no secret that corruption abounds in Russia, China, Nigeria, America, and many other countries. We could ride by the mansions of politicians who got rich in or after they served in government, such as Obama, Clinton, Biden, Schumer, Pelosi, Bush, Harris, McConnell, etc.

I met a guy at an Arby's one day while in the parking lot stretching and walking a bit before the ride home on my Hog. A large man with a long white beard was studying my 2013 Harley Breakout from every angle. I approached him and asked if he had a Harley. He said he used to have a Yamaha and loved it but never bought a Harley.

He wore an NRA baseball cap, and I gave him my campaign very conservative business card. He scanned it and quizzed me a bit.

"Let me ask you this. Should there be any limit on the Second Amendment?" he inquired.

"Very, very little. Perhaps a background check. There should not be hardly any limits on our right to bear arms in my humble opinion," I answered.

He liked that answer and said that I have his vote. Our conversation immediately returned to cars and motorcycles. Then he launched into a story of his brand-new 1972 Plymouth Barracuda. The fat rear tire on my bike reminded him of the hot rod cars of our youth. Many of them had fat rear tires and skinny front tires. We agreed that this is an awesome setup for a car or motorcycle. He loved all the chrome on the bike and was dumbfounded by the way most younger riders prefer black wheels and bikes.

He said he did a long burnout on this way home from a tire shop in 1973 and ended up with two flat rear tires. A mechanic had just replaced the original tires and put too much soap or water between the tire and the wheel. When he dogged the car and spun the tires like crazy upon leaving the shop, the tires broke the seal with the wheels. Ever since this experience, he waits a couple weeks after a tire change to do burnouts. He has not had a flat since 1973.

As I put on my helmet and jacket to ride my beautiful Hog home after a good chat with the NRA guy, I think back to my childhood days in Florida. We lived in Apopka, Florida, from 1965 until 1975. I remember watching the surfers at New Smyrna Beach.

It occurred to me that I am like the surfer who just cannot catch a wave. I keep meeting good patriots and handing out campaign flyers or pamphlets and business cards, but the emails and support are just not coming in. I am not catching fire. I will keep trying to catch that wave for the two thousand signatures to get on the GOP ballot for May 2022. I am a military man, and perhaps politics is not for me. Time will tell, and I really could go either way. I will stay faithful and strong with God, Jesus, and the Bible.

I drift back to riding or trying to ride the cheap, short Styrofoam surfboard in Florida my mother bought me. It could only be used in shallow water, and it hurt to hit the hard sand. I dreamed of somehow buying a real, huge, fiberglass surfboard one day to impress the chicks.

We need to cut the welfare to the bone. Welfare to the bottom 20 percent of earners increased by 269 percent from 1967 to 2017. Middle income earners' wages increased by only 154 percent over the same time period. This is why so many hard workers are upset with Democrats showering welfare for votes and why so many blue-collar workers voted for Trump twice.

Many low- and middle-income people live in the same neighborhoods. The hard workers see the lazy and drug idiots just hanging out on the porch while they are returning from working all day like a normal person. Welfare should be targeted and only short-term.

There should be no welfare for lazy folks. Hard work is the American way.

Fetterman loves drug addicts and dealers. He looks like a clown with the dirty hoodie. He is a sad clown. He is a clown who is not funny or bright. He has an elephant butt, but I digress. All he needs is the big red nose and long clown shoes. This is opinion.

That is really how Fetterman should campaign with his socialist-commie, everything-is-free welfare platform. It is a clown show. He blames guns for violence and not the fools pulling the triggers. The clown actually has dates of gun violence tattooed on his arm.

I am tired of writing about all the bad news. Are you ready for some more good news? How about just the top ten? Some people go through their entire lives being ugly and dumb because nobody ever tells them. It is so sad, but I do not have that problem anymore. The voters told me while campaigning for US Senate over and over that I am ugly and dumb. Many conservative and Christians have given up. Never give up. This is our country. (1) Government debt to GDP: Japan, 238 percent with xenophobic people, no fossil fuels, aging population, corrupt business and government folks, many atheists. Venezuela, 214 percent; Greece, 174 percent; Italy, 133 percent; USA, 106 percent or $26 trillion public debt to $23 trillion 2021 GDP. If the US behaved like drunken Japanese politicians with no fossil fuels, the public government debt could rise to $55 trillion (we could borrow $29 trillion more). The US government does not need to repay all that debt, but we do have to pay interest every year on it ($412 billion in 2021). (2) Many judges are overturning or blocking Democrat stupidity such as the open border, fake racism, fake climate change, and LGBTQ rules and laws. Jeff Foxworthy, you might be a redneck if you do not know what that means. (3) Most Americans are awake now. Many blacks, Hispanics, Dems, and independents have switched to the Republican Party in the last year. We moved some of them during the Senate campaign. (4) Many governors and mayors like DeSantis are standing up for Christians and conservatives. Life is good outside the corrupt and dirty Democrat-run cities like Philadelphia. (5) Foreigners still love the US dollar, and it has not been backed up by gold since 1971. The DC folks borrowed and spent like drunken sailors and could not back up all the US dollars with gold. (6) Most business transactions around the world in two hundred countries are in the USD and the English language. That is good for us. (7) Most Americans are Christian and work hard. (8) From my experience at the Pentagon and speaking with active soldiers, 80 percent will stand with us and our constitution if this nation devolves into another civil war. (9) Trump and his team exposed so may swamp rats in DC and beyond. (10) We will have a big red wave in November 2022!

We need more honest and competent people in government. We need to remove incompetent and immoral people like Anthony Fauci. Perhaps it was his great grandfather in charge of disease in 1898 during the Spanish-American War. Perhaps he has bad genes (the dumb gene). The US mobilized over 200,000 soldiers to end Spain's brutal colonial rule of Cuba, Puerto Rico, and the Philippines.

The United States had only 385 combat deaths and 2,565 deaths from disease. The idiots in charge had the soldiers living in filth and feces that led to typhoid fever and other diseases. They did not have clean water, or a cure, or antibiotics, so they just had to hydrate and try not to die before the fever broke.

It appears that Fauci and gang hurt and/or killed many people playing politics. They tried to make Trump look bad. They got many people to give up their freedom voluntarily with lies and exaggerations about the CCP virus. Fauci should get down on his knees every night and thank his union bosses for protecting him for over thirty years from being fired for saying and doing dumb things. Those union dues really paid off. It is almost impossible to fire bad employees in government. We need a grand jury for Fauci and friends.

Many sick politicians took advantage to move us toward socialism and communism. Whitmer, Wolf, Cuomo, Murphy, and others acted like Barney Fife on *The Andy Griffith Show* enjoying and abusing their power. They counted hundreds of thousands of illegal ballots for Biden and Harris. These children should never be in positions of power. We must stop them now. We must have indictments and impeachments. Our sacred constitution will be enforced soon. This is opinion.

They say pigs are smart. Rolling around in the mud does not help support their smart reputation. Are California politicians smart? Kamala Harris, Nancy Pelosi, and Gavin Newsom prove that the answer is definitely no. Someone said that all the hair gel is affecting Gavin's brain function.

The one-party state with communist media and Hollywood is known for group think and horrible policies and laws. Many successful people are moving out of the state and to Republican-run states like Texas and Florida.

The California politicians are trying to get the other forty-nine states to raise pigs a certain way. They want each pig to have a two-bedroom condo with room service or something like that. Under 2 percent of pigs in the United States are raised in California. Let us ignore the communist idiots in California.

Why are these dumb socialist people so confident and arrogant? I hope the Supreme Court smacks down the California folks on this one in their lawsuit. One thing is for sure. California would be much better off if pigs ran the place rather than unintelligent human beings. The hog farmers should just refuse to ship any pork chops to California if they will not yield to common sense and the constitution.

You know you have an education problem when "kidults" are buying over 14 percent of the toys sold in America. These are people eighteen and up who play with toys. Perhaps they should be working longer hours and not playing with toys so much. Are these the same people with purple hair calling Republicans names all the time instead of engaging in debate about the size and roll of government? Do these toy buyers include the childlike Facebook owner and employees who play in their online metaverse all day long?

We have good billionaires and bad. David Green started Hobby Lobby and is a great American. He promotes God, Jesus, and the Bible and just gave away his successful business. Zuckerberg uses his business to censor conservatives and Christians, and Green uses his business to improve mankind.

Green won a court battle at the US Supreme Court against Obama and his immoral friends who tried to get Hobby Lobby to pay for abortion-related drugs for employees under Obamacare. The court found that the Religious Freedom and Restoration Act violated the constitution in 2014.

This decision was good, but the judges should have thrown out the entire Obamacare welfare and taxation scheme. It is clearly unconstitutional to make someone buy insurance or force others to pay for someone's health care. Most welfare is unconstitutional and really dumb because it makes people lazy.

David Green was so right in 2016 when he advised others to vote for Donald Trump. He knew as we did that the Democrat Party is controlled by sick and ignorant partisans. Many Christians did not trust Trump to be a good conservative. We suffer so much now by allowing the Biden gang to control politics. One of the CCP fools said that no country will allow people who hate their country to control politics. He is evil but spot on for this statement.

Do you still think the 2020 election was safe and secure or the way the immoral, communist, Democrat, media, big-tech, and government intelligence folks spin it? Special Counsel Michael Gableman found rampant fraud and abuse occurred statewide in Wisconsin. He found in most of the ninety nursing homes that sick employees and others illegally assisted and probably forged many, many ballots to favor Biden and the corrupt Democrats.

Trump and other Republicans won their elections, but the Democrats committed many felonies and were declared winners by the fake media. They will burn in hell for this. The GOP folks must investigate and punish people for this.

Preying on dementia patients is so evil as to not be believable. Many Democrats view politics as a religion, and they will die for their stupid beliefs. They must go to jail. Government employees are supposed to protect the elderly, and they victimized them to help select creepy Joe.

That very ugly man Rachel Levine and Andrew Cuomo did the same thing, but the first idiot got promoted, and the second one was fired. They both pushed old folks with the CCP virus into nursing homes to infect others. Many of these innocent people suffered or died. Levine took his mother out of a nursing home and put her in a luxury hotel. He said the hospitals would be full, but during May 2020, only 7 percent of Pennsylvania's hospital beds were occupied by virus patients. Wolf, Fetterman, Shapiro, Levine, and many others should face a grand jury and/or be punished. This is opinion.

"Enormous effort and elaborate planning are required to waste this much money in DC. Big government can do nothing right," said P. J. O'Rourke. It is said that all people who love big, corrupt, social-ist, communist government have a negative IQ. What do you think? Have they read the tragic history of socialism and/or communism?

The Democrats are terrible at running anything and only make excuses for their many failures. Everyone in America gets their shot to learn, work hard, and be successful. Spare me the nonsense about the many excuses for laziness, stupidity, and/or failure. We need more God, Jesus, the Bible, tough love, and limited government.

It is shocking how many Democrats and RINOs are immoral and have no problem lying all the time. They are a terrible example for our youth. The Trump campaign challenged 8,329 absentee and mail-in ballots in 2020 in Philadelphia County, Pennsylvania, that were missing information on the envelopes. Pennsylvania law states clearly that the date and signature must be on the envelope.

The immoral folks on the Pennsylvania Supreme Court (mostly Democrats) ruled that the illegal ballots could be counted mostly for Biden based on the CCP virus and other irrelevant factors. Why are liars allowed to serve in our government? Should liars be fired and punished? Maybe it is just me. We need one of those elderly and strict Catholic teachers from the old days to rap the hands of the liars and cheaters and put them in the corner of the room (jail).

We like the odd news. Did you know that there is a woman in Turkey who is slightly over seven feet tall? She took her first flight in her life this year at twenty-five years old. They had to remove six rows of seats on the plane. This first should be followed by having our first Republican in Pennsylvania government tell us how many illegal ballots were counted in 2020?

We can dream. Let us have another first by having one of these RINOs decertify the 2020 election. One first deserves another. Can we at least expel a couple RINOs from state government for expanding government year after year and/or failing to enforce the state and federal constitutions? My nomination is David Argall in the Senate. He should really join the failing communist Fetterman campaign and get it over with. They can promote big and abusive government together and leave us alone.

My old Army buddy called from North Carolina the other day. Wallace Bradsher is a fountain of knowledge and great to chat with. I told him that some guy said, "The demand for racism exceeds the supply of racism." We get upset when people in government do not do their jobs. We would have been fired as Army officers if we did that.

He meant that the fools keep claiming that someone was racist, and then the facts come out, and we find out that the attack was fake. These folks deserve some jail time. Jesse Smollett should be put under the jail. A college student spray-painted racist stuff under a bridge and did not realize that a camera was on. She claimed that some anonymous person spray-painted the racist trash. Most Americans couldn't care less what your race is.

The Democrats have broken the covenant with the American people. They have not protected us from illegal aliens, criminals, election cheaters, and evil and immoral folks. The Democrats and RINOs cannot even perform the basic functions of government. They only care about power and money. Good America-first Republicans can make America great again.

The Democrats trying to divide Americans by ethnic group should listen to Mark Farner of Grand Funk Railroad. He wrote and performed some of the best rock and roll songs of all time. I like to listen to him tell stories.

"We should get rid of the hyphenated group names such as Asian American or African American and just be Americans and live in freedom. Also, if we did not have the Second Amendment, we would be licking the boots of our master right now," Mark explains. He is a good Christian and excellent rock and roll king. He actually convinced the anti-gun Frank Zappa to start shooting guns and join the NRA. What a man!

Thank You, God and Jesus, for always being by our side with family and friends. The Bible is the true source of wisdom, comfort, and peace. We need more God, Jesus, and the Bible. God always wins!

Do you remember the song "You Light Up My Life" from 1977 by Debbie Boone? The number one song was catchy for sure. She sang about God and Jesus. The record company hid that fact that the song was written by Joseph Brooks about a one-night stand.

The cover-up reminds me of Fetterman and so many immoral politicians covering up their mistakes and true nature just to get elected. Fetterman lies and hides that he has lived off his parents until fifty years old and said that he wants to eliminate fracking. He was against fracking and then for fracking in the only debate he would agree to with Oz. This is opinion.

After his smash hit, Brooks lured attractive women to his Manhattan office via Craigslist by telling them that he would make them a star. He had a bad ending by committing suicide in 2011 after being indicted on ninety-one counts of rape, sexual abuse, and assault, according to Rich Cohen in the *Wall Street Journal*. We need indictments for the Bidens and other corrupt politicians who violate our constitution and laws. How is the open border legal?

All men are created equal, that they are endowed by their Creator with certain unalienable rights, that among these are life, liberty, and the pursuit of happiness. Whenever any form of government becomes destructive of these ends, it is the right of the people to alter or abolish it.

This is adapted from the Declaration of Independence of July 4, 1776. Let us enforce our sacred constitution now. The fools running our government are operating outside the constitution. This has been going on for decades now. Let us get true patriots into government before it is too late. That Xu guy sure looks good.

Anyone creating confusion or uncertainty about our ballots and elections is committing treason. They must be put in or under the jail. Our government employees must be accountable to the people. The election machine owners must let us evaluate the hardware and software. They are still fighting Mike Lindell and his experts.

When I read history, it is the story of how government idiots caused so much suffering, destruction, and death. Look at the Chinese, Iranians, North Koreans, Germans, and many other nations. Let us get back to the limited government mandated by our sacred and original US Constitution to destroy socialism and communism forever.

Is Joe Biden the new Gary Glitter? That should be the headline. Biden has been caught sniffing the hair of little girls and women many times. The sex offender Gary was sentenced to sixteen years in prison in 2015 for sexual intercourse with a girl under thirteen years old and other charges. Perhaps we need an ankle bracelet on creepy Joe. Or should he be behind bars?

At least Gary had some talent with the hit song "Rock and Roll." Biden has no talent and allegedly his daughter said they used to take showers together in her diary. At least Joe has that going for him. Why did so many Americans vote for this fool? Trump did a fantastic job.

Here another idea for punishing creepy Joe. Let us pack him up and ship him out to the odd *fundoshi* festival in Inazawa, Japan. Big crowds of sweaty men strip down to their underwear and headbands and try to touch a holy man at the festival. The *Wall Street Journal* had a funny picture of this crazy event.

We could shave his nasty little head and then airdrop Joe into the middle of the crowd in Sea Ridge Solar Speedo briefs. He loves the human touch. That would be awesome and would keep him away from the girls and ladies for a while. I am sure they would appreciate it. We should also include Hunter on this trip.

CHAPTER 4

THE CHARMING REDNECK

I spoke to a strong woman at the gas station one day. She was pumping diesel fuel into a huge Chevrolet. She had a wonderful Southern accent and looked about fifty years old. Her bumper sticker read "FJB." I had to chat with this conservative person.

"I am guessing that you are from Boston, Massachusetts, with that great accent," I asked her between the pumps.

"Are you kidding? I am from South Carolina," the woman replied.

"I was just joking and ask people all the time where they are from," I told her.

"Where do you think I am from?" I asked.

"I don't hear an accent from you. You don't have one as far as I can tell," she explained. I thought this was so funny because I have a heavy Southern accent from Virginia and Florida, and most people guess that I am from Texas. She went off on a rant about the Biden gang restricting energy production and driving prices up.

I learned during this senate campaign that so many folks get elected and then do not do very much. They become experts at getting elected and at not doing their jobs so as not to offend anyone.

They love to sit in Harrisburg chatting and doing nothing for the common man and woman.

Tim Twardzik and David Argall come to mind. They represent me in the Pennsylvania house and senate and refuse to provide good answers my questions about the 2020 election. How many illegal ballots were counted? It is a simple question. Why do they refuse to answer it in a direct way? Here are some emails to and from them. Their answers do not satisfy me.

(dave224422@yahoo.com)
To Senator David Argall
Friday, May 28, 2021, at 9:41 p.m.

Can you throw out all illegal ballots from the last election? We believe that Trump won. Peter Navarro's report notes the following:
10,000 ballots arrived after election day
8,000 dead voters
202,000 over votes
7,000 out of state voters
etc.

*****

To Senator David Argall
Thursday, Aug 12, 2021, at 2:11 p.m.

Hi, David,

Some folks on frankspeech.com said that the voting machines in most states were hacked and that the logs were deleted to prevent an audit. Can you audit our elections now and help throw out any fool in office who cheated and put them and all criminals in jail? We believe that Trump and many other GOP folks won their elections and the Democrats are promoting socialism, communism, racism, antibiblical crap, and sloth.

David Xu

*****

To Senator David Argall, Rep. Tim Twardzik
Friday, September 10, 2021, at 9:39 a.m.

We need answers now. Over 440,000 mail ballots in Pennsylvania went missing or unde-liverable, according to the Public Interest Legal Foundation, while the known Democrat election cheaters claim Biden won by 81,000 votes. We need a full audit asap because it seems obvious that Trump won. The socialists and RINOs are ruining America.

*****

To Senator David Argall, Rep. Tim Twardzik
Sunday, November 28, 2021, at 8:00 p.m.

Dear David and Tim,

Our country cannot move forward with legitimate elections without first fixing the fraud in the November 2020 election. Our state inter-ests and our legal votes must be protected. You can do that. Please bring this case to the Supreme Court to save our state and our country! The Pennsylvania DOS in 2019 refused to allow another government person to ensure that our election system was secure. Many illegal ballots were counted. Audit everything and stop the steal!

David Xu

*****

To Rep. Tim Twardzik, Senator David Argall
Sunday, November 28, 2021, at 8:21 p.m.

Read the attached Lindell evidence and tell me how we can trust our elections. Do your job and throw out all illegal ballots now!

David Xu

*****

To Rep. Tim Twardzik, Senator David Argall
Monday, January 3 at 11:30 a.m.

Tim and David,

How many illegal ballots were counted for Biden and others during our 2020 election? Why have you not answered me? I have asked you this several times now. This is your job, and I volunteered for your campaign. Do not be lazy or dumb. See frankspeech.com and peternavarro.com for help. These patriots submit that hundreds of thousands of ballots were counted illegally. We should know 100 percent the legal ballot count on election day! Most Americans do not trust our elections, and you must fix this now, or there will be violence in my opinion.

David Xu

*****

To Senator David Argall, Rep. Tim Twardzik, James, Nancy Xu
Saturday, January 22 at 5:39 p.m.

Hi, David and Tim,

How many illegal ballots were counted in our last election? How many ballots were legal? It appears to many of us that Trump and other GOP folks won if you obeyed our laws. Did Wolf and his team commit crimes to help creepy Joe get elected? It is your job in the state and federal constitution to regulate elections. It is not up to the judicial or executive branch folks to pervert or make laws and rules and cheat. Will you vote to certify or decertify our election? I believe that if we cannot trust our elections, there will be more and more violence and chaos. God bless a capitalistic and free America!

David Xu
Candidate for US Senate from Pennsylvania

****

To Rep. Tim Twardzik, Senator David Argall, Nancy Xu
Tuesday, February 15 at 8:04 p.m.

Tim and David,

Can you answer my questions from weeks ago? How many illegal ballots were counted in the 2020 election? It appears that many folks must go to prison. Why are you ignoring me? We must destroy socialism, communism, and racism with fair elections.

David Xu

*****

Cheaters and corrupt politicians
To Senator David Argall, Rep. Tim Twardzik
Thursday, March 3 at 9:27 a.m.

How any illegal ballots were counted during our 2020 election? I have asked you this several times, and you will not answer. You are in charge of elections. Are you lazy, dumb, or corrupt? We want answers now, and your salary of $94,000 should be cut. A lot of evidence points toward a Trump victory in Pennsylvania and elsewhere. See frankspeech.com and peternavarro.com.

David Xu

Tim Twardzik finally responded to my emails and questions about election cheaters and illegal ballots. His answer below is not inspiring as he says that he does not know how many illegal ballots were counted. There are some GOP partisans who admit that long-term scum in the Pennsylvania house and senate make deals to avoid competition in elections. The Republicans will make a backroom deal with the Democrats to not run anyone in their general election race. This saves the establishment fools a lot of money and the uniparty thrives with this corruption. Someone should ask our RINO buddy Argall if this is true. He has been in the Pennsylvania government over thirty-six years and should know. I bet this happens in DC and around the nation. Can we please have term limits to remove the fools?

Many folks need to be hauled before a grand jury now for election cheating and the cover-up. Anyone who cheated or allowed cheating must be punished to save America from the communists. At the very least we should throw them out of office.

From Tim Twardzik
To David Xu
Monday, March 21 at 1:10 p.m.

David,

I do not have direct knowledge of how many illegal ballots were counted in the 2020 election. I was not in the legislature when Act 77 was enacted. Unfortunately Governor Wolf, Secretary Bookvar, and the Pennsylvania Supreme Court modified Act 77 and removed security of ballots, signature validation, extended the deadlines, and implemented drop boxes opening up the election to the speculation of cheating and illegal ballots.

I reviewed Act 77 with many members of the House of Representatives. I learned that the way Act 77 was put in place by the legislators was unconstitutional. I joined thirteen other members of the House to successfully sue the State of Pennsylvania in Commonwealth Court, and the Court declared mail-in balloting unconstitutional. The Pennsylvania Supreme Court is now reviewing the case on appeal. This was done to protect future elections, and I am doing my best to protect our constitution and make our elections easy to vote and hard to cheat.

Rep. Tim Twardzik

Why did the RINOs not sue in federal court to obey our constitution and election laws? We must remove all fools who are not doing their jobs in government. Also, why are the people in the Pennsylvania house and senate making $94,000 per year? It appears that they need a salary cut. What do you think? We have the largest full-time legislature in America with 203 in the house and fifty in the senate. We should take the advice of former governor candidate John Ventre and reduce the number of legislators. We should also reduce their salary and benefits.

The US Constitution puts state legislators and the US Congress in charge of elections. It appears to me and many others that Trump won in 2020. Are Twardzik and Argall doing their jobs to obey and enforce our state and federal constitutions? I do not think so. Why are they working full-time in passing stupid laws and increasing spending almost every year? These jobs should be part-time as they used to be.

Argall reminds me of the joke by Senator John Kennedy: "He is so dumb I am surprised that he figured out how to make it through the birth canal."

Perhaps we should get back to 1790 when Pennsylvania only had one legislative body instead of two. That would save some serious tax money and enhance our freedom. Fire the idiots! Nebraska only has one legislative body that works very well. It is human nature to spend someone else's money more freely than your own money.

I spoke with a lady at Tractor Supply. She had farmer clothes on with dirty boots. She drove a big truck. I just knew that she would support my platform. She was very upset about the fools pushing

CRT, socialism, sloth, and calling everyone a racist. She worried about her Christian children.

"We are not perfect, but the Democrats are crazy. What is wrong with them?" the good Republican explained to me.

She reminded me of the true story from Virginia when I lived down there. We had tiny one-room churches down there, where the preacher and his family lived next to the church. The church would have a sanctuary, foyer, and two bathrooms. That is it. Some of the preachers were like stand-up comedians. Think about a Jerry Seinfeld who loves God and Jesus.

The preacher was wailing about how great Jesus was during a sermon on Sunday morning. He was fire and brimstone, but hilarious. "Jesus Christ was the only perfect person ever to walk the face of the earth. If fact, if anyone here thinks they are perfect just stand up in the pew and walk to the aisle. Just go ahead and do that right now," the slim preacher proclaimed.

Sam, the local politician, stood up. His wife put her head in her hands and wondered what crazy or inappropriate thing he would say. He could really make folks laugh. Everyone knew he loved to drink vodka.

"Sam, did you really stand up? Do you really think you are perfect like Jesus?" the preacher asked. He just knew that Sam had a good line for the congregation. What wild thing would he say now?

"No, preacher. I just stood up so my wife can get to the aisle," Sam said.

The place shook with laughter. Sam was a big drinker and a great storyteller. He brought down the church that day. Even his sweet and chubby wife had a good laugh.

We need much better leadership in the US government. We are at rock bottom now with Biden, Harris, and other fools. We need a leader like George Washington who rejects mandates on the American people. The general was really into medical freedom. When he was on his deathbed, the three leeches just were not improving his outcome. The nurse said, "Hurry. Hurry. We need to give the general a booster leech. He is turning green. Quick, we need a booster leech now!"

"No, no, no, the general did not sign the consent form. He is really into individual medical freedom and against all mandates. He does not want the booster leech for himself or others. His teeth are always green," the doctor explained.

The general died the next day. Three leeches were enough for this old soldier. This is an example of great leadership from a deathbed. It is much harder to exhibit great leadership from your deathbed than from your regular bed. We must stop all the mandates from the Democrats and RINOs now in the name of President Washington.

President Washington said that a free people should be armed and disciplined. He would be appalled by the way many Democrats are letting criminals run wild in American cities such as New York, Chicago, and Philadelphia. The MCA Universal Studio owners and managers said that many parts of LA are too dangerous and that fact is driving the good law-abiding citizens to the fake and safe city amusement park to have fun. They can plunk down $160 per day to have good safe fun without stupid criminals hurting or killing them.

George Washington is rolling over in this grave watching fools run the United States government. The ever foolish and weak Obama withdrew all US forces from Iraq in 2011, thereby helping ISIS create a huge caliphate. The Trump team came in and destroyed this sick terrorist homeland.

The ever corrupt and dumb Biden surrendered in Afghanistan in 2021, thereby killing thirteen American soldiers and wounding many more. The Taliban love Joe Biden and his stupid friends. I guess the old saying still rings true. The US Constitution was written by geniuses so the nation could be run by morons.

We do not have much time to stop the communist Democrats from destroying our capitalistic and free America. They have already borrowed over $30 trillion and pay $400 billion each year in interest on that debt to buy votes from lazy or dumb voters. They are teaching our kids to live for the moment and not prepare for the future and retirement. We should deport the bad Democrats and RINOs to Venezuela. Let us cut the welfare and pave the roads.

The greedy unions are a big problem in America. We should make it illegal for any government worker to join a union. Government spending on K-12 has tripled since 1970. Only 34 percent of fourth graders can read or do math at grade level. Fire the lazy and immoral teachers and other government employees.

Many union workers are okay, but they give dues monthly to union bosses who give over 90 percent to Democrats who love huge and corrupt government. It used to be illegal for government employees to join a union. Even the corrupt liar FDR was against it at one point. Let us recapture the magic now to avoid going down the dangerous road to socialism and/or communism. Too many people vote for reckless politicians who give them free stuff every month. This is childish and dangerous for the long-term success of America.

Perhaps we should force any union teacher promoting socialism or communism to join the running of the bulls in Pamplona, Spain, in July. They could get some great exercise and try to avoid being the seventeenth to die in this glorious event since 1910. I wonder if the bull could tell the difference between the union participant and the nonunion participant. Perhaps the union person would be larger and slower than the nonunion person.

So many government employees (including politicians) lie daily to gain and maintain their jobs. They remind me of the commies in China under the idiot Chairman Mao. The CCP took over in 1949 and implemented their ruinous version of communism. By 1957, China was far behind the industrial production of Western democracies.

Mao and his team made all the villages and farmers produce steel or pig iron. They did not know what they were doing. Their products were low quality and worthless. They neglected farming and lied about their production, and the commie government leaders demanded more and more production. The focus was not on growing food.

This stupidity and immorality led to over 40 million Chinese dying of hunger. The Great Leap Forward is a testament to the stupidity of socialists and communists. Helen Raleigh describes this episode very well in her books. Xi and his gang are incompetent and illegitimate leaders in China today.

DAVID XU

The CCP rulers released a dangerous virus from a lab in Wuhan and have not even been punished. The CCP zero COVID policy was always stupid, but the government idiots only have four ICU beds per 100,000 people in China. The USA has thirty-five beds per 100,000 citizens. What kind of leaders fail to have enough hospitals for the common folks? Selfish, dumb, and narcissistic communist folks rule like this. They always have and always will. We should deport Fauci and friends to China today.

The American commies are acting just like Mao with their unrealistic new green deal delusions. They are trying to mandate electric cars before the enabling technology and infrastructure are in place. We must defeat the AOC-type fools and enjoy fossil fuels until other technology comes along. Look at the Europeans being squeezed by Putin now with their energy supplies. It seems like the socialists from Sri Lanka to California to Germany never follow truth and reason and common sense.

Why did the Democrats just renew the $7,500 tax credit or discount for upper-income fools to buy an electric car? Answer: The Democrat government idiots are wasting tax money on their family and friends for votes in the next election and giving money to communists in China for battery supplies because they love communism.

Only 6 percent of cars sold in America are electric, and the average cost is $62,000. That rules out 90 percent of Americans. Our nation and the world is not ready for this stupid push for electric cars. Over one billion people on earth do not even have enough power for their homes, much less for a car. The vehicles will only go one hundred to two hundred miles on a charge anyway. What do you do with that huge battery when it is used up?

The people running Toyota in Japan are trying to educate the Democrats on the fragile power grids, but their minds are closed for business. Perhaps the climate change folks would think before they speak if we waterboarded them 183 times like KSM after the 9/11 attacks? Snowflakes will not realize this is a joke.

I met a very nice voter named Johnny in Ashland one day. He used to be a miner and then a heavy equipment operator before he retired. He is seventy years old now and very friendly.

"Do you live here? I love the tin roof. Does the rain make too much noise for you?" I asked him.

"Not at all. The metal is on top of the old shingles. We saved money by keeping the shingles. That used to be my house across the street where I raised my three children. Those shingles are thirty years old now. I moved into this place five years ago after my mother died. One day my father walked over and gave me a check for $16,000 and said he was giving it to me because that is what he paid for my brother to go to college, and I did not want to go. They were the best Christian parents," Johnny said to me.

We need more hard workers like Johnny and his parents. They worked hard and then drove to Atlantic City on weekends. They met Trump several times at the Taj Mahal hotel and casino and loved it. Many Indians used to love that place. Johnny loved the way Trump exposed all the anti-American socialist folks in the District of Columbia.

"I think Trump did a great job, but he always puts his foot in his mouth. He does something great and then says something dumb. I think DeSantis would be better now, but I will support Trump if he runs again," Johnny explained.

I am a late bloomer as a politician. Nancy says I never bloomed at anything (so sweet). Do you remember William Blaxton? Do you want to hear about a late bloomer? This guy brought the apple to America in 1622 and grew them near Boston. The fruit probably began in or near Kazakhstan.

He enjoyed reading books and solitude and did not marry until age sixty-four. This late bloomer actually had a kid when he was sixty-five. Wow, they should have frozen that sperm. I put off marriage until age forty-one, and this guy put me to shame. This Blaxton guy had good genes.

All this talk about diversity, equity, and inclusion is really driving some people nuts. The National Hockey League (NHL) leaders just apologized for 84 percent of its workforce being white. Perhaps they should just focus on hiring the best players and managers and winning games.

Why are these people so dumb? Can we implement an IQ test for these positions? How about a standardized test at the fifth-grade level? Okay, how about a grueling five-hour interview requirement to ensure a minimum level of brain function? Could it be that one segment of the vast society does not like hockey? Is it possible that a group actually thinks hockey is a dumb children's game?

"Experts Decry Shocking Lack of Diversity on Kenyan Marathon Team," the Babylon Bee dutifully reported with a good picture of their all-black awesome runners.

The Congressional Black Caucus has been around since 1971, but they cannot seem to invite any black Republicans. Byron Donalds in the US House has not been invited. He just happens to be a MAGA Republican. The racists (blacks supporting a white guy) in the caucus are backing the very white incumbent Frank Mrvan over the great military veteran GOP candidate Jennifer Green. She just happens to be black.

Perhaps the Democrats should focus on stopping America from being a sanctuary for illegal immigrants, sex traffickers, drug dealers, and gang members. Most Democrats are against law-abiding American patriots with guns.

Many American fools want a system like China. This system is a disaster, just like the old Soviet communist central planning. Do you remember when the Russian idiot leaders dictated which products were produced and how many? They used to make millions of shoes of low quality that nobody wanted or needed.

The commies in China are carrying on the stupidity of central planning today with dire results. They are hiding economic data more and more to bury their mistakes. They have severely damaged their environment to make money and pay bribes to government idiots.

They killed too many baby girls and now do not have enough women or babies to sustain the population. They finally eased the one-child policy to rectify this dumb policy. Their working-age population is decreasing, and the average age of the country is increasing.

Their lockdowns hurt and killed many good people. They are locked in their house and watched on cameras like zoo animals. Many folks have mental problems because of the communist mind control. Investors in and outside of China have to guess at economic data, which leads to uncertainty, which leads to less investment, which leads to fewer jobs and a lower standard of living. The folks at Twitter and other places censored the Barrington Declaration, which pointed to evidence that the lockdowns were really stupid and would hurt many people.

Investors want two things: high return and low risk. They will invest in countries using these metrics, and China has fallen out of favor. The Chinese government idiots have taken over or control many companies to use as slush funds for lavish lifestyles of CCP leaders and their families. They say when someone gets elected in China, the whole family goes to heaven. I believe that most Chinese are good and want nothing to do with their corrupt government employees and leaders. Only 8 percent of the population belong to the atheist and evil one-party regime.

The CCP has taken the freedom away from the folks in Hong Kong. The British were kicked out of their colony, and perhaps that is fair. Why did the Chinese allow the British to take over Hong Kong in the first place? The weak always suffer under the strong and evil folks. The people in Hong Kong protested and blocked streets when they should have kicked the CCP out if they were strong. The same thing will happen in Taiwan if they are weak and stupid. The woke and dumb people will be destroyed by the strong and smart people. The world has always been this way. I pray to God that our military folks can protect us in spite of our woke political appointees put in place by Biden like Milley and Austin.

The housing sector in China is going down because too many fools borrowed too much money speculating. The greedy government and real estate people worked together to make money and destroy the environment. They were myopic and did not think long-term. The apartment vacancy rate is at least 14 percent and climbing, and many builders have filed for bankruptcy. Central planning is always worse than a free market in allocating scarce resources to the best use. Thank God we live in the awesome capitalistic America. We just need to fire and arrest all the socialists and commies trying to pervert our free markets like the CCP did. Government is always more wasteful than private companies. A business owner must watch his money, and the politician just flushes money down the toilet.

The unemployment rate for young Chinese is very high. They have not fought a war since 1979 when Vietnam aligned itself with the Soviet Union and made Chairman Deng mad because China had supported Vietnam against the Americans. The CCP indoctrinate the young folks with communist propaganda, but the smart ones see that capitalism is a much better system for individual freedom and success. Most people do not want government people controlling them.

The CCP uses lockdowns to prevent protests, riots, and challenges to its rule. Many Chinese are sick of the tyrants spying on them for control. You do not see many women in the Politburo. The CCP's *People's Daily* propaganda machine declared in 2019 a "people's war against the United States."

Most of the mothers in China do not want their only child killed in a dumb war started by Fat Papa Xi and other fools. It appears that he should push himself away from the kitchen table more often. Why does he eat so much? He may not be fat. He may just be bloated as the guy screams in the TV commercial. They call him the Chinese Oprah.

The Chinese people would do well to fire Papa Xi. This boat anchor is dragging the ship toward the ocean floor. He is trying to rule another five years after his failing ten year regime. Do they have smarter candidates? Is this dolt really the best one to make China stronger?

Papa Xi has failed in economics, with the CCP virus from Wuhan, and in so many other areas. He says dumb stuff all the time that offends many people from other countries. The closest problem for us is that the CCP has corrupted many American politicians, journalists, college employees, big tech, and businesspeople. These useful idiots have taken CCP cash and sold out America. They must be fired and punished. Perhaps we should deport them to China and put them on the no-fly list. Biden is the worst traitor.

Ye Jianming allegedly gave Hunter $10 million and a three-carat diamond worth $80,000 for introducing him to Joe Biden, according to Hunter's laptop. Ye is a Chinese spy for the CCP and the China Energy Fund Committee (CEFC). He is close to Papa Xi. What did the Chinese get in return for their Biden investment? That is the question for the Bidens and other idiots. Sam Faddis, retired CIA, found these nuggets for us. Have the agents at the CIA, FBI, DOJ, and DIA looked into this probable corruption and influence peddling? Where is the grand jury?

Never forget that Mao, Xi, and others in the CCP have killed over 100 million Chinese plus over 400 million babies with abortion, and they are just getting started. Most Chinese would not follow him to the bathroom if given the choice. They would flush Xi down the toilet if they could.

Speaking of toilets, did you hear the government idiots in San Francisco planned to spend over $1.7 million on one toilet for a park? The Democrats have ruined that place with massive welfare, drug addicts, failing schools, lockdowns, drug dealers, and criminals.

Most Democrats want to control how we work, travel, congregate, eat, demonstrate, hire, fire, speak, and celebrate. We must elect honest and accountable people like David Xu to stop this stupidity. Most of their proposals are unconstitutional and illegal. Government should only do what private firms cannot do.

The Democrats are so arrogant that they want to tell us what kind of car we can buy. The firefighters will tell you that to put out a fire from an electric vehicle takes ten times the amount of water than putting out the fire from a fossil fuel car. It can take over twenty hours to put out the electric car fire.

This is America, and we will buy whatever type of vehicle we want. Can someone muzzle the dumb socialist communists and make them use deodorant and mouthwash? While we are at it, can we force them to get a real job in the private sector and get off welfare?

It is time for another reminder of why we are very lucky to follow our Founding Fathers. They warned about the dangers of big business in bed with big government. This tale involves a dumb

CEO named Jeff Immelt and a really dumb politician named Barack Obama.

Immelt ran General Electric into the ground from 2002 until 2017 while flying around the world playing big shot on not one but two corporate jets. He had two just in case one broke down. The inside joke was that the second jet carried his ego. I am so glad that I never bought the stock with this fool wasting so much stockholder money on lavish free trips.

This guy is relevant for this book because he was on Obama's Council on Jobs while GE avoided taxes by shifting profits and workers oversees. Both the leftists and conservatives were outraged. Immelt pushed the climate change crap for Obama also. He shut down the light bulb factory in Winchester, Virginia, laid off the workers, and moved production overseas. Then he lobbied the corrupt politicians for tariffs on his competition.

Immelt gave Obama a tour of his factory in New York and thanked him for the federal taxpayer subsidies while the CEO made millions. This is the CCP model in China where the business folks and politicians are joined at the hip and ignore the common citizens and their issues and concerns.

Immelt used to preach about how smart he was to other employees of GE at their beautiful corporate retreat in Crotonville, New York, on the Hudson River. GE is finally selling the training academy or playground for lazy and stupid corporate leaders now.

Immelt visited Obama and the White House gang over thirty times. That beats Jeffrey Epstein's seventeen visits with the Clintons. Are we finished with corrupt, lazy, dumb, immoral, and greedy business leaders and politicians hanging out on our dime? We must destroy the CCP model in America now. This is opinion.

If we had honest people running the government, we would know everyone who knew or should have known about Epstein and many others who sexually abused girls. Fox News reports that he paid more than twenty victims through accounts at JPMorgan Chase. Did Jamie Dimon, Obama, Clinton, etc. know about or participate in crimes?

Some Democrats and Republicans are keeping the Epstein crimes covered up. We just heard that a French modeling scout by the name of Jean-Luc Brunel allegedly killed himself in a French prison in 2022. He was awaiting trial for supplying Epstein with girls and young women. There are court documents that say that Epstein paid out over $1.5 million to recruiters such as the dead French guy from JPMorgan accounts. Why did the JPM folks allow this? Where were the moral or Christian employees? Epstein was a registered sex offender in Florida by 2008. This is opinion.

It appears as though many folks should be in or under the jail for abusing girls and women. Where is the guest list for Epstein island? This is opinion. Are the people lying when they say that Epstein killed himself in the Manhattan prison during 2019? We want the truth, and we want it now. Do the Democrat political leaders really care about women?

The big, fat governor of Illinois Pritzker and friends are trying to amend the state constitution to allow corrupt unions to have more power than the good taxpaying citizens. The government union idiots would be protected with long-term contracts, multiyear salary increases, and lifetime pensions. Pritzker looks like he is overdue with triplets. Can we get a pediatrician to check him out? Perhaps he is a she as the leftists shout.

The progressive governor and friends have passed a law to do away with cash bail and other procriminal stuff that is effective during January 2023. The Illinois people better stop that law or more good people are going to be shot. These Democrats love lazy union people and criminals. We love nonunion hard workers and law-abiding citizens with guns. Arrest all criminals to make America great again.

I sure hope the Republicans vote that crap down in this one-party disaster of a state. The teachers in Illinois go on strike all the time and control the dumb politicians. The unions and Democrats are violating the constitution by trading votes for campaign cash. Shouldn't the politicians incarcerate or execute the criminals instead of promoting lazy union employees? Can we remove this state from the union? They can be a voluntary member of the Cuban federation.

Pritzker's comrade Fetterman reminds me of that village idiot in Iran who has not taken a bath for sixty years. He is ninety-three years old and thinks that a good bath may kill him or make him sick. I think he wears a hoodie like Fetterman. This could be the next move for our village idiot when he goes down in flames for this senate seat.

Sometimes we should just listen to normal, hardworking soldiers. I saw a typed paper sign on the men's bathroom wall at the Fort Indiantown Gap ID office recently as follows: "Flush once you are done! After the flush, check what you flushed went down! If it did not, use the plunger! If you can read this, you are smart enough to use the plunger. The next guy in line thanks you for making this happen!"

You can learn a lot listening to soldiers. Someone put a lot of time into this sign. Good ideas have nothing to do with rank or going to college. This soldier really believes in exclamation marks to emphasize something important such as disgusting and rude soldiers.

It will be a miracle if we have fair and honest elections thanks to the Democrats and RINOs. Some counties in Pennsylvania are alerting mail-in voters about mistakes, and some counties are not. All ballots are supposed to be treated the same. This is common sense and a legal principle. Ballot curing is about correcting ballots and could lead to manipulation and cheating.

Over 70 percent of mail-in ballots are from Democrats. Many of them will cheat if given the opportunity. We must exclude all illegal ballots from immoral idiots. The cheaters should be arrested immediately. There was massive cheating in 2020, and the Pennsylvania uniparty people have done almost nothing to prevent it from happening again. Ballot curing is required in twenty-five states. I think it should be outlawed. It is not government's job to keep us from doing stupid stuff.

We do not need to help fools vote. Perhaps only landowners should be able to vote. That would be old school and awesome. We can only dream. Many ignorant folks who do not pay taxes vote for larger and more corrupt socialist government every year. This is a recipe for disaster for any nation. All citizens must have skin in the game. There should be a tax on apartment renters to pay for government programs. Real estate owners get abused with high taxes to fund welfare for many lazy folks who live in apartments and use those government programs.

Here is another example of climate change stupidity from our friends in Scotland. They have many windmills to generate power, and that is fantastic, but it seems like they did not plan ahead. Over seventy windmills had to be powered by diesel generators recently when the temperature dropped.

Correct me if I am wrong, but diesel generators pollute much more than natural gas or nuclear power plants. Why are the socialists and commies so weak at living in the real world and planning ahead? The gas and nuclear plants are great during the winter with or without wind. Perhaps the United Kingdom should just let the Scots go to form their own socialist paradise with blackouts all the time.

CHAPTER 5

THE RHINESTONE REDNECK

Picking a guitar was a lot easier than picking
cotton. I'd have to pick cotton for a year
to make what I'd make in a week in LA.
—Glenn Campbell

Trump was right on so many topics. I always wondered why he mentioned the fake media all the time. I thought he should ignore them and cut back government. Over 92 percent of journalists in America are Democrats, and most spew propaganda rather than facts. This is a huge problem because many citizens watch local, state, and national journalists who lie and do not cover the facts. Every story they do is biased. They love huge, corrupt government, and their jobs depend on the corrupt politicians and access to scoops. Many journalists have never had a real job and are fresh out of college where socialism and communism are promoted by ignorant professors and managers. The US Constitution rejects this crap.

I noticed this on WNEP in Wilkes-Barre during November 2021. The good folks in Virginia had a sweet red wave election, and I made sure to watch the news that night. The local idiots on

WNEP ignored this massive rebuke of woke, socialist, communist Democrats in my home state of Virginia.

The Democrat journalists seem to find time to cover anything negative about Trump and the Republicans but had to keep this conservative and Christian victory quiet. I guess the Democrat owners and employees of news stations would like to keep the corrupt propaganda media industrial complex going a few more years. They speak positively about what ridiculous people like Wolf, Shapiro, and Fetterman do or fail to do. The American communist media folks would make the Chinese communists proud. Many Democrats do not know that the Biden gang has let millions of illegal aliens walk into America at our Southern border.

MSNBC has idiots on all the time saying how racist and bad white people are. Why are these racists on TV? Comcast owns it and NBC, the Golf channel, and other networks. Are these people trying to start a race war as Charles Manson tried to do?

There was a radio station in Rwanda that had MSNBC-type fools telling the Hutus that the Tutsis were all racist and horrible. After several months, the Hutus went wild and murdered over five hundred thousand Tutsis in 1994. Immoral Bill Clinton and friends did almost nothing. They froze like a deer in the headlights. Dumb and sick journalists anywhere can prey on ignorant people and feed them lies. The US Democrat media people have been lying about Trump and Republicans for years and promoting violence and racism.

This makes me sick and must be exposed and stopped. The FEC people could punish partisans pretending to be journalists for one thing. The DOJ should not allow racists on any media platform. Racism is illegal in America. Did the Democrats forget that?

All the free advertising for socialist Democrats is a huge advantage in political races. Most of the local and state journalists would not cover me at all while running for the Senate when I contacted them. The Democrats get union dues and feed it to the TV stations for political commercials to dupe the average citizens. They want to hide all the dumb and bad things that the government is doing. Many people do not know that our Southern border is wide-open thanks to the Democrats like Biden and Harris.

Kari Lake in Arizona is great at exposing the immoral media folks. She will turn the camera around and show them making fools of themselves all the time. She was a network anchor and saw how many sick Democrats took over the industry many years ago. She worked in TV for over thirty years and decided to run for governor. I sure hope she wins. She is the communists' worse nightmare, and that is why they lie about her every day. Basement dweller Katie Hobbs and friends have perverted the elections in Arizona and should be investigated.

When I realized that even the local journalists were so biased as Democrats, I did not want to buy any advertisements from them. I do not want to support with our money any socialists or communists. I love capitalism and hate huge, corrupt government. We only ran two ads on TV during the entire senate campaign costing about $600.

Many normal Democrats and independents would not have voted for creepy Joe if the local journalists had done their job and covered the Hunter laptop story. They really hurt America by covering for corrupt Biden just because he is in their socialist Democrat Party. They told common folks that Biden was a moderate when they knew or should have known that he is controlled by the radical left. People like Biden and Harris will do or say anything for power or money. They are nasty folks.

Nancy and I needed a break from the campaign and IT work, so we headed to Nashville for a week. Peter Serefine had invited me to be on his show, and we met online on Thanksgiving night. He is a good conservative who served in the Navy and delivers mail too. The show is *Liberty Lighthouse* and very well done by this intelligent veteran. His beard steals the show.

We had a nice one-hour conversation about the corrupt Democrats and RINOs spitting on the constitution for decades. We dreamed of shutting down many departments such as Education, Interior, Commerce, and HHS. He sang a silly song about the fool Fauci and his gang pushing vaccines and mandates.

The Biden gang fired or forced out over 8,400 Americans from our military for refusing the experimental vaccine. These Democrats are a danger to our national defense and should be fired and punished. Most of the fired people were strong Christian warriors who do not trust government idiots and who can blame them. We do not trust fools who reject our sweet original constitution. The situation would be much better if everyone embraced the Bible or at least those principles.

Peter asked if I had considered running as a Libertarian party candidate because my platform is so conservative. I told him that those people can split the conservative vote and help elect horrible Democrats. That happened in the 1992 presidential election with Ross Perot. He ran as an independent and took votes from Bush and helped the immoral Bill Clinton gain power.

I voted for Perot because he was better than the RINO Bush. Perot wanted to cut spending and taxes and would have done a fantastic job in my opinion. The Clintons really hurt America with their bad example of unethical behavior and many scandals. He could have killed Bin Laden before 9/11 but was too busy watching golf to bother with the missile strike.

Peter complained about a lack of competition in the United States. I thought about how much power the politicians have allowed Jeff Bezos to have. He can and in fact did cancel Parler by kicking over 10 million members off the social media site during 2020. He can keep your book off Amazon, thereby severely limiting your book audience. Social media is the new public square and must be protected by the constitution. Free speech is a must for a free America. I would help clean this up from inside the US Senate.

Bezos and his team can censor your book cover as they did to my book *Redneck Dystopia*. They did not like bullets on my cover. Have they not heard of the American revolution with guns or the Second Amendment? Bezos can make you look very bad in the *Washington Post* or completely ignore you if you are a conservative Christian person working to make America great again by destroying socialism, communism, and racism. How much money has Bezos given the corrupt American politicians? I want to see the list of beneficiaries of his largess. The government folks should protect rednecks. Our rights are guaranteed in the constitution. This is opinion.

"If you call a man a redneck today, you're also calling him ignorant, but that ain't no big thing if you're a redneck too. In that case,
you're both just good ole boys wherever you live in this country,
although a Southern drawl will usually leave no doubt," said Gene
Odom. Gene is a great and strong patriot from Jacksonville, Florida.
He was a childhood friend, US Army soldier, and bodyguard for the
awesome Ronnie Van Zant of Lynyrd Skynyrd. This is my favorite
band of all time, and I saw the tribute band at the Sturgis Bike rally
back in 2018. I love the word *redneck* and proudly consider myself
one. I met Gene one time, and he is a fantastic storyteller. He was
severely injured in the plane crash in 1977 that killed several people.

How much pollution does Bezos create with his rockets? Why
does he get to ruin the environment when most Americans help protect the environment? Perhaps the politicians should stop the billionaires and millionaires from polluting so much? Perhaps the politicians should be forced to meet via Zoom and stop flying so much
and destroying our environment? Perhaps we should make them pay
for their flights, hotels, and meals? Joe and Hunter come to mind
with all their free trips thanks to the taxpayers. How much damage
does Elon Musk do to the environment with his rockets?

We toured Andrew Jackson's home in Nashville. He was a great
redneck president who shut down the corrupt Federal Reserve bank
and had open houses at the White House for the common, normal person. They had to stop due to a drunken brawl. Jackson was
awesome.

We needed a break from the cold weather and booked a cruise
with Norwegian Cruise Lines. Nancy and I had never taken a cruise.
Our crazy neighbor Phil predicted that we would gain ten pounds
each. He was close.

America would be a better place with more folks like Phil. He
worked hard with aluminum for many years and now restores Honda
motorcycles and Ford Broncos. The man is very generous and can fix
anything. We are lucky to have such a neighbor cruising around on
his spotless blue Harley-Davidson Sportster.

We walked up to the steakhouse one night on the huge ship.
The server asked if we wanted the twenty-five- or thirty-ounce steak.

I told him that I had a couple muffins and ice cream about three with my coffee, and I was not that hungry. I usually get the eight- or ten-ounce steak at home. I told him, "I will have the thirty ounce."

I gained six pounds and Nancy four during the one-week cruise. There was an incident in Manhattan when we tried to board the ship. I left a 9 mm bullet in my jacket the last time I shot targets on the farm in Pennsylvania. The metal detector found it before we walked to the COVID testing center.

We were suddenly surrounded by several security guards in tight uniforms. They looked very concerned about the bullet and this redneck person and his wife. I explained that everyone has guns where we live, and we shoot people just for fun.

"I shot a young man last week just for walking through my yard. I just shot him in the leg. It will barely leave a mark," I told the impressive security guards.

One guy said, "Wow, I would love to see this magical place you speak of. Were you in the Army?"

We had to wait in the VIP lounge for about an hour for them to rescan our luggage and complete a background check. I would not have minded much, but the food sucked. Most of the crew were from the Philippines and very professional and helpful.

I was thinking about how sad it is that having a bullet or gun is so odd and scary for so many folks. Many judges and politicians have not obeyed and enforced our sacred constitution over many decades. We must remove these fools from government and prosecute them if necessary. We must get back to the constitution somehow before America is lost forever.

Nancy was laughing and threatened to deny knowing me. She threatened to go with the sexy, younger man with no ammo to the ship pool for cocktails. Thank goodness she stayed with me and enjoyed the pastries. Most of the crew members were very good at customer service. You could tell they loved their jobs and worked hard. Most Americans are like that, but so many are entitled and lazy now.

I was glad to be in America where we can carry guns most places. I was glad not to be in Guatemala where the prosecutors put defendants in a cage in the parking lot outside the courthouse for days before the trial. They get the media folks to come take pictures and video to humiliate the alleged criminals. I did notice that many folks in the Obama and Biden regimes such as Antony Blinken praised the socialist-communist Guatemalans who treat innocent people like dogs.

Eric Clapton is a great musician and complained about our lazy, entitled youth recently. He is right on target. Most Americans do not like the long-term welfare and lazy folks who milk it for all it is worth.

We cruised to Charleston, Orlando, and the Bahamas and had a grand time. The food was fantastic and everywhere. We never had buffets for breakfast, lunch, and dinner. It is dangerous for most folks who love to eat.

I must give credit to the few journalists, reporters, and others who cared enough about my campaign to ask questions or interview me. Kevin Menne is one such person. He asked for an interview on his YouTube channel in January 2022. He interviews candidates from across America to inform the voters and does a great job.

Kevin is a banker full-time and talk show host part-time in Cincinnati, Ohio. I could tell that he is pretty conservative and wants more limited government like most Americans. We spoke about the Federal Reserve employees who enable big, corrupt government by printing and borrowing trillions of dollars to buy votes. We should downsize the Fed and fire many of the 780 economists who are Democrat to Republican 10 to 1. They are spin masters with statistics for the socialist Democrats.

The economists for the board of directors is 48 to 1 Democrat to Republican. Congress created the Fed in 1913, and we must cut it back now. They have brought us to the brink of ruin with the socialist Democrats and RINOs with decades of myopic or short-term behavior.

I was walking around getting signatures in Ashland one day in March and met an old lady. She was hard of hearing and said the CCP virus vaccine had reduced her hearing ability. She yelled about lazy young people on welfare living in an apartment complex next to her house.

She said that many young folks on her block get high all day and live on welfare. They make fun of people who work hard and pay taxes. She is surrounded by these sick people funded by corrupt Democrats buying votes and running toward socialism. The drug and alcohol people will be thrown in prison or worse after the Democrats do not need them anymore. Socialists and communists always do this. But this crowd does not read history. They do not read anything and will pay a steep price for their ignorance. They are too dumb to realize this and vote for Republican outsiders like me before it is too late for America.

The old woman insisted that I guess her age. I tried to avoid this game and did not want to offend her by guessing too high. I finally guessed that she was between sixty and seventy years old. She proudly said that she is eighty-six years old. She looked great for that age.

She went on and on about how she and her husband worked hard, paid for their kids, prepared for retirement, and gave to charity for decades. She demands that our youth do the same. Nothing is free. She signed my petition to get on the ballot. We need more Americans like her.

She complained about the big-city Democrats paying lazy folks to move to rural areas and infecting the community with bad culture. We must promote hard work, God, honesty, education, personal responsibility, selflessness, obligation to defend our country, and giving to charity to save America.

I saw the following on the Schuylkill County GOP website. We would be in good shape if all Republicans acted on these beliefs. Instead, so many RINOs get elected and then do nothing. We are Republicans because...

> We believe all Americans are endowed by God with an inalienable right to Life, Liberty, and the pursuit of Happiness.
> We believe in a free marketplace, and that the freedom of all Americans to fulfill their talents

and ambitions has provided the greatest prosperity of any nation in the history of the world.

We believe the best government is that which governs least; the proper function of the government is to do for the people only those things they cannot perform themselves.

We believe stable economic growth is achieved by sound monetary policy and by spending every dollar necessary, but not a dollar more.

We believe in equal justice for all, regardless of race, creed, religion, gender, or color.

We believe America is the safest from threats of foreign aggression when we have the strongest possible military, and when we actively confront—rather than passively appease—our aggressors.

We believe the fraternal bond of Americans is strongest when we celebrate our shared, uniquely American culture.

We believe that the traditional family is the cornerstone of our society.

We believe in personal responsibility, volunteerism, rugged individualism, civility, decency, and morality.

We believe that only through the Republican Party can these ideals become active and successful principles of government.

We have a leadership problem in the United States. Only about 30 percent of the 36 million seventeen-to-twenty-four-year-olds meet the military standards now. Most young folks are fat, on drugs or alcohol, weak, lazy, or dumb thanks to adults like Biden encouraging them to be that way in exchange for free stuff. Many good and young Americans see the immoral politicians running our government and military and will not sign up to serve under them. Moral hard workers do not want to work for a fool.

Where is Calvin Coolidge when you need him? He was the US president from 1923 until 1929 and cut a lot of wasteful spending. He is my favorite president who destroyed the lazy union police in Boston in 1919 while he was the Massachusetts governor. They went on strike and let criminals run wild, and Calvin put them in their place. No government employees should be able to join a union and/or go on strike. They work for the taxpayers.

Coolidge was VP under the ever-frisky President Warren Harding from 1921 until his death in 1923. Harding is the guy who said, "It is a good thing I am not a woman. I would be pregnant all the time."

There were many immoral folks in the Harding administration and a number of scandals. He appointed friends and acquaintances to high office, and it did not work out very well. His Veterans Bureau chief Charles Forbes did some illegal stuff, fled to Europe, and then served prison time for his scandals.

Harding had one thing right: his praise of the sweet United States Constitution. He said, "The constitution is the very base of all Americanism, the Ark of the Covenant of American liberty, the very temple of equal rights."

I like Coolidge for his love of the constitution also. He said, "If all men are created equal, that is final. If they are endowed with inalienable rights, that is final. If governments derive their just powers from the consent of the governed, that is final. No advance, no progress can be made beyond these propositions."

He would be shocked by all the fools spitting on our sacred constitution for the last few decades. I agree with him that political freedom requires moral government folks with self-control. He would lock up Biden, Harris, Pelosi, Clinton, Obama, and Schumer. The corrupt crowd always says that personal character does not matter regarding a candidate or politician. Yeah right.

I think all politicians should serve in the military to qualify for the ballot. This would weed out many fools who would never make it through basic training. Some bad apples would get through such as climate fool Kerry or RINO McCain, but at least they would have to put their lives on the line for the sacred constitution for a few years as many of us have done. It just brings your commitment to the original document to a higher level for most soldiers and veterans.

I called my mother one day to chat. She lives in Myrtle Beach, South Carolina, and loves the beach and sun. She is a bit eccentric and has a life-size cardboard cutout of Kris Kristofferson in the passenger seat of her Smart car. She is a superfan.

"I was complaining to Nancy last week about how tough it is to get elected. The voters treat me like a used car salesman or telemarketer," I told Mary Penn.

I would love to hear her response. I remember when you were complaining about working the graveyard shift at the Pentagon during 2008. She suggested that we make posters and banners and protest in the Pentagon parking lot. She said the poster should say, "LTC Xu is being abused by the Pentagon leaders. Please stop the madness and rescue him from actual work."

"She had no sympathy for you and your high-level Joint Staff Pentagon job. She does not take any crap from you or anyone. I love that about her. She is tough," Mary Penn said.

We love to laugh but must realize that Biden and other corrupt socialist fools do not represent those of us who went to war for this great country. We must destroy them in politics now or destroy them later in war. Our constitution will be enforced one way or the other under God. We pray for the peaceful option and obedience to our constitution. That is the ultimate rule book. Biden is foolish when he proclaims that the Second Amendment is not absolute.

Let us move the discussion from the Pentagon to 935 Pennsylvania Avenue NW. Where is the Federal Bureau of Investigation (FBI) when you need them? Why are they protecting Hunter, Joe, and James Biden from criminal prosecution yet finding plenty of time to target parents angry about fake racism being taught to their children by union teachers?

Shouldn't the agents be targeting and arresting Chinese agents in America stealing technology in every conceivable industry? Why did Biden and Christopher Wray stop arresting Chinese spies at

American universities? Trump and his team had them in their sights. Could it be that the CCP has many sick secrets on the Bidens? Why were the Bidens allowed to take millions from the commies in China through the Upenn center? Hunter made a lot of money in China for many years with no observable knowledge or skills.

China uses state-sponsored hackers with worldwide intelligence operatives to take secrets and technology from Western companies, universities, and citizens. Why are the CIA and FBI employees focusing on imaginary white supremacists and not protecting us from evil, dumb, and sick Chinese idiots? Many Chinese citizens are good, but the CCP crowd must be eliminated in America.

Shall we arrest all the professors at American colleges who help the Chinese spies steal secrets? What do you think? Harvard and Columbia come to mind. These professors and administrators are insulated from the private markets and personal accountability and should be laid off before they harm any more students.

The commies at Harvard and UNC will face the US Supreme Court soon regarding their discrimination policies. They love to drop academic standards for students with certain colors of skin for some dumb reason. People should advance on merit or not at all.

The folks running the Thomas Jefferson high school in Virginia are discriminating against hardworking Asian students in the name of equity. Governor Youngkin and gang are going to stop it. It looks like at least seven schools withheld national merit awards while the kids applied to colleges. There are empty jail cells for these sick people.

Why do the teachers unions support the college folks using affirmative action or discriminatory policies? It is because most students from bad union-run government schools are not ready for a job or college. Most Americans agree that our country should be totally colorblind and teachers should get back to the basics.

We must remind the professors that if a nation and economy stagnate or decline, investors and their capital will go elsewhere. The investors are looking for a high return with low risk. They do not care if the professors are obsessed with gender fluidity, fake climate change, or communism.

In running for the US Senate, I channeled the American Indians near the Olympic National Park in Washington state. This is a stretch but bear with me because I am a legend in my own mind. There is a tribe out there that still hunts whale in small wooden boats in 2022. The youngest member of the hunting party has to dive into very cold water and sew the mouth of the whale shut so it does not sink while they pull it onto shore.

I was like this brave and/or dumb Makah Indian in Neah Bay. I dove into freezing water without caring about my personal comfort or safety in order to win the Senate seat for all the We the People conservative Christian Americans. I took the bullets for the team, and it was awesome. The voters treated me like a used car salesman instead of the strong and brave American Indian every day. Thank you very much.

I saw the childlike Fetterman on TV the other day. He would be a rubber stamp for the Biden children running US policy. They think speeches will solve everything and are not smart enough to foresee bad consequences of dumb decisions.

Fetterman loves to get violent criminals out of prison. He would probably release the killer of Jeffrey Dahmer in 1994. The other prisoner went to prison for murder and then terminated Jeffrey because he cut up his food to look like body parts and put ketchup on it to resemble blood. The prison killer told a *New York Post* writer that this taunting had to stop one way or the other. They should execute horrible folks like Jeffrey immediately after they commit terrible crimes.

Susan Rice, Ron Klain, and other Biden fools made horrible decisions regarding inflation, energy production, Afghanistan surrender, and our Southern border. They do not understand a complex world and just want to virtue signal all day long. They are dumb children for sure. We love smart and Christian children.

Biden and other fools really believed that they could boss around the Saudis to pump more oil while strangling American oil production. They have sent billions to the Islamic terrorists running Iran while harassing the Saudi people for killing an Islamic terrorist supporter *Washington Post* writer by the name of Khashoggi during 2018. They cut my boy up into little pieces inside the Saudi Arabia embassy in Turkey. This is the foreign policy of the other childlike idiot Obama. The Obama gang loved the Muslim Brotherhood (terrorist group) for eight years over Christians, Islamic moderates, and conservatives. Khashoggi was a member.

Let us have three cheers for the Illinois union schoolteachers. In 2019, over 64 percent of third graders could not read at grade level. The dumb CCP virus lockdowns and masks only made the situation worse.

The government employees are trying to cover up their horrible performance with the kids, but most Americans now see that immoral and dumb socialists and communists should be removed from the classroom and campus asap. They are destroying the future of these kids. The Illinois administrators are delusional and rate over 90 percent of the teachers as excellent or proficient.

The overpaid Chicago union fools have gone on strike four times in the last seven years for higher pay and benefits. The children suffer so much under childish and greedy parents, administrators, and teachers. The atheist Democrat Party is a train wreck. We need more God, Jesus, the Bible, and limited government!

Do you want more good news? According to the Young America's Foundation, 32 percent of self-identified liberal students and 56 percent of moderate students said there are too few opportunities to hear from conservative speakers on campus. They cited a study by UNC trying to gain insight into the 19 million college students and 25 million high school students in the great United States of America.

We must reach out to these voters and potential voters. They realize that their woke, insulated, leftist, overpaid instructors are ignorant about what made America great, and it was not dumb government programs. It was hardworking citizens and business owners who hate big and abusive government giving out massive welfare. We need to downsize these colleges and government in general.

How is John Durham doing with his investigation and prosecutions of sick deep state folks? The FBI had Danchenko on its payroll for over three years ending in October 2020 (just before the rigged 2020 election). This was years after the FBI idiots knew that the dossier was unverifiable. Why are the deep state traitors not in jail? When will we have justice?

When will the government idiots decertify the election and switch creepy Joe for Trump? So many judges are weak and will not stop the lawlessness. The US Supreme Court members are supposed to rule against all actions that are outside the constitution. Why are they letting politicians violate our constitution and laws?

So many in the media lied to help creepy Joe and other socialist fools get elected. They are traitors to the great United States and should be punished. We cannot allow a communist media in our nation. The CCP loves it, but this is America baby, and we need an independent press.

The media hid the report by the DOJ Inspector General Horowitz explaining the FBI's corrupt actions for several years. Why was his report not declassified as Trump wanted? The voters deserve to know the truth about the traitors. The Republicans must expose all this when they retake the House and Senate and White House. That would really be the best.

We need to ensure that only honest and accountable people are allowed in our government by the people. I love the Army values as follows. These values always made sense to me in uniform and still today. Is it too much to ask that our government employees be honest, work hard, and enforce the original constitution? Will someone please fire the lying Pelosi, Schumer, Biden, Harris, Fauci, Milley, etc.?

We often thank God for living in the great rural United States of America and not in some filthy Democrat-run criminal paradise, such as Philadelphia. We would be fish out of water dealing with drug addicts and dealers running around night and day living their best life. Wawa just shut down a couple stores over there because flash mobs were looting and destroying the stores. Perhaps we would feel like the very old college students on campus at Arizona State University.

Retirees pay at least $440,000 down and $4,000 per month to live on campus and go to classes with the other younger college students. The old folks must not be too bright because now they are complaining about the 24/7 noise at a school that was rated the nation's top party school by *Playboy* magazine in 2002, according to the *Wall Street Journal*.

The retirees filed a lawsuit to quiet things down. One old lady said that she had never heard of electronic dance music before and prefers Christmas music and Broadway show tunes. This bunch needs to get back to the retirement home to get some rest and relaxation and then die while listening to show tunes.

The young students protest about the lawsuit and noise complaints by the old people with signs that say "Just Buy Earplugs." Perhaps the college scene is not for these 260 elderly folks. What were they thinking?

What do Pope Francis and creepy Joe Biden have in common? They are both weak and/or corrupt. Francis has plenty of criticism for the United States and capitalism but made and maintains a secret deal with the CCP for selecting church leaders in China. The 2018 deal lets the atheists only allow bishops who will remain silent on human-rights abuses and other immoral behavior and crimes by the sick Chinese communists.

Francis and Joe have undermined the moral authority of the Catholic church and the American government in exchange for power, money, and their great positions. Can we please replace these fools with good folks such as Pope John Paul II and Calvin Coolidge? We need leaders who fight like crazy for the Bible, God, honesty, kindness, freedom, our constitution, and Jesus against atheist mafia-like corrupt idiots.

Do you want more crime? You should really move to a Democrat-run city. Democrats run twenty-seven out of the top thirty American cities with the highest homicide rates, according to the Heritage Foundation. You can find us outside the socialist dumps in MAGA country enjoying our success, freedom, and money.

We need more conservative Christians in government to outlaw dumb stuff. For example, under federal law when a Native American child is put up for adoption, priority goes to other Native Americans. This puts the tribe's interest ahead of the child and is clearly unconstitutional. This injects race into the situation for no good reason.

Why has this stupidity gone on so long? The uniparty folks do not care about these kids. The best possible home for the child should be the top priority and not the tribe. Many tribes have drug addicts and alcoholics lying around everywhere also due to bad leaders. Perhaps that should be considered in these situations. Do you remember Stanley Weber? He was an Indian Health Service pediatrician who was convicted of sexually abusing boys over two decades. Did they execute this fool and his protectors? Did they shut down this unnecessary and dangerous welfare program?

The *Wall Street Journal* reported extensively on a program for wayward kids in Somaliland (an independent state within Somalia). Parents with children older than fifteen years old can have them put in prison for up to six months to straighten them out. This is the perfect program for Hunter Biden. This program helps people get off drugs and alcohol and stop them from doing other dumb stuff.

Some parents in Minnesota have taken advantage of this program by moving back to Africa to help their dumb kids. Over 170,000 people living in America are from Somalia and Somaliland. Perhaps Ilhan Omar's parents can ship her and her brother and spouse back to Somalia to take advantage of this outstanding program. This would keep her from voting in the US House for bigger government.

The leaders of Somaliland are really into parental rights and discipline. Hunter is fifty-three years old, and there is no maximum age for this program. This is perfect. Why did George W. Bush appoint Hunter to the Amtrak board of directors in 2006? Perhaps W is a RINO from hell and needs a six-month visit to Somaliland. He is seventy-six years old, but maybe he can still learn from his many mistakes.

THE FIRST OFFICIAL REDNECK FOR US SENATE

08/12/2021 14 : 31

PAGE 1 / 4

FEC FORM 1	STATEMENT OF ORGANIZATION	Office Use Only

1. NAME OF COMMITTEE (in full) (Check if name is changed) Example: If typing, type over the lines. `12FE4M5`

DAVID XU REDNECK FOR US SENATE

ADDRESS (number and street)

x ◄ (Check if address is changed)

ASHLAND — CITY ▲   PA — STATE ▲   17921 — ZIP CODE ▲

COMMITTEE'S E-MAIL ADDRESS

◄ (Check if address is changed)

COMMITTEE'S WEB PAGE ADDRESS (URL)

x ◄ (Check if address is changed)   www.davidxuforsenate.com

2. DATE   M M / D D / Y Y Y Y   08 12 2021

3. FEC IDENTIFICATION NUMBER ▶   C C00786046

4. IS THIS STATEMENT   x NEW (N)   OR   AMENDED (A)

I certify that I have examined this Statement and to the best of my knowledge and belief it is true, correct and complete.

Type or Print Name of Treasurer   Xu, David, , .

Signature of Treasurer   Xu, David, , .   [Electronically Filed]   Date   08 12 2021

NOTE: Submission of false, erroneous, or incomplete information may subject the person signing this Statement to the penalties of 2 U.S.C. §437g.
ANY CHANGE IN INFORMATION SHOULD BE REPORTED WITHIN 10 DAYS.

Office Use Only				For further information contact: Federal Election Commission Toll Free 800-424-9530 Local 202-694-1100	**FEC FORM 1** (Revised 06/2012)

I thought a gimmick like naming my campaign "Redneck" would draw free media attention. I was wrong. Many folks in the local, state, and national news are liberals or leftists promoting socialism or communism. This is the first official Redneck campaign in US history for senate. Thank you very much. August 2021.

Nancy Xu promoting David Xu for Senate

@easyeddie7475

We made campaign videos on the beautiful cliff walk in Newport, Rhode Island. The mansions there are unbelievable. Some of our videos are still on YouTube and Rumble. August 2021.

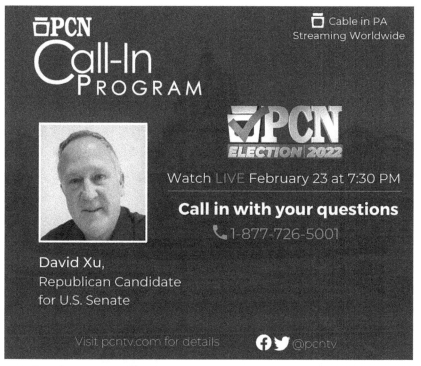

Phil Beckman interviewed me on PCN TV. I think he was taken aback with my very conservative and Christian platform. February 2022.

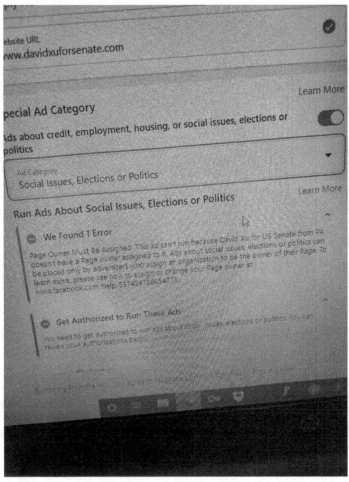

The Facebook folks censor Christians and conservatives and would not answer my emails for help. I wanted to get into the senate to force them to obey our sacred constitution.

Nancy and I campaigned at the Schuylkill County Fair and met some great folks. Ninety-nine percent of the county GOP committee people would not help me at all or to get signatures to get on the primary ballot. Most of the committee members in the entire state should be replaced with MAGA or real Republicans. August 2021.

MAJ David Cox, USA
"With appreciation for your service to the Joint Staff and our Nation."

PETER PACE
General, United States Marine Corps
Chairman
of the Joint Chiefs of Staff

I learned a lot about the swamp while working on the Army and Joint staffs at the Pentagon from 2006 until 2009. General Peter Pace was pretty good. Many generals and admirals are weak, immoral, dumb, and/or political yes men and women (e.g. Austin and Milley). I wanted to change the promotion rules from the senate to get honest and accountable generals in our military. October 2006.

We are very upset with all the election cheating and tried to wake normal citizens up to this threat from socialists and communists. See www.frankspeech.com

I wrote Redneck Dystopia when Pocahontas was leading in the Democrat party primary. This book has her beating Trump in 2020 and ruining out great nation. I cannot believe that so many voters are okay with her lying about being an American Indian to get jobs.

It was so nice to drop out of the senate race and get back to my wonderful and normal life of traveling and writing books (Easy Riders, Redneck Dystopia, and Orphans in the Barn).

Norm, Sabrina, and Kenneth Diehl were great supporters of
my campaign. They let me put a banner up in Saint Clair on
Highway 61. Sadly, Kenneth died during 2021. He always
kept his deceased wife Tina's motorcycle jacket and helmet on
the wall at their great auto shop. These are great people.

Nancy and I love to walk around Washington, DC. Our nation was at its peak with more limited government and God. Can we please get back to the limited government mandated by our golden constitution and the Bible?

We toured President Andrew Jackson's Hermitage estate in Nashville and loved it. This Redneck did a fantastic job in the Army destroying the British in New Orleans during 1815 and as President from 1829 until 1837. November 2021.

We visited the beautiful Gaylord Opryland Resort. Peter Serefine had me on his show one night from our condominium. He does a great job standing up for our constitution. ZZ Top was in town, but I was too tired to go. November 2021.

Here is Nancy promoting her man. We had Redneck and a non-Redneck versions of banners, shirts, and business cards. We made several videos around our barn. We love the traditional red and white colors. There is an apartment upstairs. My book "Orphans in the Barn" is set there.

THE FIRST OFFICIAL REDNECK FOR US SENATE

September 08, 2021

Mr. David Xu

Penalty - Notice Letter

Report: Candidate Report
Filed on: 09/01/2021
Report/Response due on: 07/02/2021
Penalty occurs on: 08/01/2021

Previous Correspondence Sent:
Invitation to File - Candidate Report (sent on 09/01/2021).

Please respond by 10/08/2021.

Dear Mr. David Xu,

You are receiving this letter because you were more than 30 days late in filing your financial disclosure report. More information about your late report can be found in your eFD account. Section 104(d)(1) of the Ethics in Government Act of 1978 requires filers to pay a $200 penalty if they file a report more than 30 days after the due date. Please send a certified check or money order in the amount of $200, made payable to the *United States Treasury*, to the Select Committee on Ethics, Hart Senate Office Building, Room 220, Washington, DC 20510.

In **extraordinary circumstances**, the Select Committee on Ethics (the Committee) may waive the penalty, but the Committee will generally not grant more than one penalty waiver to a filer during his or her Senate employment. A waiver of the penalty must be requested online via eFD within 30 days of this notice and must indicate the specific, extraordinary circumstances that led to the late filing of the required report. The Committee will review your request and respond to you in writing. Payment of the penalty need not be made while a Committee decision on your waiver request is pending.

If you have any questions regarding this letter or your financial disclosure requirements, please contact the Committee at (202) 224-2981.

Sincerely,

/s/

Shannon Hamilton Kopplin
Acting Chief Counsel and Staff Director

| 0068224 | 11-24 | **CASHIER'S CHECK** | SERIAL #: |
| Office AU # | 1210(8) | | ACCOUNT#: |

Remitter: DAVID XU
Purchaser: DAVID XU
Purchaser Account:
Operator I.D. ps002010
Funding Source: Cash

September 8, 2021

PAY TO THE ORDER OF *****UNITED STATES TREASURY*****

Two Hundred and 00/100 -US Dollars **   **$200.00****

Payee Address:
Memo:

WELLS FARGO BANK, N.A.

VOID IF OVER US $ 200.00

NOTICE TO PURCHASER-IF THIS INSTRUMENT IS LOST, STOLEN OR DESTROYED, YOU MAY REQUEST CANCELLATION AND REISSUANCE. AS A CONDITION TO CANCELLATION AND REISSUANCE, WELLS FARGO & COMPANY MAY IMPOSE A FEE AND REQUIRE AN INDEMNITY AGREEMENT AND BOND.

NON-NEGOTIABLE

Purchaser Copy

Senate fine

FB004 (10/19) M4200 00166798

The US Senate people fined me $200 for a late financial report that I did not know about. I always wondered if this is legal to fine someone not actually in the senate. The government idiots gathered our financial information with this scheme. September 2021.

I gave a speech to the great veterans at the AmVets Post 293
in Lebanon. They do the right thing and allow beer during
their meetings while the Frackville group does not. I noticed
that many veterans are oblivious to the growing threat of
internal enemies pushing socialism and communism.

I spoke at the New Covenant Church in Bloomsburg. The Christians were so loving and nice. Stacey and Webb Kline were great hosts. Many people signed my petition to get on the ballot. March 2022.

Nancy and I drove from the New Covenant Church to State College that night and Pittsburgh the next day in snow for a candidate forum. The other Republicans did not show up and I wonder why. It was a great time to answer questions from the liberal or leftist perspective. March 2022.

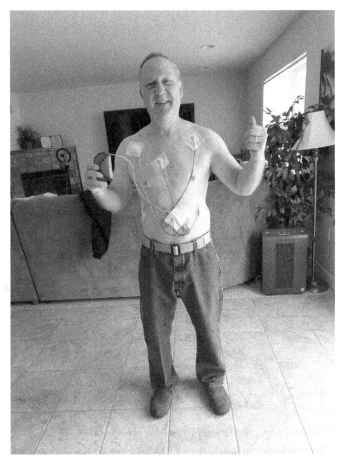

I had my heart checked due to chest pain (from the Pfizer vaccine?). This was during the 18 day period to get 2k signatures to get on the ballot. The government and party idiots moved the dates at the last minute. I think the period should be much longer to help normal, common people get on the ballot and give voters better options. March 2022.

DAVID XU

BALLOTPEDIA

SEARCH THE ENCYCLOPEDIA OF AMERICAN POLITICS   🔍

David Xu

David Xu (Republican Party) ran for election to the U.S. Senate to represent Pennsylvania. He did not appear on the ballot for the Republican primary on May 17, 2022.

Xu completed Ballotpedia's Candidate Connection survey in 2021. Click here to read the survey answers.

Biography

David Xu was born in Danville, Virginia. Xu served in the U.S. Army from 1983 to 2014. He received his MBA from James Madison University in 1990. His professional experience includes the Army Reserve and working as a community college program head and instructor. [1]

Elections

2022

See also: United States Senate election in Pennsylvania, 2022

BP	This page was current at the end of the individual's last campaign covered by Ballotpedia. Please contact us with any updates.	
	David Xu	
	Republican Party	
Education		
Graduate	James Madison University, 1990	
Military		
Service / branch	U.S. Army	
Years of	1983 - 2014	

I answered many questions to get on Ballotpedia. Voters should go there to research candidates to weed out the RINOs, socialists, and communists to MAGA. Did you notice the Masters shirt?

I had a book signing at the Laconia Bike Rally in New Hampshire. It is always great to meet the crazy bikers. The hill climb at the Gunstock Ski Resort is awesome. June 2021.

We only ran one homemade advertisement on TV twice due to the expense. This is our masterpiece that ran on WFMZ in the Philadelphia market for about $600. Owen Gabbey declared it "visionary" in the Pittsburgh City Paper as a joke. That is the nicest thing anyone ever said about me. February 2022.

We tried to make our videos funny. Here is Nancy crying about me going down in flames in the primary. I peaked at 1% in the polls. Very manly! March 2022.

This is my concession speech on our front porch. I was relieved to get out of politics forever. It is a nasty business for sure. Too many voters stay uninformed and do not read much. March 2022.

◁ YouTube removed your content

From: YouTube Community Guidelines (no-reply@youtube.com)
To: david.pa.xu@gmail.com
Date: Tuesday, March 15, 2022, 04:53 PM EDT

YouTube

Hi Easy Eddie,

Our team has reviewed your content, and, unfortunately, we think it violates our **misinformation policy**. We've removed the following content from YouTube:

Video:

We know that this might be disappointing, but it's important to us that YouTube is a safe place for all. If content breaks our rules, we remove it. If you think we've made a mistake, you can appeal and we'll take another look. Keep reading for more details.

How your content violated the policy

Content that advances false claims that widespread fraud, errors, or glitches changed the outcome of the U.S. 2020 presidential election is not allowed on YouTube.

How this affects your channel

We must force the big tech idiots to obey the constitution for free speech in the public square or our constitutional republic is over. The YouTube folks removed my speech at the New Covenant Church because I mentioned all the election cheating going on. It is still up on Rumble.

Gwyn Fowler had me on her Rumble show. She does a great job of standing up for conservatives and Christians and covers many events around the state. February 2023.

TALK OF THE TOWN | David Xu, Author: "Easy Riders: The Older Ones" | WHHITV

Robyn Zimmerman interviewed me on WHHI on Hilton Head Island about my book "Easy Riders." Robyn, Susan Green, and gang run a top notch local TV station down there. April 2023.

We The People of Coal Country

We stand with God and our constitution

We are proud Americans in Schuylkill County, Pennsylvania making a bold statement that we will not stand for the abuse of power going on now. We will defend the constitution against all enemies foreign and domestic. Our sacred constitution rejects socialism and communism and will be enforced soon with the limited government it mandates. America is capitalism. We will always help each other. Huge and abusive government is the problem. WTP are strong. We are NOT servants!

I started We The People of Coal Country during 2022 to educate and motivate the voters in Schuylkill county. Over 50k in the county do not vote. We must get better people elected to save our country.

I have been vacationing at Hilton Head my whole life. The people there are fantastic and the island beautiful. We enjoyed the golf tournament at Harbour Town in Sea Pines. We bought a condo during 2022 and love it there. April 2023.

Big Daddy at Ocean City, Maryland. We thank God and Jesus for a wonderful life in the greatest country ever to exist with family and friends. We can turn this ship around by getting honest, conservative, Christian, smart, and accountable people elected. "That Redneck David Xu for US Senate is the real deal," a voter once said.

CHAPTER 6

THE FIGHTING REDNECK

THE BITTER END, JANUARY THROUGH MARCH 2022

> I have never had a message for anyone
> in my entire life. Except maybe to
> give out my room number.
> —Bon Scott of AC/DC

I began to have lower abdominal and chest pains in January. I hoped it was just stress from the campaign or indigestion. It sucks getting old, but I felt like I was doing something important for the future of our great nation. Running for office definitely put me outside my comfort zone of being a rough and direct veteran.

The doctor was 90 percent sure that my heart was okay. I had to wear several sensors on my upper body a few days and lie inside an MRI-type machine for a while. My heart checked out fine, and I continued to campaign. I do it for the love.

I submitted the complaint below to the FEC folks about Oz on January 10. In my opinion, Hannity on Fox and Kelly on Newsmax were promoting Oz instead of interviewing him. They looked like schoolgirls with a crush. I updated and resubmitted the complaint again in March because the FEC did not respond in January.

January 10, 2022, and March 18, 2022
Re Mehmet Oz (second complaint to the FEC folks)

Hello, FEC Manager,

What is the status of my complaint? I am concerned about the following regarding Mehmet Oz running for the US Senate seat in Pennsylvania. Is he paying for the fluff interviews on Fox News, Newsmax, etc.? His friends Hannity, Kelly, and others resemble campaign spokesmen instead of objective journalists. They look like schoolgirls with a crush.

Is Oz in the Turkish army? Is he a Turkish citizen? If so, this is a national security risk. I served thirty years in the US Army. Also, is Oz using his TV show to further his senate campaign? Does Oz live in NJ? These things have been reported in the press and do not sound right. Let us stand up for our thirty-page golden original constitution and the limited government and capitalism it requires and reject socialism and communism, and corruption together. This is opinion and fact. Thank you, and we thank God and/or kind Christian folks!

Sincerely,
David Xu
Former first official redneck candidate for US Senate in history (www.davidxuforsenate.com)

I drove over to New Hope solo on February 9. Nancy wanted a break from the boring campaign speeches. Maria Miller invited me over to one of her meetings. She and her friends started a conservative Christian group New Hope for Our Nation to help inform the public and support candidates.

She is very nice and helpful. She and her husband have a beautiful luxury home and estate of about sixty acres with a big pond. I spoke about cutting back government and getting back to our sweet constitution.

There were about twenty good people there at Giovanni's Pizza restaurant. A medical doctor spoke of being fired for prescribing a drug to fight COVID. The hospital leaders had a policy of not promoting this drug for some dumb reason.

Dasha Pruett spoke before I did and went on too long. I did not sleep well the night before and was not at my best for sure. She is running in the primary for US House. I am not sure but think her husband was drunk.

He had some funny lines, such as, "See this face? See this face? This is the new face of the Republican Party right here." He pointed at Dasha's face. I imagined him squeezing her face while spouting this nonsense.

I was thinking that he is probably a liability for this campaign. That is going to turn people off, and she should leave him at home with the vodka next time. Of course, this is just speculation or opinion on my part.

Dasha spoke passionately about election integrity and the need to prevent cheating. In April, Levittownow.com reported that many signatures on her petitions were forged according to the people whose names appeared. She dropped out of the race after this came out. She said that being a native Russian and the Ukraine war would limit her appeal to the voters. A candidate for the US House needs one thousand signatures to get on the primary ballot.

I bet many spouses turn off voters without realizing it. Many candidate spouses are not thrilled about all the dumb and arduous things you must do to get elected. Nobody needs a drunken spouse going around saying dumb things. Boy, I am lucky that Nancy does not drink and thinks before she speaks.

I met Carol Ann, and she is very sweet. She offered to help me anytime, but I did not want to bother her. She wore a necklace that I had never seen before. It was an air purifier about the size of a cigarette pack that kills the CCP virus and other things. This group of patriots are helping to get us back to limited government.

The group spoke of a frisky candidate who spoke to them a while back. He was caught taking pictures under the table of a young woman in a dress. Thank goodness he lost in his run for governor or senate or something. He is too horny like JFK.

Nancy and I drove down to Hamburg in the rain on February 17. The Berks County Patriots invited us down to have a table and meet voters. Many boring speeches were given that rainy night. There must have been three hundred folks there.

It was frustrating because the idiots in the state government would not allow us to get signatures. They postponed the signature period because they could not agree on the new voting districts due to the 2020 census. Is it too much to ask that all government idiots do their jobs? The folks in the Pennsylvania house and senate make about $94,000 per year. This is absurd. I bet they would do their jobs if we threatened to cut their pay.

Clarice Schillinger gave an uninspired talk. She spoke of being a housewife and then noticing that the schools have been taken over by sick folks pushing woke crap on the students. I guess she thinks this qualifies her to be lieutenant governor.

She spoke of being a teen mother and many wild nights in her youth. I wanted to ask her to elaborate on those summer nights but thought the question may offend some of the RINOs at the event. We met Sam and Kelly who help run the group and they are nice.

Some guy asked Clarise about helping to raise money for a BLM group. That is a bad look for someone claiming to be conservative. She said that they wanted to reopen the schools during the dumb lockdowns, and they worked on that together.

A young man about thirty years old was handing out flyers about some US Senate candidate. I told him that I am running for US Senate also and that I am better qualified than his candidate. His eyes lit up due to being impressed upon meeting another candidate for this high office. I should have told him that any idiot can run by registering with the FEC and burning a few hundred dollars.

It made me think back to driving around in a light-green Chrysler K car at Fort Lee, Virginia, while in the Virginia National Guard. I would drive this car from the armory in Danville, Virginia, to bases for duty sometimes because my car had a lot of miles on it and I was a broke college student. I wondered why soldiers and entire formations were stopping to salute me early in the morning on the Army base. I was only a brand-new second lieutenant after graduating from officer candidate school (OCS). I was thinking, "Boy this is nice. I am getting plenty of respect here and now. This sure beats being an E4."

I walked around the car after getting to work and noticed the front bumper. The cover on the two-star license plate had fallen off. If anyone other than the general was in the car, they covered the plate. The soldiers thought I was a two-star cruising around. The US government bought many low-quality K cars to bail out Chrysler Motors back then. Lee Ioccoca, the CEO, made out like a bandit.

Dave White went on and on about how great a businessman he is. He is running for governor and anti-Trump. Good luck with that. The Trump team did an outstanding job. I saw some people falling asleep after gobbling down too many cheap hot dogs and cake. His parents had many hot summer nights and fourteen children. Now that is impressive.

The organizers would not let me speak, but we met many kind and normal Christian people there on this night. They are sick of big, corrupt government.

The event was held in the Hamburg Field House. This old place was made from a bridge that was torn down. You can see the bridge beams that hold up the roof of the building. It is huge with and old hardwood floor. The bathroom stalls are very old and small. They must have had only midgets and children in the building back then.

The Pennsylvania legislators, Supreme Court folks, and executive branch fools argued for years over voting districts. They refused to set and announce a three-to-four-week period for candidates to get signatures to get on the ballot. The period was supposed to begin on February 15 and end on March 8. These fools did not do their jobs again and must be fired.

They finally set our petition period as February 25 until March 15. This is a shorter period than planned for previously.

Many of us think they did this to favor establishment Democrats and RINOs or the uniparty idiots over people like me who want to cut back government and have accountability and honest government employees and politicians. We need outsiders who love and obey our state and federal constitution. We need Christians and conservatives to take over government soon before they destroy America.

We delivered and mailed many petition forms and instruction letters to about four hundred folks and groups. My only chance was that these folks I had met before would get several signatures for me. I found out on March 14 that many of them were not into it. They did not do anything to get my ideas or me on the ballot.

I will try not to take it personally. Many folks just do not trust strangers, candidates, or politicians. I fully understand that. They really did me a favor to ease me to quit on March 14. I love my life with Nancy and enjoy the good life after working hard for several decades.

I was disappointed that several veteran groups did not send in any signatures. The so-called leaders down near Fort Indiantown Gap would not put my petition out even though it was fully voluntary to sign to get me on the ballot. I guess they do not care about the many corrupt politicians in DC destroying America. Perhaps they did not want to offend any Democrats. We are in a dark time now and need folks to stand up for the constitution. This is not the time to be a sheep. They could have announced the petition and covered up any signatures.

Op-ed for the Lehigh Valley commentator (they never ran it):

David Xu, redneck for US Senate
Ashland, Pennsylvania, 17921

February 20, 2022
The Lehigh Valley Commentator

Re Redneck Dave Xu for US Senate from Pennsylvania

Hello, Editor,

I like your periodical. Please keep promoting capitalism and rejecting socialism and communism.

Sincerely,
David Xu
www.davidxuforsenate.com
dave224422@yahoo.com

Redneck David Xu for US
Senate from Pennsylvania

You might be a redneck if you believe that the constitution is thirty pages and many Supreme Court decisions should be ignored. Our socialist judges think the document is three thousand pages long. We should go by the original document. It is not a living document to assist socialist and communist judges, deep-state traitors, and politicians in ruining a great, capitalistic, and free America. Think Ginsburg. Redneck Dave Xu for US Senate.

You might be a redneck if you believe that the US government politicians should cut spending now. They have already run up at least $120 trillion in unfunded liabilities. Why can't they just run the government on $4 trillion per year, stay off TV, and shut up? Think Obama. Redneck Dave Xu for Senate.

You might be a redneck if you want term limits for our folks in the House, Senate, and Supreme Court. How about six years? Think Schumer at forty brutal years in government and Pelosi at thirty-four long, long years in the House.

You might be a redneck if you support a balanced budget amendment to our sacred constitution. Our founders would die if they saw how wasteful, huge, and corrupt our federal government is now after 246 years of folks spitting on our constitution by approving many, many dumb laws. Think Obamacare.

You might be a redneck if you demand that every voter show an ID and all illegal ballots not be counted. We must audit the elections from November 2020 and January 2021 to ensure that the correct folks are in office right now. Will ten days be long enough for that audit? Twardzik and Argall will not answer my question, "How many illegal ballots were counted during our 2020 election?" Many of us believe that Trump and other conservatives won their elections.

You might be a redneck if you want a convention of the states as allowed in our constitution. We need thirty-four states to call a convention and then thirty-eight to approve amendments to take back power from the corrupt full-time and long-term politicians in DC. Why are the House,

Senate, and Supreme Court jobs full-time now? They used to be part-time positions. Nobody needs to be passing laws all the time. Ask your politician to support a convention of the states.

You might be a redneck if you support breaking up big tech and big media. About half the country are being lied to now. Are you being shadow-banned? Did Trump do anything positive for the working, law-abiding citizens? He and his team were awesome for the United States. Was that virus man-made? Did Joe commit crimes with Hunter? Is Joe capable of being president? Did Kamala bail out violent criminals from BLM or *antifa* in 2020? Where is the evidence that most Americans are racist? I cannot find any evidence to support that lie, and I am from the South. Why are the lazy, union, or racist teachers still employed? We need to force news organizations to hire only real objective journalists. Too many journalists are liars and socialists or commies. The First Amendment should apply coast to coast.

You might be a redneck if you want a border wall. It should be tall with razor wire on top. We love immigrants who work hard but do not care for illegal aliens demanding free stuff from the socialist Democrats. Taking taxes from hardworking citizens and giving it to criminals in our country is not moral or fair. We must lock up all criminals stop the drugs coming from Mexico and China.

You might be a redneck if you want to ensure that the Supreme Court remains with only nine members. FDR got the party started for the Democrats trying to pack it with socialists and big government freaks. Many horrible nations such as Venezuela have done that with tragic consequences.

You might be a redneck if you want to reduce the power of the Federal Reserve bank. These arrogant folks increased interest rates to hurt Trump and lowered rates to help Clinton and Biden. They are buying $120 billion of treasury bonds, etc. each month to support our huge, abusive, corrupt government. They print US dollars like drunken sailors devaluing each one in our bank accounts. They brag about how smart they are from Jackson Hole every year on luxury trips paid for by the US government. Redneck Dave Xu for US Senate from Pennsylvania.

I use the word *redneck* as a compliment. To me, it means someone who works hard and plays hard and probably lives outside the big cities. They love limited government and reject socialism and communism. They do not study wine and cheese. They do not like wine and cheese. We called one another rednecks all the time in Southern Virginia and Florida growing up.

Most of the talk about systemic racism is exaggerated or a lie. I can count on one hand the racists I met or heard about in my forty years living in the great southern United States of America. Many folks are getting rich and famous lying about systemic racism. Please join us on gettr, gab, mewe, clouthub, Twitter, and FB. God bless America and the American redneck! Redneck Dave for US Senate.

David Xu
First official redneck candidate in
history (see FEC website)
www.davidxuforsenate.com

Candidate for US Senate from Pennsylvania, US Army retired, thirty years, Airborne, LTC, Pentagon and combat duty, Artillery; and author of *Easy Riders: The Older Ones*, *Redneck Dystopia* (Pocahontas wins), *Orphans in the Barn*, and the *Easy Eddie* series of books on Barnes & Noble, Amazon, and many retailers; IT business owner; college program head and instructor; real estate investor; Christian; volunteer

I connected to PCNTV with Zoom on February 23 for their call-in show. Phil asked me questions for thirty minutes. The questions had a Democrat or RINO bent to them. I just hammered the message of cutting back government to obey and enforce the constitution.

The questions from viewers and Phil asked about systemic racism. I told them that I have not seen any evidence that racism is systemic here in America. The fools promoting that false narrative never offer any proof because there is none. They are only seeking money, power, or fame with this nonsense. Many people never leave the big city and are ignorant on the topic and just agree with liars. Racism is abhorrent and is not accepted anywhere in America.

I had a dream at the beginning of March. I was a mouse who crawled into a bird cage and ate too much seed and could not fit between the bars to get out. The birds pecked at me, and it hurt.

I imagined the months ahead if by some miracle I made it onto the ballot. If the good voters gave me two thousand signatures, I would have to continue in this odd contest. Half of me wanted to drop out, and half of me wanted to get on the ballot and continue into the spring.

Most of the campaign was fun, but the long, boring speeches at the luncheons were brutal. One guy in a tight suit spoke of how smart a baby he was. He threatened to show his baby pictures in a PowerPoint slide show. The old woman next to me said, "I am surprised he figured out how to climb through the birth canal."

We drove up to Clifford on February 26 for a Lincoln Day event. We love the bad food and mediocre speeches. The GPS lost the signal, and we had no cell phone coverage. We came in a little late. There were about 150 Republicans there. We gathered a few signatures.

My favorite voters were two blue-collar guys toward the back of the dining hall. They heard my pitch and instantly signed the dumb petition. We need more business owners and hard workers like these muscular guys. One owned a construction business, and the other worked in construction. They wore jeans as I did. Many folks were in business casual or suits and ties.

All the candidates took group photos in a separate room before the stump speeches. This jackass in a tie running for lieutenant governor shook my hand but did not look at my face. I released and waved him off. If I ever see this fool again, I will inform him that if he does that crap in coal country, he will get punched in the face.

The master of ceremony informed the speakers that we cannot criticize the other candidates. I was thinking that takes all the fun out of it. I had new material. It would be wasted. People love a good insult. What is going on here?

I asked him just before I spoke if I could hammer Democrats, and he said that was fine. I told the Fetterman joke about his lack of brain power. "He is my favorite of the Democrats, but he is not quite ready to climb that tree of knowledge if you know what I mean." He reminds me of the turtles that survive under ice for weeks by barely maintaining consciousness. They threatened to remove anyone who insulted the other candidates. Now I would love to see that.

I was thinking about the old lawyer boxer from Philadelphia. George Bochetto would never make it. He rails at the carpetbaggers all the time. It is a good thing that he skipped this event.

I bet the old guy in the back $20 that Kathy Barnette would not make it past thirty seconds. She is tough. I like that. She bashes Bartos, McCormick, Oz, and Sands 24/7 and is very entertaining for sure.

The weather was awful that day. It was snowing and cold. I almost insulted David McCormick, who was seated behind the lectern, while I spoke but did not want to be kicked out.

"Is this weather not the best? You cannot beat that weather. Do you know where they have great weather? Connecticut. New Jersey is good, but Connecticut weather is the best. They have the best weather over there," I almost said to the crowd of Republicans and RINOs. This is a bit from *Seinfeld*. I would turn around and stare at McCormick after the punch line. If I had to do it over again, I would have gone for the cheap laugh and risked my ouster. The crowd could have used it after the bad food. I do it for the love…and the stupid signatures to get on the ballot.

McCormick is viewed with suspicion for being a member of the Democrat Party until 1996. He said Trump has a lot of responsibility for the January 6 event. He has said many dumb and dangerous things, such as, "When China succeeds, the United States succeeds." He has helped Bridgewater Associates make a lot of money off the CCP and China.

His work with the commies in China should disqualify him from public office here. McCormick and his latest wife, Dina Powell, worked for the ultimate RINOs Bush I and II and love the World Economic Forum folks who want one world government (socialist, of course). The big government loving Democrats at Goldman Sachs hired Dina in 2007 despite her having no background in finance. This is opinion and fact.

This skinny guy in a tie complained about others saying, "Let's go, Brandon." He thinks it is uncivil and was traumatized when he had to explain to his daughter who Brandon is. I think his name is Coleman. He is a waste of time and very weak. He is a beta male when we need alpha males to take back our country from many sick people. This is opinion.

I spoke about twenty minutes before Coleman and always end the talk with "Let's go, Brandon." This always gets a laugh and means that we have a corrupt fool in the White House supported by lying communist media folks. I guess this triggered this RINO imbecile.

I remember what my older brother Al always said. "All cats are gray in the dark," crazy Albert explained. He referred to bringing beautiful women home or not so beautiful women home after a wild night at the cowboy bar and grill in Orlando. He was fine either way when the lights went out. Any extra-large, medium, or small honky-tonk queen will do. Our friends in the We the People groups draw a bright line between conservative Christian Republicans and RINOs. They are *not* the same.

Nche Zama yelled at the crowd for five minutes when the light turned yellow. He walked to his table and screamed some more campaign crap. Some in the crowd did not like the dictator behavior. It was killing him to sit down and shut up.

Zama seemed a little too desperate to be the next governor. He lost by a wide margin to Doug Mastriano on May 17. I voted for Doug and not the strongman wannabe.

Another guy spoke about how great he would be as lieutenant governor. His cellphone went off during his stump speech. This pointed out one of the many flaws in his argument. He did wear a nice suit and tie for the occasion.

Nancy and I drove over to Morgantown, Pennsylvania, on March 5 for the trucker rally. These awesome Americans are protesting against CCP virus mandates such as vaccines and masks and huge, corrupt government. We saw many "Trump" and "Let's Go, Brandon" flags hanging off trucks and cars in the strip mall parking lot. These people realize that weak RINOs will always be destroyed by socialists and communists in the Democrat Party. We need to totally remove the RINOs and socialists from all levels of government to save America.

I met so many great citizens while running for the US Senate. One such couple was Sabrina and Norm Diehl in Saint Clair. They own and run a small auto repair shop. They display a huge Let's Go Brandon banner on the fence beside Highway 61. Norm received a nasty letter from a woman who disliked the banner. He displays her childish letter on the wall in his office as a badge of honor.

I met Kenneth and Norm Diehl back in April 2021 when first starting the US Senate campaign. They let me fly a David Xu for limited government and US Senate banner on their fence beside the highway. This hardworking father-and-son team wanted to help remove the immoral and lazy folks from government and supported me like nobody's business. Ken, the awesome Harley rider, passed away at the end of 2021. May he rest in peace.

Sabrina and Norm collect and deliver Easter baskets to poor children during March and April every year. They understand the damage done by huge, expensive, and corrupt government. We need more hardworking Christians and conservatives like them. I highly recommend Diehl's Auto Shop for tires, etc.

We walked around speaking to very nice folks and getting signatures to get on the ballot during the trucker rally. We cleaned up. I love the people who after hearing my brief pitch say, "Give me that pen. Where do I sign?"

"I am David Xu running for US Senate. I want to cut back government at least 10 percent and get back to the limited government mandated by our constitution. Is that enough? Do you want more?"

"No, give me that damn pen. That is enough for me. You sound great. Why have I not heard of you?" the informed voter said.

"Thank your local TV station and other media folks. These Democrats and RINOs will not cover me unless I spend a lot of money on advertising. We do not believe in that," I told the voter.

I noticed an old man staring at me. He looked irritated and nervous. His jaw was tight and face red. His wife was well dressed, smiling, and friendly. It looked like she was enjoying all the angry and hilarious conservatives and Christians having a great time standing up for limited government and against corrupt politicians such as Biden, Harris, Pelosi, and Schumer.

"Do you have a million dollars?" he said.

"Yes, we do. Do you mean for this Senate run? I do not think so. Do you have a million dollars?" I replied.

He stormed off, and his wife signed my petition to get on the ballot. She deserves better than this rude, old, bitter, and ugly guy. She deserves a younger, more intelligent, and attractive man.

I should have given him the *Seinfeld* line. In the show, a woman heckled him during his stand-up show. He went to her office and booed and hissed at her while she was trying to work. Also, a prisoner heckled him during his last show in the prison, and Seinfeld said, "Do I come down to your cell block and grab the license plate out of your hand?"

I should have said to this ugly old man, "Do I come to your old folks' home and tell you how to do your job? Okay, then do not tell me how to campaign." He was implying that we do not have enough money to win. The truth is, Nancy and I have plenty of money but not for a silly political campaign where others are burning tens of millions of dollars.

The worker on a train told me one time that a customer told him he handled a situation wrong. He told a woman that she should not have a normal bike on the train. Only bikes that fold in half are allowed. The male customer thought the train worker was too abrupt with the biker. He told the irritating man, "Have you ever seen me at your office telling you how to do your job?" The irritating man had nothing to say.

We stopped at a Weis Markets grocery store. I like that place, and Nancy worked at the headquarters in Sunbury and really liked the employees. "I peed here," was written on the bathroom wall. Did Fetterman write that? That seems like something he would do. Has he smoked too much weed? Maybe it was laced with something strong, and he blew a fuse.

One young couple wore costumes of the Statue of Liberty and Uncle Sam. Another couple had US flags painted on their faces. I wish all Americans were like this crowd, and we could turn back the clock and recapture the great America with limited government and freedom for all.

Some candidates and their volunteers were stressed out. A woman getting signatures for Doug Mastriano tried to butt in and get a signature from a voter we were talking to. She raised her voice in an aggressive way and irritated the voter and Nancy and me. I wonder if she was getting paid, and we were getting between her and some cash.

I saw Rick Saccone in a tight outfit trying to work the crowd. He looked like mental patient to me. He was aggressive like a fat wild animal that just got out of a cage. The previous week he was yelling into a microphone at a Lincoln Day meeting. I was thinking that he is turning off most people. He hurt my ears, and that is tough to do. I shot artillery for sixteen years.

Trump came to a rally for Saccone years before, but he lost to the lying Conor Lamb. Trump said that we must run the right kind of candidates. Was that a swipe at Saccone? Trump said that Lamb lied so much that he sounded like a Republican to get elected. I noticed that Lamb has voted 99 percent of the time with Pelosi and other socialist fools after his election. You would put yourself at great risk to get between Saccone and a ballot or a ham sandwich.

We met some awesome bikers. I love bikers. They will tell you what they think and do not give a crap what you think. A tall man had a German or Austrian accent, and I asked him about it. I like to guess where people are from. Many people do that with me and my Southern accent. I guessed that he was from Germany.

"Do you ask everyone you meet where they are from?" he said to me. He was very upset and glaring at me.

"Yes, it is a fun game to guess where folks are from, and I love different accents. Usually people ask me where I am from before I have the opportunity to ask them. We had two hundred Germans in my unit in Kuwait in 2003. The German politicians would not let them go into Iraq, and we all thought that was stupid," I informed him.

He agreed and said he moved to America from Germany for one reason, to get away from those dumb politicians and socialism. He and his nice wife are US citizens now, and they signed my petition. They rode very nice Harley-Davidsons.

I walked toward a Smart car in the parking lot to ask for signatures. The driver quickly rolled up his window and sped away. I was thinking, "Wow, this guy never wants to see another idiot running for office again." We had a Smart car a while back and loved it. My mother still has one and is obsessed with it. She has a life-size cardboard cutout of Kris Kristofferson in the passenger seat wearing a seat belt. People think she is a mental patient. She is just a superfan.

We met Ericka at the trucker rally. She spoke eloquently about how the immoral and childish politicians like Biden and Obama had politicized most government agencies and how many Americans do not trust anyone in the government now. Ericka, her family, and friends are fighting to take back our government and country. She volunteered to get many signatures for me to get on the ballot. She mailed many signatures to us later.

Nancy and I drove over to Bloomsburg to the New Covenant Church on March 8. The local We the People group were having a meeting, and we just had to go. They usually meet in an awesome horse training center but not when the weather is cold. I needed two thousand signatures, and many good folks would be there.

My friend Dan told me to be bold. He thought I was too reserved during interviews and speeches. I told him that I was just trying to be humble, but it is hard for such a successful and handsome person to act like they are humble.

Our friend Dave suggested that I downplay the redneck angle. He thinks it may lead some voters to think that I am not serious about getting into the Senate and making a difference. I explained to him that I am dead serious about voting in the Senate to get back to the constitution and just used the redneck theme to get attention in a crowded GOP primary. He always said that nobody worships Trump as the dumb Democrats suggest. They just loved his policies and that he stood up for common, normal Christian people like us.

I am reminded of what Winston Churchill said when asked about Mahatma Gandhi. Churchill wanted to keep India in the kingdom and did not care for Gandhi at all.

"Gandhi is great. He walks around in a sack and he is so humble," the person said.

"And he has a lot to be humble about," Winston replied.

We met so many awesome Christians and conservatives. They spoke of being worried for our country with the stupid children in charge of the government. The preacher and his wife were so nice and supportive. Amy and Rick Dilena are on fire for God, Jesus, the Bible, and the constitution. Nancy and I are the same way.

We spoke Jacob Bailey and his wife. They are helping take back our country and getting signatures for me. They see through the empty promises from corrupt politicians buying votes from lazy and ignorant folks and moving America toward sick one-party rule.

Webb Kline and his wife, Stacey, own a successful transportation company and love capitalism and limited government. They and others started this We the People of Columbia County group about one year ago, and it has grown so much. Webb wears a camel hair robe with a big leather belt around it and sandals. He dines on locusts and wild honey. I called him a wise man for giving us great advice for starting our WTP group. Okay, I made up the camel hair outfit. I told our group that we need a wise man in a cave while introducing Webb at our meeting. John the Baptist wore an outfit like that in the Bible, and it just sounded righteous.

These voters want to get back to the limited government mandated by our constitution. We all love God, Jesus, and the Bible and our capitalistic America where everything is based on merit. Gary, Craig Reichart, and so many other strong Christians are making a difference.

Craig does a lot of research on the candidates. I met him while I was out getting signatures to get on the ballot. His office had some great banners on it. One said, "Let's Go Brandon."

"Have you had the CCP virus or the vaccine? I had the Pfizer vaccine during 2021 and the virus during January 2022. Nancy had the Moderna vaccine. Getting the actual virus was no big deal for either of us. I kind of regret getting the vaccine. It may not work at all. We could have had mild symptoms without the vaccine in our blood," I informed Craig.

"I had the virus twice. The first time it was no big deal. The second time I got really sick, kind of like the flu. I will never get the vaccine. It is from the New World Order, World Health Organization, and/or the World Economic Forum idiots. I believe that they are giving mostly safe vaccines with deadly ones interspersed. It is like a lottery. I bet you had the safe one," Craig explained.

I hope and pray that the vaccines are safe but would not be surprised if Craig was correct. I just think Trump and many insiders would know about it if sick criminals were trying to kill folks in order to depopulate the earth. I noticed many members of this group do not trust our government folks at all and will never get a vaccine.

I spoke with a salesman at the Bloomsburg Harley-Davidson shop one day while out campaigning. He looked shell shocked or very stressed out sitting in the corner of the showroom. He said that he refused to get the vaccine because he did not trust the CDC fools and then contracted the actual virus and had to spend a couple weeks in the hospital. He took the vaccine after he recovered and regretted his delay. It is a shame that so many people in the government say or do dumb things so often that many Americans do not trust them in the least. Fauci and so many others must be removed and punished.

The Columbia County folks educated me on the need to get true Republicans into GOP committee slots to defeat the RINOs. Many slots are empty and most of the sixty-seven county GOP organizations will not support outsiders who want to severely cut back on government. Each county has many slots that help vet candidates and elect good conservatives and Christians.

Most Americans agree on the Bible and constitution, and we must get back to that. We do not have to agree on all the issues. People just want to be free to live their lives the way they want to. Hard work is the key. Limited government is required for this.

I greeted an old, chubby man in the parking lot. He had a MAGA hat on and veteran pins.

"I like that hat. Were you in the Eighty-Second Airborne?" I asked him.

"What?" the man responded. He was irritated.

He obviously does not take any crap from anyone. He was probably thinking, "Who is this idiot with the campaign posters in his hand?" He has seen many candidates and politicians lie to get elected and then proceed to ruin our capitalistic America while getting rich themselves. It is funny how that works.

I did not mind. I actually prefer this kind of person over a fake nice person. Many military folks like me are like that. I think it is hilarious when they snap at you. I like people with very direct communication. It helps reduce misunderstandings. They can get you killed in the military.

"I love that hat and think Trump did a fantastic job. I noticed your Eighty-Second pin," I clarified.

"No, my son was in the Eighty-Second, but I never served. I tried to but failed the physical in Richmond," the old man responded in a friendly voice now.

"That is amazing. I took the Army physical in Richmond, Virginia, in 1983. We spent the night in a bad part of town with criminals walking around shooting guns. I was in the Eighteenth Airborne headquarters at Fort Bragg, and the Eighty-Second was one of our four divisions during 2002," I told him.

Nancy and I met some nice and impressive candidates and voters during my Senate run. Andrew Shecktor spoke before me and was really impressive. He is running for the US House and knows that RINOs are so bad for America.

Andrew is a technical person who worked in electrical engineering and IT for years and then was elected to the Berwick Borough Council. He wants to elect folks who represent the people and not special-interests and only rich people. He spoke of the criminal acts by Biden and gang in allowing millions of illegal immigrants to walk into our awesome country from Mexico.

I met a guy supporting Kathy Barnette. She is running for my US Senate seat and seems okay. He was getting signatures for her to get on the ballot as Nancy and I were doing. He did not know I was an actual candidate and her competition.

"Can you sign for Kathy? She grew up on a pig farm and is a great conservative," the man explained.

"I would, but I am running for that Senate seat and need some signatures too. Will you sign my petition? She is good, but I am better," I explained to him.

"I don't know about that," he said with a laugh.

I spoke of the need for honest and accountable politicians and all the election cheating during 2020 and the GA runoff election in 2021.

"I am between 99 percent and 100 percent sure that Trump won and at least one of the candidates in GA."

I received an email on March 15 from the good socialists at YouTube informing me that they removed the video of my speech for violating their misinformation policy. They helpfully explain that I advanced false claims that widespread fraud, errors, and glitches changed the outcome of the US 2020 presidential election. I guess the Google partisans ignore all the evidence to the contrary on frank-speech.com and peternavarro.com and many other places.

We need better judges who will rule that the entire constitution applies online. The internet is the new public square, and many big tech folks should be punished for spitting on our constitution and civil rights. I posted the video of my outstanding speech on Rumble. It is still there today.

"If freedom of speech is taken away, then dumb and silent we may be led like sheep to the slaughter," General George Washington said in 1783. Biden and other fools have censored many Americans for a long time and should be punished severely.

Along those same lines, the idiots at the FTC should never have allowed Google to buy YouTube. It is too much power for socialist, communist fools pushing one-party rule in the great United States of America.

After the Bloomsburg event, Nancy and I drove to Pittsburgh for a forum at the University of Pittsburgh (the ultimate socialist bubble). We drove a couple hours the same night. I was sucking down coffee and about to fall asleep at the wheel and asked Nancy if she could drive. She said to put the pedal to the metal and take small sips.

"Can you drive? I am falling asleep. This coffee is not doing it for me. My cup is almost empty," I informed Nancy while rubbing my eyes and shaking my head to stay awake.

"Take small sips. When you run out, just wet your lips with the coffee until we get there," Nancy said to me. What a sweet woman! She has developed quite the acid tongue during the Senate campaign. I really dig it.

We were exhausted and stayed at a hotel on the way in State College. We chatted with so many awesome folks in Bloomsburg at the church. They lifted our spirits. It snowed that night and the following day on our trip. We were worn out from a speech and three-hour drive from Bloomsburg.

The next day I was waiting for my coffee at Dunkin' Donuts and needed a boost. The employee was announcing the drinks for customers to pick them up at the counter. "Extra-large hot coffee, twelve sugars, six creams." The overweight FedEx guy looked so excited to get his pick-me-up. I suddenly felt wide awake and so happy that my coffee and sugar addictions were not as bad as his. I was thinking, "How long is this guy's shift? How many more miles does he have to go? I do not think he is going to make it. Does he get that drink every day?"

The other three Republicans did not show up. Two leftist moderators asked me ten different ways how I would help illegal immigrants. I had ten different answers on how we liked legal immigration and disliked illegal immigration. I told them how we must cut welfare and any other incentive not to work and fill up the 10 million open jobs we have right now. We must light a fire under the young people to work and make products and services and live the American dream. This country is not great because of expensive and ridiculous government programs such as universal basic income.

Visiting the University of Pittsburgh felt like a forced march through hell. The students and others who asked me questions seemed devoid of good judgment and biblical wisdom. It was like being in Dante's hell to see so many ignorant and weak college students being manipulated into voting for corrupt Democrats such as Biden, Harris, Fetterman, and Wolf in exchange for free tuition, food, welfare, birth control, rent, health care, cable, phones, etc. It sucks to be dumb. The socialist Democrats and RINOs are not elites. They are known as government idiots around here. These folks belong in Venezuela, China, or Cuba.

"Do you have an extra dress and high heels?" I asked Nancy as we walked out of the University of Pittsburgh building. I wanted to dress up in disguise so the leftist college students would not harass or attack us. They may have eggs to throw. I wanted to embrace the spirit of Confederate President Jefferson Davis on the run at the end of the civil war. He dressed up like a woman to avoid the Union soldiers coming to arrest him on May 10, 1865, in Irwinville, Georgia. Davis and his entourage had to flee Richmond for Danville, Virginia, (my birthplace) during April.

We were lucky that we visited the lovely liberal college bubble during spring break. I could have become the GOP's only drag queen for the day. Perhaps that would have hurt me in the polls. I could have gone from 1 percent to negative 1 percent in the next GOP primary poll. That was a close call.

Back in January, Betty and Olivia invited me to the March forum in Pittsburgh. The email is the only one I ever received with pronouns in the signature block. I told Nancy that I should probably sit this one out. I figured it may be an ambush with leftists and maybe violent protesters who hate conservatives and Christians who want to cut welfare to the bone. We have seen many criminals injure or try to injure Republicans on TV. They are like the Brownshirts in Germany working for Hitler and the Nazis in the 1930s. They were socialists too.

January 24, 2022

Dear Team Xu,

I'm writing today to invite David Xu to participate in a live in-person discussion on foreign policy. This event will feature active Pennsylvania US Senate candidates for the 2022 election and is slated to take place in Pittsburgh the first week of March. *Please let us know if you are interested in joining this timely discussion and we can work together to finalize a date and time that is best for the majority of the candidates.*

This forum is hosted in partnership with Women & Girls Foundation, Casa San José, PUMP, and World Affairs Council of Pittsburgh. All candidates for the 2022 Pennsylvania US Senate election are invited to participate in this forum, where each candidate will have the chance to speak and respond to both prewritten and audience-generated questions presented by our moderators. The US Senate is integral in shaping foreign policy, making this event an incredible opportunity for candidates to share their ideas and positions on US foreign policy with prospective voters.

The tone of the forum will be strictly nonpartisan and will be facilitated in a fashion to encourage an insightful and thoughtful exchange of ideas on foreign policy. Each candidate will receive equal time to respond to all questions addressed to them, and audience questions will be moderated. *Topics will include immigration, climate policy, human rights, and diplomacy.*

We look forward to hearing back on your interest and availability. We are also happy to schedule a quick call with you if that is helpful. Further information, including the format of the event, will be provided prior to the forum in a follow-up email.

Thank you for considering this invitation, and we look forward to your participation.

Many thanks,
Betty

Betty Cruz
PRESIDENT & CEO
she • her • ella

I responded with my own redneck signature block below and credit them for inviting me anyway. It was spring break, and everyone was cordial to the redneck and his lovely wife.

January 28, 2022

Hi, Betty,

I would like to share my views on those topics with our youth. Many union teachers are brainwashing our kids and promoting trans, commie, lazy, immoral, and/or dumb lifestyles. They should teach math, reading, writing, critical thinking, and morals. Legal immigration is great. Illegal is very bad. Most climate change talk is exaggeration in order to gain or maintain power and money. I want to get back to the limited government mandated by our sacred thirty-page constitution. We must cut welfare and promote hard work. Socialism, communism, and racism suck!

David Xu
First official redneck candidate in
history (see FEC website)
There are only two genders. Take a guess.
http://www.davidxuforsenate.com

We arrived at the university at noon. The event organizers informed us that the three other Republicans did not show for various reasons. I guessed that they figured out that most of the folks involved were liberals or leftists and loved big, corrupt government and free stuff. I spared them my usual routine of how we need to cut back on college loans and make the students work unpaid or paid jobs. We also should make many folks serve in the military to protect all Americans. Freedom is not free, and many people have forgotten that.

The MIA Republicans were good for me. I was the only one there and did not have to sit through all their comments. I felt sorry for Erik Gerhardt, the libertarian candidate. He had to join the Democrat forum from several dumb Democrats promising free everything for anyone with a heartbeat.

The Democrats and RINOs remind me of the *Seinfeld* line, "Many people go their entire lives being dumb and ugly because nobody ever tells them." Perhaps we need to tell them now that we are taking our country back from fools.

Meeting the ignorant college students and leaders reminded me of the 2018 Program for International Student Assessment (an international evaluation of math, reading, and science skills of fifteen-year-old students). The Americans scored below students from China, Japan, the EU, Germany, and the United Kingdom. We must fire the lazy, dumb, immoral, union teachers now before it is too late to maintain American exceptionalism.

Two moderators asked me questions for an hour, and that was it. They asked me ten different ways how I would help illegal immigrants. I rejected their setup and informed them that we support legal immigrants and not illegal immigrants and that English should be the mandatory US language.

My wife Nancy does not go around demanding that Americans speak Mandarin. Why do folks demand that we speak Spanish in our own country. English should be mandatory in the United States. Why must we sit through the dumb outgoing messages at Lowes, government agencies, and elsewhere in Spanish. Just learn the language and get on with making great products and services in the land of milk and honey. This is America, baby.

The people who submitted questions to the moderators complained about prison conditions. I told them that we have two choices for violent idiots. We can put them in prison, or we can kill them. They want Guantanamo Bay closed. I told them that Cuba was the perfect place for Islamic terrorists, and they do not deserve protections under the Geneva Conventions because they do not wear uniforms and kill for no good reason. Prisoners should live in tents without cable and air conditioning. Our prisons are too nice and too expensive for the taxpayers.

Also, the government fools who do not prosecute or arrest criminals should face grand juries and go to jail if appropriate. These people are growing like weeds in many big cities and terrible for America. They are violating their oath to our state and federal constitutions.

I am reminded of the Seinfeld bit about prison. He and George were fascinated by prison life. "What is the deal with solitary confinement? Do we really need a prison within a prison? Isn't the sodomy and weightlifting enough punishment?" Seinfeld explained.

I told the moderators over and over that we need to cut welfare and end any incentives for people not to work. Capitalism depends on mostly young workers who work hard and provide ideas and also middle- and upper-income folks who provide the capital or money. All income citizens can then live in harmony in our great meritocracy. The Dems are attacking capitalism when they buy votes from people making them lazy and stupid.

The moderators wanted to help the Ukrainians. I told them we should have been selling them weapons for years, but Biden, Obama, and other fools only gave them blankets when the Russians invaded in 2014. Obama and the Democrats are weak and foolish here and abroad.

I told them that I am worried about hypersonic missiles landing in the United States much more than any other nation. Also, that I do not trust Biden and gang to protect us with the Southern border wide-open and being obsessed with woke nonsense.

Criminals and drugs are pouring across our Southern border killing over 100,000 people every year now. Biden and many need to be impeached and charged for crimes. The Chinese and Mexicans should be punished for pushing all the drugs into America through our Southern border. The Trump border wall would stop this crap.

I could tell by the faces in the forum hall that they could not believe what the Senate candidate was saying. It was amusing to me to try to educate these folks in this immoral, socialist bubble known as the college campus.

They were concerned about climate change and racism. I informed them that most of the talk of climate change and systemic racism is exaggeration and lies. I have seen no evidence that we must move to socialism and communism because of these false narratives pushed by corrupt politicians and ignorant others.

The police killed about one thousand unarmed folks last year. Under ten were black. They arrested about 10 million. This is not systemic anything. Many of the deceased were resisting arrest. We support our law enforcement, and we must arrest all the criminals and put them under the jail house.

Americans have been good to our environment. Our emissions went down in the last twenty years while more cars and people worked and played. This is amazing, and we need to protect our planet and drill, baby, drill for energy independence. Trump had us on the right track in so many ways.

The United States gets 61 percent of our electricity from fossil fuels, 19 percent from nuclear power plants, and 20 percent from renewables. This why we say "Drill, baby, drill." We must ignore the climate change communist liars and power on with our awesome nation.

I thanked the cops and security guards on the way out of the university. I told them that they had it tougher than us soldiers with the rules of engagement. We shoot at any threat in the combat zone, but the cops have to be more careful who they shoot. Also, the cops have to work for immoral politicians who care only about themselves and their bank accounts.

I had an idea to improve the mental ability of Fetterman. He seems mentally challenged for sure. Scientists are raising pigs like crazy to be organ donors to humans. Perhaps we can remove Fetterman's peanut-sized brain and upgrade him with a large pig brain. That is bound to help my oldest boy with critical thinking. Pig hearts have worked for a short time in brain-dead people.

Fetterman and other fools on the Pennsylvania Board of Pardons successfully urged Governor-Dictator Wolf to free Raymond Johnson (aka a son of the devil) from prison in 2019. Johnson and another man shot and stabbed a man to death in York County back in 1973. He walks free today thanks to Wolf and Fetterman. Perhaps the electric chair would have been more suitable for Johnson and the taxpayers.

Scientists are using gene editing to create pigs with organs that the human body accepts. With a new, improved pig brain, perhaps Fetterman will not say things like, "We can let out a third of the prisoners without increasing crime." On the downside, he may gain weight and become more grotesque if that is even possible. His shape could go from turtle-like to piglike in a few weeks. Does that make sense?

We love the Babylon Bee. They had a different take on Fetterman. Here is their headline about my man: "Neck Lump Has Gross Politician Growing Out of It." The writers helpfully explain that the hoodie makes perfect sense now to hide the disgusting politician and save the campaign for US Senate. The neck lump's campaign is embarrassed by Fetterman.

Fetterman should really move to Manhattan and get his parents to pay for an apartment. The police over there are handing out pamphlets in the subway telling citizens about personal safety tips. Why are they ignoring all the stupid criminals and bothering good taxpayers? They may as well grab a guitar and play for tips. This is almost funny, but not really because so many people have been attacked on the subway since the ridiculous Democrat Party "Defund the police" movement.

We should deport Fetterman to New York state. The Democrats up there established a $200 million slush fund for people who were arrested for drugs in the past. Each drug fool can now borrow at 14 percent from the government idiots to start a cannabis business. Fetterman could start a pot store after he is thrown out of the Pennsylvania government and is destroyed in this senate race by my man Oz.

I dropped out of the race on March 14, 2022. What a relief. I had tears of joy. Below is my front-porch speech and post on the campaign website. It was a sad and happy day. The angry and brutal voters and party members scared me straight. I vowed to never run for any office ever again. Nancy and I laughed over the many funny and odd things that happened during the campaign and then grilled some awesome rib eyes.

I remembered one woman at the cash register in a retail store placing my campaign flyer in the trash can as I turned to walk out of the store. The voters are angry and brutal, my friends. I like that. I respect that. She did not have time for another liar trying to get elected.

March 14, 2022

I did not make it. I have decided today to suspend my campaign for US Senate from Pennsylvania. Nancy and I have been at this about a year and met so many great, kind, generous, and Christian folks. This was always a guerrilla redneck campaign self-funded with about $4,000, blind faith, and duct tape for an old soldier with some health issues. We used to call each other rednecks all the time in the South. Us rednecks love capitalism, limited government, and the freedom to work hard and play hard. We despise full-time and long-term fake politicians in suits and ties. They remind me of that bumper sticker, "No human being is worthless. They can always serve as a bad example."

I have never begged anyone for anything and did not want to start now by begging for campaign contributions or even signatures to get on the GOP primary ballot. I wanted to see how far my platform and ideas would go and promote capitalism and our great American meritocracy along the way. We had a lot of fun with great people across the state. I learned a lot about myself. No, just kidding, I learned nothing about myself. I hate myself.

Let us destroy socialism, communism, and tribalism now to save America from the radical leftists. Let us cut welfare and government spending before they bankrupt America. Let us remove all corrupt, lazy, and immoral Democrats and RINOs (the establishment or uniparty) from our government now. They only care about ruling over others and making a lot of money. We love God, Jesus, the Bible, and the original constitution. We need normal, common folks in DC with accountability and honesty. We need union, lazy folks out of government. Thank you, volunteers, for all your help. Thank you, voters, for all your cruel observations and very creative insults. I will carry that pain and good humor with honor for all my days. Sometimes silence is louder than thunder, and perhaps you gave me the highest compliment in saying that I do not belong in the group of corrupt politicians in DC (Hollywood for ugly people). Better days are ahead. Most Americans hate big, corrupt government. The constitution will be enforced soon. America is the greatest nation ever to exist. It is exhausting being with you. I am hungry now. Let's go, Brandon!

The Senate ethics committee folks ask for our personal financial information from time to time. They fined me $200 one time for being late with their silly reports. Here is their latest request after I dropped out of the race. I believe that they are violating our constitution and laws in requiring this information from Nancy and me.

I am not a member of the US Senate and do not have to follow their stupid rules that are designed to keep normal, common folks out of government. This is yet another example of big, abusive, and corrupt government in the good old USA. We must have term limits and accountable, honest politicians.

Big government working with big business is a socialist and corruption disaster. John Adams and George Washington warned us about this back in the 1700s. We remember Enron giving money to the Bushes in Texas and many other politicians and hiding hundreds of millions in losses and debt. Perhaps W would not have been a governor or president without all the corporate cash.

Arthur Anderson audited Enron for sixteen years before both companies filed for bankruptcy amid convictions of financial crimes, obstructing government investigations, and destroying evidence. Many politicians took the easy money from these corporations and had a great time getting elected and looking the other way until it all came tumbling down in 2001.

The idiots in Congress passed the Sarbanes-Oxley Act in 2002 to show they were doing something about the criminal activity that had ignored for so long. The government folks are always the last to do anything. They usually miss huge clues to the crime until after many innocent citizens get hurt. This law imposed a lot more unnecessary cost on big corporations, which just jacked up their prices on consumers.

The geniuses on the US Supreme Court overturned the criminal conviction of the company Arthur Andersen in 2005. One problem was the that the prosecutors should have charged individuals with crimes and not the company itself. Good job, Democrats and RINOs, in wasting so much government and citizen money. Trump says drain the swamp.

We must get back to hardcore American-style capitalism, which has lifted more people out of poverty than any other system devised by man. The socialists and communists must go now. The intelligent adults must take back the American government from the dumb children such as Biden and Harris. Princess Charlotte and her brother Prince George would do a much better job of running our government than what we have now.

The Obama-Biden regime folks were frightened of the Tea Party folks and began labeling all conservatives and Christians as terrible Americans in 2009. The Biden-Harris regime people continue this disgusting behavior today. Many totalitarian regimes throughout history have done this to dehumanize their political opponents. Obama and friends promoted fake racism every chance they had also.

It always ends with many good folks going to jail or being executed. The socialists and communists have killed over 100 million so far. The American socialists and communists will do the same if we do not destroy them at the polls and in the public square now before it is too late.

We must teach our youth about the horrors committed by socialists and communists. They will go down in flames soon. The Chinese commies have destroyed many churches and killed over 60 million people so far. They threaten good people all the time these days. AOC would look better in an orange jumpsuit with Bernie. How on earth did these people graduate from a college? Why did Twitter have a CCP idiot on the payroll recently? The Facebook, Amazon, and Google owners and managers have censored good conservatives for years, including myself. They should go to jail tonight for violating our sacred constitution. This is opinion and fact.

I find it amusing that the Google folks pulled out of China in 2010 after refusing to censor for the CCP. These same Google fools censor Christians and conservatives like crazy in the great and free United States of America. Let us lock them up for violating the constitution and break up big tech. Google had no problem making money with and for the CCP until 2022 when they finally shut down their translation service in China.

We need to fire many, many government idiots and cut taxes. Over four hundred of them were at the school in Uvalde, Texas, in May and waited over an hour to kill the killer. No government employee should be allowed to join the corrupt unions. A serious reading of the constitution would prevent most of the US government. Vote GOP!

President Reagan knew how to handle lazy and greedy government union folks. The Air Traffic Controllers threatened to go on strike in 1981. Reagan warned them not to do it and that he would fire them if they made the foolish move. They did indeed go on strike, and Reagan followed through and fired all 11,000 of them. The Russians could not believe it and realized that Reagan embraced peace through strength. The ever-weak Biden cheers on the incompetent and lazy union members, and Hunter took in millions from Russian government and corrupt people.

Let us not forget that the Democrats caused murders to rise by 30 percent in the United States in 2020 with their stupid defund-the-police movement. They want the voters to forget their riots and marches now before the next election. We love the police, and they abhor the police. The Democrat Party today is mostly a mafia-type organization that will cut off your arm to gain or maintain power. Think CCP.

Why have the corrupt American politicians allowed foreign investors to buy over 37 million acres of agricultural land? This should be zero. The CCP folks have stolen US agricultural technology and trade secrets for many years. High-tech seeds and food production are kind of important to a society. Perhaps the American government folks are stupid and corrupt and the Chinese government folks evil and too lazy or dumb to do their own research? We need adult GOP leadership now to put America first.

Nancy and I were chatting with our neighbors Deb, Dan, David, and Jay Zaharick. You really want these folks on your side in a fight or campaign. They work hard and play hard and ride ATVs. They despise big, corrupt government and dumb politicians in ties. Dan said he liked my redneck theme. David thought I should downplay that theme so everyone would know that I am a serious candidate. I went with Dan's advice on this one and never looked back.

Here is some more good news. Over 70 percent of Americans want the border closed, more limited government, low inflation, criminals arrested, blind justice, secure elections, and conservative Christian values. Vote on election day for the GOP candidates to overcome the Democrat cheaters!

More than 2,600 US government idiots reported owning or trading stocks that stood to rise or fall with decisions their agencies made, according to a *Wall Street Journal* investigation. The journalists analyzed over 31,000 financial disclosure forms for about 12,000 senior career employees, political staff, and presidential appointees in the US government from 2016 until 2021.

How much corruption must we tolerate? When will these corrupt fools be fired and/or arrested? Why are so many hardworking Americans ignoring this? We must get back to the limited government mandated by our sacred constitution now.

The American communists have learned well how to live like kings on the taxpayers' money from the Chinese communists or CCP. We need more judges who will rule as unconstitutional many government programs. The dumb and corrupt judges just rubber stamp many programs under the general welfare clause, which is meant primarily for national defense.

Speaking of national defense, General Michael Flynn would have been a fantastic National Security Advisor to Trump if the deep state had failed to get rid of him. I believe that Flynn could have stopped the Russia collusion hoax and a lot of the lies and exaggerations surrounding the CCP virus. I bet he could have publicized the Hunter Biden laptop and all those crimes and unethical behavior *before* the 2020 election.

Obama and other fools knew that Flynn would have access to all their lies and crimes. The Democrats schemed with FBI Director Comey to destroy Flynn within a month of his appointment by Trump. Many folks must be put in or under the jail for treason and other felonies. We have a constitutional republic and a cancer inside it made up of socialist Democrats and RINOs from hell.

Biden and other communist fools are engaged in widespread illegal discrimination against white and Asian Americans. Their equity crap is code for excluding citizens based on skin color. These racists should go to jail. Vote GOP!

One of Biden's first illegal executive orders was to mandate racial equity, whatever that means. Why are judges, prosecutors, and other government folks allowing these idiots to discriminate 157 years after the Civil War? The Democrat Party is full of sick communist people.

"Biden's restaurant relief program excludes white male owners. They will not be considered for three weeks when the program is expected to be depleted," the Daily Wire explained on May 12, 2021.

"Equity redistribution is utopian socialism destroying personal responsibility and property rights leading to impoverished living standards," Bob Bishop said in The Gateway Pundit. We better wake up the many Americans who are oblivious to the disgusting behavior of most Democrats nowadays. Did you notice that many employees in and out of government cannot count to ten or perform basic tasks due to politicians and their stupid programs?

CHAPTER 7

THE RELIEVED REDNECK

AFTER THE GUERRILLA CAMPAIGN, MARCH
2022 TO SEPTEMBER 2022

> I have a problem with the silver medal. It's
> like, congratulations, you almost won. Of
> all the losers, you're the number one loser.
> —Jerry Seinfeld

I think I know how Abraham's son Isaac felt at the altar on top of the mountain when God provided a ram to sacrifice instead of poor Isaac. Abraham actually promised to off his son there in Moriah. He built the altar, and he was going to use it.

I had a similar feeling when I dropped out of this senate race. It was such a relief to know that the corrupt media and political folks would tell lies and dig us dirt about one of my competitors and not me. I was spared from being sacrificed on the altar of the government church. I felt joy and relief to get back to my wonderful life on the farm. Perhaps everyone has skeletons in their closet, and it is usually best to keep them in there.

(juliet_michaelsen@ethics.senate.gov)
To dave224422@yahoo.com
Wednesday, March 16 at 4:37 p.m.

Good afternoon,

Earlier today, you received an email from financial_disclosure@ethics.senate.gov stating that the due date for your upcoming Financial Disclosure Report was April 17, 2022. The correct due date for the report is *May 16, 2022*.

The due date has been corrected on your account at efd.senate.gov. We apologize for any inconvenience. Please do not hesitate to contact us if you have any questions.

Sincerely,
Juliet

Juliet Michaelsen
Financial Disclosure Specialist
Select Committee on Ethics
220 Hart Building
United States Senate
Washington, DC 20510
(202) 224-2981 (Office)

*****

(dave224422@yahoo.com)
To Michaelsen, Juliet (Ethics)
Wednesday, March 16 at 8:34 p.m.

I dropped out of the Senate race. Must I still file your silly reports? They seem to be illegal as I am not a member of the Senate. We must get back to the limited government mandated by our constitution. Our government is too big and abusive. Socialism and communism suck!

*****

Michaelsen, Juliet (Ethics) (juliet_michaelsen@ ethics.senate.gov)
To David Xu
Thursday, March 17 at 9:59 a.m.

Good morning, David,

Thank you for your email. Based on the information provided, we have disinvited you from filing this financial disclosure report.

Best,
Juliet

Did you notice the wording? She disinvited me from filing the report. I did not know it was optional before when I sent our 401(k), IRA, real estate information to these deep-state folks. Perhaps we need to disinvite them from our next pig roast or tractor pull in glorious coal country (Ashland, Pennsylvania).

Let us not be like the weak and cowardly Chinese nationalists who gave up and fled to Taiwan seventy-three years ago. The communists destroyed the corrupt, weak folks and took their guns and ammo. Let us not be like the weak and socialist Europeans who still buy oil from the evil and aggressive Russians and Iranians. Let us rise up and destroy the socialists, communists, and killers in Russia, China, Iran, North Korea, Venezuela, Cuba, and the United States of America now.

The uniparty of Democrats and RINOs are buying the votes to gain and maintain power. They are using tax money from the hard workers and capitalists in America to buy voters and their souls with welfare. The lazy idiots enjoying the free stuff now will be thrown in jail or executed later. This is always what socialists do after gaining power and the guns. They do not need the voters after they gain political power. Read about Mao, Xi, Putin, Erdogan, Castro, Lenin, and Chavez.

The strong will always abuse the weak. That is human nature. The American patriots will prevail. This is always the case here. Let us wake up the folks who are still asleep as if it is 1980.

We must remove all anticonstitution folks from government before they waterboard us. Do not forget that KSM was waterboarded 183 times. We do not want to be like that fat and hairy idiot in the dirty T-shirt. Those commies love to torture people. They put the whole family in prison in China for criticizing the government idiots. We cannot have that in America.

As I write this book in March 2022, we have multiple crises going on here and abroad. We have the evil Russians killing the poor Ukrainians. The Democrat Party idiots at the Federal Reserve are finally raising interest rates after lying about inflation being temporary for months and months to help the Biden regime move us toward socialism before most Americans wake up.

We have surging commodity prices due to the Fed printing money and the politicians still paying people not to work, still imposing CCP virus restrictions, and cutting American energy production in the name of fake climate change. All the while, we have dumb children running the entire United States government and calling everyone else a racist or a terrorist. Something has to give.

I pray that we can remove these fools now with grand juries, impeaching, and expelling from Congress and with the November 2022 midterm elections and get back to more limited government and the constitution.

I joined Nextdoor (a local social media website) to spread the word about the commies taking over America. The fools (opinion) who run it banned me for two weeks for the following post during April 2022: "Please vote for people who will put the disgusting criminals in or under the jail. Murders went up 30 percent last year in America and gun thefts went up 29 percent in 10 major US cities over the past two years. We do not have a racist problem. We have a criminal problem."

Devin and Shawn Hartman are the best. They defended me and my right-wing propaganda. They are great patriots who homeschool their kids in an outstanding way to avoid the CRT madness and other immorality in the government schools. They helped set up and run our county group at the following website. We meet in our barn once per month (www.wethepeoplecoalcountry.com).

Perhaps the Nextdoor folks love criminals and specifically criminals who steal guns? Many Democrats are like the kids at Dream Lake Elementary School in Apopka, Florida. I grew up there from 1965 until 1975. They enjoy calling others names (such as racist) and avoiding the hard work of being an adult. This is opinion and fact.

Meanwhile, it is so nice to live the good life here in coal country with such great Americans. I love the trucks and deer rolling and running around. We had some black bear visit a few months ago.

I hope that our We the People groups can stand up and win like the paratroopers who missed their drop zone in France on June 6, 1944. These fifty-two brave soldiers were led by Sergeants OB Hill and Ray Hummel who were just barely in their twenties. They had no heavy weapons, officers, or radios, but they still killed many Germans and stopped them from reinforcing other enemy units.

These great patriots were rescued after fighting hard for five days. We need more brave, Christian, and strong Americans now to incarcerate or kill all socialists and communists and take power from the corrupt fools in the District of Columbia.

There are no rules or laws unless someone enforces them. Do you want Christians and conservatives to enforce them? Or do you want ignorant socialists and communists within the corrupt Democrat Party to rule? We started We the People of Coal Country in Ashland, Pennsylvania, to get back to our constitution and Bible during March 2022. The website is wethepeoplecoalcountry.com.

"You cannot bring that camera crew in here. The owner of the property does not want them here," the men informed Carla Sands and her campaign aide. She had just arrived at an event for candidates to speak to the voters in Allentown during April. What she found out later was that the men worked for Dave McCormick, another candidate for the same US Senate seat. They lied to Carla to keep the Showtime camera crew out of the event. The owner of the property and the event organizer Tom Carroll had no such rule. Did McCormick know about this lying? Does he support the dangerous goals of the World Economic Forum?

Carla drove down the road and did an interview and returned to speak to the voters. I guess this is an example of why they say politics is cutthroat.

Sam and Linda Brancadora, founders of the Berks County Patriots, invited me to join other WTP group leaders to vet or chat with candidates and relay their answers and our opinions to our members. We do this to help educate our voters. We are just trying to get conservatives and Christians into government positions and immoral, socialist, communist, stupid, union folks out of government.

We met with Carla Sands on April 14 in Blandon at the local GOP headquarters in a strip mall. Sam and Linda had the virus and could not participate. It was our loss for sure. Some Hispanic Christians were making a joyful and loud noise for Jesus next door. The walls are thin.

Carla was mostly impressive but seemed not to know how corrupt the Federal Reserve bank folks are in enabling massive US dollar printing, borrowing, and spending to buy votes when I asked her about it. The ten-to-one Democrat to Republican economists at the Fed love big, expensive, and corrupt government.

She is a bossy thing. She barked at her young worker to ask the Hispanic church members next door to support her US Senate campaign. The young lady said she did not want to interrupt their church service with a political request.

She said that she would eliminate or drastically cut back the Department of Education. This deep state operation loves unions and woke nonsense and is terrible for America. Many union teachers only care about their pay and benefits and not the children and their education. They loved the dumb virus lockdowns and not teaching our youth while continuing to be paid.

A staunch Kathy Barnette supporter asked Carla about her statement that Kathy lost to a Democrat by 20 points two years ago for the US House. The supporter believes like Kathy that the Democrats' side cheated during the election. Carla said that the cheating did not change the outcome and that there is no way for Kathy to beat Fetterman in November. We disagree with this opinion for sure.

Carla talked about her faith in God and Jesus and said that many preachers had endorsed her. She seemed sincere about the greatness of God and Jesus and the Bible. We can agree on that for sure.

Carla is good at dropping names. She casually mentioned that Ric Grenell had introduced her to a Showtime producer, and it would be great for her campaign to have a cameraman follow her around for a day. She just happened to mention that Betsy Devos told her that the entire Department of Education could be wiped out, and the United States and its youth would be much better off.

I found out after meeting with Carla that she called Tom Carroll and asked him to convince Kathy Barnette to drop out of the Senate race. I think this showed poor judgment because Tom has supported Kathy for a long time. Any person with common sense would not ask a loyal friend to do that. This is opinion.

Eight WTP group leaders met with Kathy Barnette on April 29 at Sam and Linda Brancadora's luxury home. Kathy, her daughter, and campaign aide Kristin came. I asked her what she would cut, and she said that they should eliminate the Department of Education. Kathy was impressive as a normal, common, conservative Christian person. She has had some success of getting voters to switch from the Democrat Party to the GOP. Nancy and I helped with that during my campaign too.

Peggy Buhalo was at the meeting and as always thoroughly prepared with excellent questions for Kathy. Peggy runs the Patriots of Lancaster County and is tough as nails and also one of the nicest people I have ever met. She will call a liar a liar without regard to their position or status. The world would be a better place with more Peggys.

Kathy will appeal to many black voters who for some odd reason only vote for other black people. She described meeting with some Amish folks and encouraging them to vote. I encouraged many Amish to vote, but most said that they would continue to abstain. That is too bad because their values align with ours in the GOP coming out of the Bible and constitution. We made a decision the next week to cut her a check and endorse her with our WTP of Coal Country group.

Many We the People groups created a declaration on April 30 in Allentown to stop election cheating in Pennsylvania as follows. Sam Faddis (retired CIA) is the brains behind this project. The dumb or corrupt Republicans in the Pennsylvania house and senate voted for Act 77 that allowed the corrupt Democrats to cheat during the 2020 election and install the fools Biden and Harris. They are ruining America as I write this book and must be stopped. In my opinion, Governor Wolf and many others should be impeached and/or arrested.

Election Integrity Declaration

Whereas electoral integrity is essential to the functioning of a constitutional republic, and

Whereas, the move to mail-in and drop-box voting in Pennsylvania has seriously undermined the integrity of our electoral process.

We the People of the Commonwealth of Pennsylvania do hereby demand that the Pennsylvania state legislature immediately return the Commonwealth to in-person voting on election day, with the exceptions as noted in the PA election code prior to ACT 77, with photo identification, proof of US citizenship, state residency and hard copy paper ballots.

Attested to this _____ day of April 2022.

Dr. Herb Kunkle spoke, and he is very impressive and funny. He said his father always said after he retired that he was "retarded now." Herb wants to elect and support patriots to office who are courageous, conservative, obey the constitution, and have common sense. He calls this the four Cs. About ten of us are focusing on people in the Pennsylvania house and senate. The house has 203 and the senate fifty folks. About 110 in the house represent us, and about ten in the senate are good conservatives.

Leah Hoopes and Gregory Stentrom were there. They have gathered a lot of evidence of election cheating in Delaware County, Pennsylvania. They presented McSwain, Shapiro, and others with the evidence, and they did nothing. Shapiro actually sent agents to their houses to harass them for turning in election cheaters. How about that for effective governance?

The socialist Shapiro is now running for governor against our man Doug Mastriano. Let us destroy the corrupt Democrats in November 2022. Leah and Greg's book *The Parallel Election* is great.

They found over 120,000 ballots that probably contributed to creepy Joe's alleged 81,000 victory. It is shocking that many alleged felonies have not been properly investigated. At least forty-seven thumb drives were mishandled or erased. The law requires that all election records be kept for twenty-two months.

It gives Democrat voters a bad name when their party leaders are not interested in probable crimes by their members. The party leaders just shout insults and lies at the conservatives, Christians, Republicans, and other honest people who are 99 percent sure that Biden and Harris cheated big time.

Greg was a poll watcher on election night in 2020 in the counting center in Delaware County. He saw many ballots separated from their envelopes. This destroys any chance of a good audit. He had to wait about five hours before the supervisors even let him in the counting center. We need to get rid of big ballot counting centers where idiots can cheat.

Greg also saw people running the election uploading USB cards into voting machines over twenty-four times. He informed a deputy sheriff and clerk of elections. What did they do with this information? Greg saw many folks working alone with ballots. They should have worked with someone and/or been observed at all times.

McSwain was told about a lot of probable election cheating, but he did not follow through.

Greg and Leah filed a lawsuit on November 18, 2021, that said they can prove that November 3, 2020, election, data materials, and equipment were destroyed including but not limited to V-drives, return sheets, machine tapes / proof sheets / result tapes, mail-in ballots, ballots destroyed, voting machines, hard drives, paper documentation, Blue Crest data, and correspondence concerning the election. What did the judge do with this information?

I pray to God and Jesus for Greg, his family, and friends. His son, Brian, took his life on February 6, 2021, at thirty-three years old. He called his father a Nazi before he died. I thank God for Greg and Leah for exposing election cheaters. The probable cheaters must face a grand jury now.

Al Martin from Arkansas is going around the country trying to pass a Twenty-Eight Amendment that removes Biden and Harris and elects people who actually obey the constitution. His proposal is below.

Amendment 28

Reasons for Enacting the 28th Amendment:

The impeachment process has proven to ineffective and flawed to remove a sitting President from office regardless of the offenses committed.

Amendment 28 is necessary because there currently exists no other method in the Constitution to remove a President from office who is derelict of duty, corrupt, incompetent, or lawless.

Amendment 28 is necessary because the Constitution provides no other method to remove a lawless, incompetent and or corrupt administration from power.

Amendment 28 is necessary because there are no effective restraints in the Constitution to prevent a President from engaging in foreign or domestic abuse of power.

Amendment 28 is necessary when the other branches of government fail to prevent the President from excessive use of their Executive Orders.

Amendment 28 is necessary to give the citizens of the states the ultimate power and authority to remove a President and their administration should they be corrupt, derelict of duty, incompetent, or whose actions pose a threat to the citizens lives, freedoms, or property.

Amendment 28 is necessary because the citizens of the republic have no other recourse to remove a rogue and lawless President than by vote every four years.

28th Amendment to the Constitution:

Section 1. The States, on the Application of three fourths majority of the Legislatures of three fourths of the several states, shall have the right and authority to call a National Referendum to Recall the President of the United States, including the Vice-President, and his or her cabinet, should the President be derelict of duty, treasonous, incompetent, corrupt or violates their sworn duty to preserve, protect and defend the Constitution of the United States.

Section 2. The States, upon three fourths majority of the Legislatures, shall convene to determine the date and conditions of the Referendum, and the term of the New President which will not be less than two years and not more than four.

Section 3. Coinciding with the National Referendum to Recall the President, the Vice-President and his or her cabinet, a national election will be held at the exact time to elect a new President.

Section 4. The National election of a new President will be determined by majority of the electoral college.

Section 5. Upon the assembly and vote of the Electoral College, the Recalled President, and Vice-President will be removed from office and replaced by the newly elected President and Vice-President as determined by the Electoral College.

Anne Applebaum put it this way in the *Atlantic*, "There is no natural liberal world order, and there are no rules without someone to enforce them." She makes a great point as many leftists, and liberals just assume that someone will protect them as they lie idle on drugs and/or alcohol soaking up free stuff paid for by hard workers. Perhaps they never even contemplate this reality.

"Mr Putin's attack (in 2022) on Ukraine demonstrates that many people in the West had grown complacent about the peace and prosperity brought about by the liberal order that has prevailed in recent decades," Francis Fukuyama. I noticed this decades ago when I joined the Army in 1983. Most soldiers are recruited in the South, as I was from Virginia. I noticed that many folks in the Northern big cities did not care and even lift a finger to defend our constitution and nation. This group has only gotten bigger over the last few decades.

A recent poll found that over 60 percent of Democrats would not fight if we were invaded. I believe that we need a draft to force people from all counties to serve two years in the military. Freedom is not free. It could be a lottery because we do not need all young folks to serve in the military. If you are not willing to fight and die for our freedom, you should not enjoy it. This is America, baby! Love it or leave it.

President Reagan said, "Freedom is never more than one generation away from extinction." We are dangerously close to this because of many socialist college employees teaching our youth about the joys of socialism and communism. These fools have never lived in a socialist or communist nation and should be fired and put in jail for preaching this garbage in our capitalistic and great America.

Decades of political corruption in America have eroded public trust. The government idiots are playing with fire because if we are invaded, many Americans would not fight. I want to get into the US Senate to live by the Bible and constitution and restore the public trust. We will be lucky if several nations do not combine to invade us while we have fools running our government and Pentagon.

My guy in the Pennsylvania senate David Argall is still not doing enough to arrest all the election cheaters and save our nation from the sick socialists and communists. Perhaps he is content with his $100,000 pension for thirty-five years of wasting tax money in the Pennsylvania government? Here are some more emails to my representatives in the Pennsylvania house and senate Tim Twardzik and David Argall from May 2022. It is six months before the midterm elections, and we are worried about the Democrats stealing another election. It seems like most Republicans in our government are still asleep and must be removed.

From David Xu
To Rep. Tim Twardzik, Tim Twardzik
Wednesday, May 4 at 9:04 a.m.

Tim,

Did Trump win? We believe that he did. How many illegal ballots were counted in 2020? Did you read or watch the massive amounts of evidence of election cheating on frankspeech.com, 2000 Mules, rigged movie, etc.? Why did you certify the results? When will the audit be completed? Can you remove, impeach, or prosecute the many election cheaters? Use your position to stop the sick socialists, communists, and other fools before they impose the CCP model in America. Under 8 percent of the Chinese belong to the corrupt CCP who have all the guns but rule the others with an iron fist. We must get back to the constitution and Bible to save America. Sorry to be blunt, but it seems like our Republicans are asleep. Can you reduce the number of folks in the Pennsylvania house to sixty-seven or less from 203 and cut the salaries for everyone in the Pennsylvania senate and house? The $92,000 per year is outrageous. Your job should be part-time for sure. The voters are angry, my friend.

David Xu
http://www.wethepeoplecoalcountry.com

*****

From David Xu
To Senator David Argall
Tuesday, May 3 at 11:22 p.m.

David,

How many illegal ballots were counted during the 2020 election? You should know this and should not allow any illegal ballots. This is your job. Act 77 was stupid and illegal. I have asked you this several times. Can you answer the question? Do you agree that your salary is too high at $92,000? You will be replaced if you do not do your job.

David Xu

Election cheating
Yahoo/Sent

*****

David Xu (dave224422@yahoo.com)
To Senator David Argall, Sam Brancadora, Webb Kline
Wednesday, May 4 at 8:49 a.m.

David,

Did Trump win? We believe that he did. How many illegal ballots were counted in 2020? Did you read or watch the massive amounts of evidence of election cheating on frankspeech. com, 2000 Mules, rigged movie, etc.? Why did you certify the results? When will the audit be completed? Can you remove, impeach, or prosecute the many election cheaters? Use your position to stop the sick socialists, communists, and other fools before they impose the CCP model in America. Under 8 percent of the Chinese belong to the corrupt CCP who have all the guns but rule the others with an iron fist. We must get back to the constitution and Bible to save America. Sorry to be blunt, but it seems like our Republicans are asleep. Can you reduce the number of folks in the Pennsylvania house to sixty-seven or less from 203 and cut the salaries for everyone in the Pennsylvania senate and house? The $92,000 per year is outrageous. Your job should be part-time for sure.

David Xu
http://www.wethepeoplecoalcountry.com

The FEC deep-state actors finally responded in May to my January complaint about Mehmet Oz. Six of us WTP group leaders chatted with Mehmet Oz on May 13 on Zoom. Nancy and I were vacationing at Myrtle Beach, South Carolina, and visiting my mother and other family members.

Oz impressed me with his knowledge of the corrupt Federal Reserve folks. Janet Yellen is the worst and was promoted for her devotion at the Fed to the corrupt Obama-Biden administration with the title of treasury secretary now. Mehmet understands that our nation owes over $30 trillion from decades of idiots buying votes with tax money. Yellen was caught meeting almost exclusively with Democrats while at the Fed. Also, she irritated her neighbors in DC by having many security guards in black SUVs retrieve here worthless butt from her house every day as if she was a queen or world leader.

I asked Oz if he regrets supporting the Sultan Erdogan and the group dictatorship of Turkey. Oz was in the Turkish army back in the 1980s and is still a citizen there. I informed him that we had a deal with the Turks to use their bases for our invasion of Iraq during 2003, and then more radical Muslims won elections and reneged on their promises. I was supposed to work there, and Turkey is listed on my combat order.

This led to long supply lines because we had to pump everyone through Kuwait. Many Americans were injured or killed because supply lines are hard to defend. Do you remember Jessica Lynch? Oz said that he was only in the Turkish army for a few months and said he has disagreed with many decisions of the Turkish government over the years. I served in combat in Kuwait during 2003.

Mehmet was good with people during our Zoom meeting. I see why he had a silly TV show. He called everyone by name, which most people like. I remember reading that tip in Dale Carnegie's *How to Win Friends and Influence People*.

The government fools running the election love the mail-in ballots. Unfortunately, criminals and idiots love the mail ballots also. They were still counting them on May 20 (three days *after*) election day. Oz had a lead of 992, and McCormick sued to count ballots in undated envelopes. He thinks this is a great idea, like the Democrats, but there is the minor fact that it is illegal. Some federal judges said that it is fine to violate the law and count these ballots. They should be arrested. This unnecessary mess reminds everyone of all the cheating before, during, and after the 2020 election. Many folks need to be in or under the jail for this crap. Socialist France just had an election during April 2022 and counted all the ballots and announced the winner ON election day. Imagine that. I am 100 percent sure that Trump and Pence won that election.

I had Ed Durr join our WTP of Coal Country meeting via Zoom on June 2. It was great, and three medical doctors and our group members asked probing questions. I asked Ed if the establishment GOP folks helped him win the New Jersey senate seat during November 2021. He said that he went to them at the beginning of his campaign, and they worked together. I tried this in Pennsylvania, but the Republican committee people would not help me at all. Perhaps they have better conservatives in New Jersey, but I doubt it.

Ed Durr is very impressive. He pulled off one of the biggest political upsets in American history in 2021. Fifty-nine years old, Harley rider, tractor trailer driver for Raymour and Flanigan, we just bought a king bedroom suite from them. GED from Gloucester High School, elected over a union boss in the Senate who was like a weed in Hitler's bunker for twenty years during November 2021. Ed smoked this bad big-government, union-boss politician with only $3,000 to get 52 percent of the vote (33,761). Boy, I thought we were tight with the $4,000 US Senate campaign. Sweeney wasted $305,000 and a lot of union dues on his failed campaign for 48 percent of the vote (31,562). The margin was 2,199. They say Steve Sweeney is humble. That reminds me of the Winston Churchill bit about Gandhi. Someone told Winston how great Ghandi was and so humble in the sack and sandals even though he was a lawyer. He has a lot to be humble about. Sweeney has a lot to be humble about and running for governor in 2025.

Ed supports a ban on CRT, gun rights, limited government, and low taxes. I tried to shoot my pistol while at Fort Dix and had to wait one to two weeks to buy ammo. This is unconstitutional and illegal and really stupid. What made you run? Did the establishment GOP or RINOs help you get on the ballot or after the primary? They are worthless in Pennsylvania in helping outsiders like us get into government. I think it is fantastic for anyone to run especially if it is a long-shot guerrilla campaign. We are so lucky to have been born in a democracy or constitutional republic. Do the New Jersey Democrats cheat with mail-in ballots and drop boxes and no ID? Did the union boss and gang dig up dirt or uncover skeletons in your closet? They lied about Kathy Barnette and Doug Mastriano here in Pennsylvania.

Ed the truck driver ran for the New Jersey house in 2017 and 2019 before smoking the union boss Democrat Stephen Sweeney in 2021. The most impressive thing is that he only spent about $3,000 to Sweeney's $305,000. I guess the good citizens of New Jersey were finally sick of huge and corrupt union government.

David McCormick finally conceded to Mehmet Oz on June 3 after the government idiots counted mail-in ballots for eighteen long days. One judge said it is okay to count the ballots with no date on the envelope. This dumb judge is ordering people to violate Pennsylvania law. There were only 800 votes separating the two on June 3. I wonder how many illegal ballots were counted this time.

Trump's endorsement of Oz really helped him prevail over the World Economic Forum king McCormick. Over seventy We the People groups are still hounding the lazy or corrupt RINOs in the state legislature to go back to paper ballots, voter ID, and in-person voting on election day only. Photo ID and proof of citizenship would be great also.

I wonder if McCormick felt like the guy who had the tattoo at twenty-six years old "No Regrets." And later he regretted getting the tattoo. McCormick wasted over $14 million on his failed campaign to convince voters that he is America first when he put China and the CCP first for many years and made billions of dollars.

The dimwitted John Fetterman will face off with Oz in November for this Senate seat. Fetterman had a stroke in May and looks terrible with enormous breasts and torso. He looks like a tick in sweatpants and a hoodie if you want to know the truth. He is a socialist/communist who wants to legalize drugs. The lazy government union workers worship him because he wants to grow government even more.

On the bright side, most of the local, state, and federal government is still run by conservatives and/or Christians, and life is good for hard workers. They still arrest the criminals out here in rural America (Ashland, Pennsylvania). The Democrats have not ruined our great America outside some of the big cities. Myopic and lazy fools do not protest or beg the corrupt politicians for free stuff out here paid for by hardworking taxpayers.

I thought about Witold Pilecki as I escaped from this sick world of politics by dropping out of the race. He arranged for his own arrest in Poland in 1940 in order to go to Auschwitz to report on the conditions there and help the resistance kill Nazis. He eventually escaped the concentration camp. What a man!

You would have be crazy to volunteer for a senate run with very little chance of success and a high chance of personal attacks. My goals were similar to Witold's in that I wanted to learn about our political process and the actors from the inside and take out anti-American RINOs and socialist Democrats.

There was a great victory in York County. It is known as the Bloodbath in York during the May primary. The RINO from hell Stan Saylor has been in the Pennsylvania house for twenty-eight years mostly acting and voting like a Democrat. Wendy Fink took him out with the help of sitting house member Mike Jones. The establishment went crazy threatening Jones for supporting conservatives and Christians. Wendy is very impressive and has no competition for the general election in November. She will help stop election cheating and get us back to limited government and our sacred constitution.

This was a wonderful event, but it is alarming how much it cost. Wendy's team had to burn over $500,000 to unseat this RINO. Saylor's team wasted over $700,000 trying to defend his seat. We are paying a great price for the political ignorance of so many voters. They do not read much and believe everything on TV, so candidates are forced to run expensive ads on networks owned by RINOs and Democrats. It is a perverse world for sure.

Wendy's husband, Jason, told me that an old woman holding a Fetterman sign told him, "I feel so sorry for you being a conservative person campaigning for her." This rude person did not know that Wendy is his wife. She just thought he was campaigning for a

Republican candidate. She went on and on, and then Jason just had to call her a commie and get away from her.

Nancy and I met Jeff Piccola in Gettysburg before the primary while I was still a US Senate candidate. I suspected that he was a RINO by his comments. He abruptly quit as York County GOP chairman on election night. He called Saylor and Gillespie fine-seasoned legislators. I bet he meant that RINOs stick together. This is opinion.

As a bonus, Joe D'Orsie destroyed the twenty-year RINO incumbent Keith Gillespie. This is the model for export to the other sixty-six counties in Pennsylvania. Argall comes to mind with his decades in the Pennsylvania house and senate. Schuylkill County, and indeed the entire state would be better off without this guy in government. D'Orsie works at a church and thanked God for the victory. We need more God, Jesus, and the Bible.

Herb Kunkle, Mike Jones, Dawn Keefer, Jim Fitzgerald all deserve a lot of credit for the bloodbath of York County on May 17, 2022. The group at www.paeconomicgrowth.com deserve our support for standing up for the Pennsylvania and US constitutions and limited government and running off these RINOs.

We had tragic news in June. Our WTP of Coal Country member Leslie Gingrich died on her Harley-Davidson Sportster on June 4, 2022. She hit a poorly covered trench on Highway 895 near Orwigsburg. Many other folks hit this pothole in the weeks before Leslie hit it. They old others, "Someone is going to die here if this is not fixed."

She was a bright light at our meetings and volunteered a lot to get better folks into government and make the world a better place. She helped Doug Mastriano win his brutal primary for governor during May 2022. God bless Leslie, her family, and friends. Her situation is a perfect example of so many government idiots not doing their jobs. Some people who hit the trench reported the danger to the government. We are lucky to have Dean Hartenstine (Leslie's fiancé) in our group now.

Nancy and I drove by the accident sight the afternoon Leslie died and noticed the trench as smooth as a baby's butt. She hit it about 11:00 a.m. The government folks sure did a great job paving the road *after* Leslie was killed. People must be punished for this stupidity.

I believe that we are in another great awakening in America and many other nations. Most people are discovering the beauty of God, Jesus, the Bible, and the glorious, limited government mandated by our sacred US Constitution. Let us continue to take back our country from socialist, communist fools. The Democrats are digging their own graves with their dumb anti-American policies.

Most Americans are tired of lying hypocrites getting elected. Nancy and I were bored and flew over to Paris for a fashion show. Just kidding, I have never been to a fashion show and quite sure I will never go to one. I have noticed that many liberals love the fashion shows and tell us to cut back on our lifestyle for the sake of fake climate change.

What they do not say is the over 85 percent of textiles go to landfills or are incinerated. These hypocrites fly in private jets to fashion shows and have the nerve to tell us not to fly or drive for well-deserved vacations after working hard and paying too much in taxes. Furthermore, industries such as paint and electronics have paid taxes to help with the environment for years, while the textile industry folks have not. Are the Democrats in government protecting their Democrats in the textile industry from higher taxes? Lizzo could save a lot of textiles if she would just slim down a bit.

As I write this book during June 2022, more and more Hispanic voters are joining the Republican Party. This is great and will help us take back our government and country in the November 2022 elections. Trump secured 46 percent of the Hispanic vote in 2020. This was much higher than the 27 percent the weak RINO Romney got in 2012. Mayra Flores, a Mexican-born American citizen, just won a US House seat in Texas on June 14, 2022. She is the first Mexican-born woman elected to serve in Congress. Better than that is the fact that she is pro-God, family, and constitution. We need more people like Mayra in government now.

It is brutal to watch the Biden Marxists try to make government a god just as Castro did in Cuba. They are making secret plans to steal the 2022 elections and we will stop them. The socialists and communists in the Biden gang, media, academia, and corporations only have a polished understanding of the sickness they support because 99 percent of them have never lived in the many poor and corrupt nations living under that crap. We must throw these folks out of government and into the garbage can of prison soon in order to save America. Most Democrat fools hate America and should be cut off from welfare and deported to wonderful places like Nicaragua or Honduras.

Watching blunder after blunder by the Biden gang, I am reminded of what the corrupt Obama regime did to millions of patriots. These geniuses allowed the CCP spies to steal over 20 million SF-86 forms filled out by people like me. They finally admitted this huge mistake during 2015, but the Chinese spies roamed around in our computer systems for two or three years before they were busted. We revealed many personal details and mistakes to the government idiots in order to get top-secret security clearances to defend America from all enemies foreign and domestic.

Did anyone get fired? Did anyone go to jail? Was anyone executed? I do not think so. The government fools rarely get punished for doing illegal or stupid things. Republicans must change this and hold them accountable in 2023 or nobody is safe. Why were our forms at the Office of Personnel Management (OPM) online for the evil CCP gang to steal?

The Obama socialist Democrat fools recklessly disregarded inspector general warnings for years about IT security deficiencies. They violated my constitutional right to privacy with their stupidity. Perhaps they were a little bit too focused on increasing welfare for lazy people instead of actually doing their jobs?

The Biden Federal Trade Commission (FTC) fools made CafePress pay $500,000 on June 24, 2022, for a 2019 breach affecting millions of customers' social security numbers, etc. Perhaps we should take some money from Obama and others who let the CCP steal our very private information.

The only good thing for me was that I refused to answer questions about the dumb things I did in high school when the investigator came to the Pentagon for my interview to renew my top-secret security clearance in 2009. I told him that he could not ask questions that far back in my life. He laughed and backed off. This idiot did not even ask about my girlfriend, Nancy (now my wife), who grew up in China, but he did ask about my pot smoking in high school. Perhaps we can remove folks like that from government and hire qualified conservative Christians who actually do a good job.

I have some questions for the government investigators. Did the investigator ask Joe Biden about all the illegal and sick things Hunter did? Joe has a top-secret clearance. Did the investigator ask Obama about campaigning for a communist in Africa? Did he ask Michelle Obama about her no-show job at the hospital in Illinois? I remember reading that in a book somewhere. Are those stories true? Perhaps creepy Joe has been bribed by the Chinese or Russians or Ukrainians? Creepy Joe and so many others really earned some jail time. It is a cry for help. Let us help them now. We do it for the love.

Many Americans are finally waking up to the enemy within. Even our men in the Pennsylvania house and senate Twardzik and Argall signed our election cheating declaration during June 2022 to stop all the mail-in ballots and drop boxes. Now we shall see if they are on our side or the corrupt RINO and Democrat side. The Democrats love these tools to cheat during elections. This is how they say they beat Trump during 2020.

I thank God that we live outside the horrible Democrat-run cities such as Philadelphia and NYC, where criminals run wild. We have fun in rural America shooting pistols and rifles. Government is more limited out here, and that leads to more freedom and lower taxes. I think I will have something that had parents for lunch. No vegan lifestyle for big daddy.

A big, fat rib eye perhaps. It could be a thirty-ounce steak like they serve on the cruise ships before our ATV ride. This is coal country. We love coal, coal miners, and all fossil fuels. Drill, baby drill! Nancy and I and so many others are just living the American dream after decades of hard work, planning for retirement, and self-discipline. America is definitely exceptional. God, Jesus, the Bible, and the sacred original constitution are great and always win. God bless our capitalistic and free America!

They say the vegetarian hates meat and the vegan hates himself. Most of these odd balls are Democrats. Are they driving themselves crazy trying to avoid delicious and succulent meat? Consider the former chief operating officer of Beyond Meat. Doug Ramsey was arrested recently for allegedly biting a man's nose and threatening to kill him.

Wow, get that man a steak fast! He is not thinking clearly on the vegan diet. The plant-based meat just does not do it for me. I want to eat something that had parents. Elaine on *Seinfeld* had that line.

The Biden regime is failing at everything they try. The price of a new car in America went up to $46,000 during June 2022. The socialist Democrats have actually restricted labor by giving out so much welfare. The vaccine and mask mandates helped reduce the supply of American workers.

Perhaps the Biden gang is failing all the time due to affirmative action. This is a cancer on the government that the Supreme Court folks green-lighted back in the 1970s. Look no further than Defense Secretary Austin. This genius had a one-day military-wide stand-down in 2021 for the problem of extremism but offered no evidence of an actual extremism problem. I would not follow this dolt to the bathroom. He was a four-star general. Wow.

They have restricted energy by stopping pipelines and fossil fuel drilling. Their ridiculous regulations hammer business owners who create jobs for people without savings. When this happens the folks with money stop investing and creating jobs for the lower educated. If you had $1 when Biden was installed as fake president in January 2021, it is only worth 88 cents now due to inflation. The politicians goosed demand for goods and services and cut supply for goods and services at the same time. Only a dumb or evil person would do this.

The dumb American Democrats are only one step behind the dumber socialists in Europe regarding climate change crap. They have bet their economies on cheap energy from Russia with the unstable dictator Putin. He has cut their energy supplies a lot due to sanctions over invading Ukraine. It is so bad that the Spanish prime minister suggested that men ditch their ties to feel cooler with the thermostat higher during a hot summer. The politicians in the Netherlands suggested that people take shorter showers.

The Europeans shut down nuclear and coal power plants for decades while building more and more wind and solar plants. These new plants just cannot keep up with demand when the wind does not blow and the sun does not shine. I guess these politicians could not plan ahead. Jimmy Carter must be enjoying this and remembering when he suggested that Americans wear sweaters at home during the winter to save power after he made a mess of our economy during the late 1970s. He is not in the fool pool alone anymore.

This Democrat-caused inflation punishes the uneducated folks with no savings. They cannot drive as they like due to high gas prices. They cannot buy great food as much. The middle and upper class will get by with their savings from working hard for decades. We need to take power from the corrupt Democrats and RINOs, cut government spending, and promote business operations and hiring. That is the American dream for all income levels. The Trump gang had this right from 2017 until the rigged election in 2020.

I believe that most Americans will vote to send conservatives and Christians to the House and Senate on November 8, 2022. They can cut spending and regulation and take power from the socialist idiots like Bernie Sanders and Pocahontas and get America back on track for success and glory.

It is June 19, 2022, and Father's Day and I bet Hunter Biden thanked his creepy father as follows. The *New York Post* and Amanda Devine report that Biden and so many others should be in or under the jail. Do you remember when Twitter, Facebook, Google, big tech, big media, and others suppressed the Hunter Biden laptop story just before the 2020 election? Those were good times for the communists.

"Thank you, Dad, for the millions and millions of dollars for drugs, alcohol, free trips, fake high-paying jobs, and prostitutes. Thank you for the FBI agents who covered up my gun crimes and other sick behavior for decades. I hereby promise to keep all your crimes a secret except for the ones already discovered on my computer," Hunter said to Joe as he created one of his childlike $500,000 paintings for a foreign customer.

Biden and other fools in and outside of government in the Democrat Party have been obsessed with environmental, social, and governance (ESG) issues over the normal, common, conservative, and Christian hard workers for decades now. The constitution calls for decentralized power and the Democrats hate that.

If obeyed, the constitution blocks the Democrats from running to socialism and/or communism. They want the Chinese model here where only about 8 percent of the population control government and the people. We must stay focused and get more conservative Christians in government and return power to the people.

The Biden gang will not even protect the Supreme Court folks or any American now. Many abortion lovers are protesting outside their homes in Virginia and Maryland. This is illegal and immoral to disrupt a peaceful and successful American dream of owning a home and land. They allow violent criminals to roam freely. This must stop soon, or we will end up like Venezuela or Cuba.

British Prime Minister (PM) Boris Johnson resigned during July 2022. You have to envy the British parliamentary system for its ability to rid itself of fools so quickly. Johnson ignored dumb COVID rules and loves big and corrupt government despite calling himself a conservative. The UK voters are sick of hypocrites like Johnson. The workers in Britain are also sick of the royal family fools and the slow, woke government health-care system. Government idiots have caused massive inflation with borrowing and spending too much to buy votes from low-information voters. Let us just call them ignorant of history and civics now.

They pick the PM from parliament, and I always thought the American system was better. I now have a greater appreciation of the British system. We must keep working to remove Biden and all socialists from government and prosecute them if appropriate. Our judges have let us down by approving many laws and rules that clearly violate the constitution. The judges should force idiots like Alejandro Mayorkas to finish the border wall and ignore Obamacare and put them in jail asap.

195

Proof comes in every day that conservatives and Christians are taking back our government and country. Craig Reichart and friends just took over the Columbia County GOP committee after the May elections. Many RINO folks on the committee statewide are tired, corrupt, lazy, or dumb and need to be replaced.

Craig even somehow managed to be elected chairman of his county. He and his good team are working now to fill about thirty empty slots out of eighty. This is typical of the sixty-seven county groups. They are so lazy that they never even bothered to fill all the slots with patriots. The RINOs control the whole thing and do not want outsider conservatives in the group. They are controlled opposition to the sick socialist-communist Democrats led by Governor Wolf and Lieutenant Governor Fetterman. God help Craig and his team make this a better place by removing bad people from government.

Nancy and I attended the rally at the Rock in Wysox on July 10, 2022. Doug McLinko and his wife put on a great conservative rally every year. This is the sixth year. The conversation was great and the fool even better. Doug and his team work around the state exposing the horrible voting records of RINOs in the Pennsylvania house and senate. Most voters do not keep up with how their candidates vote after pulling the lever on election day.

Most Republicans work hard and just pull the level for all Republicans and go back to their jobs, God, and their families. Doug is highly intelligent and understands what it takes to win in the dirty game of politics. He ran for the US House one time and would have been outstanding in the DC swamp.

Dr. Chris Unger drove up from Washington, DC, to ride with us to the rally. It is ninety-four miles from our house in Ashland.

Chris has helped many candidates and politicians uphold the constitution for decades in Maryland, DC, Virginia, Alabama, and other states. He said that Trump reminded him of many surgeons he studied under at the University of Pennsylvania and other places. They are confident, highly skilled, arrogant, have a rough bedside manner, and highly effective at accomplishing any mission.

Chris likes to stop bad legislation before it is passed. This is much easier than repealing bad laws. We are trying to count all legal ballots now and throw out all illegal ballots now. Our small group is led by the awesome Dr. Herb Kunkle. This group is a subset of the We the People coalition that Sam Faddis and others put together for the election cheating declaration of April 2022.

Herb wants older, more experienced people to lobby our legislators and help them cut back government. He is cranky in a good way. There is good cranky and bad for sure. He thinks many young folks need more experience before giving advice or being in charge of anything. He is the old guy on the Zoom call in dim lighting with the camera showing only the top of his head.

"I do not care how many times you went to Mar-a-Lago," Herb complained about a young woman activist who always bragged about flying down to Trump's estate and hanging out in Palm Beach, Florida.

Mehmet Oz spoke with a microphone that kept going in and out. The question for us is the following. "Will he vote in the US Senate like a WTP patriot or abandon us like so many RINOs?" He is a Muslim citizen of Turkey, and this will probably be a problem for the Christian citizens of the great United States of America. But perhaps he will surprise us. Trump did endorse him for some odd reason. It is sad that the best candidate rarely wins due to money and dirty politics. That redneck David Xu was the best candidate but did not have the funding to compete.

Oz is much better than the ever-foolish Fetterman, but he is too close to the Turkish dictator want-to-be Erdogan. The Russians opened up over five hundred companies in Turkey during the first six months of 2022 to help ease the pain of Western sanctions for attacking Ukraine. Oz better decouple from Turkey with his citizenship there and fast. The Biden gang threatens the Turkish business folks with sanctions, but nobody respects them.

This is a good illustration of the stupidity of Obama, Clinton, and Biden who tried to appease Russia and Putin by being weak and naive. We have children in many adult-only government positions now. Do you remember when Hillary Clinton gave the Russian foreign minister a big reset button from Staples while she was secretary of state? Wow. She has embarrassed the United States for many years now and should be locked up as the Trump fans chant at his huge rallies.

Why are Democrats so picky? They do not like fossil fuel for some dumb reason. God blessed us with the greatest energy source imaginable. They remind of the joke about the farmer who died and went to heaven.

"Did you know they are making milk from almonds down there? That really hurt my cow farm," the farmer explains to God.

"I gave them six different animals to milk. Why are they doing that? It does not make sense," God responds to the good Christian man.

"They don't like it," the farmer explains.

Putin does come up with some good insults for the Western politicians. They make fun of him for riding horses without a shirt for the journalists. "Western leaders would look disgusting with their shirts off," Vladimir explained.

Someone asked Dan Meuser about flying over to Davos, Switzerland, for the World Economic Forum powwow this summer. He is a RINO and said that he did not know how many normal voters hate or care about the globalist and socialist-communist agenda. Meuser should be replaced by a conservative Christian soon. He appears to be either too dumb and/or corrupt to represent us in the US House. This is opinion, folks. On the positive side, he did object to some of the electors for Trump during January 2021.

Does Dan Meuser use suntan cream or lie in a suntan booth for days on end? He appears to be tanned even in the winter. The tan looks fake. What is going on with this RINO? Let us have an investigation. Why is his face orange? We must have answers.

The Wisconsin Supreme Court on July 8, 2022, barred absentee ballot drop boxes outside election offices. They illegally set up over five hundred drop boxes for the 2020 rigged election. Nobody has been arrested or sent to jail for this obvious violation of the state and US constitutions. The Pennsylvania Democrats did the same thing and must be punished.

About one hundred We the People group leaders are on an email chain. Many messages flow day after day, and many are amusing.

Sometimes you even see a cat fight. During July 2022 Caroline Avery introduced herself as running for the US House on the Libertarian Party ticket. She is trying to take out the RINO Brian Fitzpatrick. One person basically told Caroline to butt out of our email chain because we should only talk about our election cheating declaration. The man who introduced her to our email addresses defended her. Another sour soul informed us that Caroline used to be a stripper. She is okay with that but is not okay that she is a nasty person who lies about opponents.

I have sympathy for Caroline in that running for office takes a lot of time, volunteers, and/or money. She is just trying to run a successful campaign, and I like her drive to connect with fellow conservatives. I had a similar situation with the Convention of the States folks while I was running for the US Senate, and a nasty email control Nazi complained about me announcing my campaign to an email group. I invited Caroline to speak to our group, without a stripper pole, of course.

Many Democrats have been cheating during elections for years and years. We need to mobilize conservatives and Christians to watch the polls as the cruise ship employees watch over the guests. I remember holding my small hand sanitizer up to compare its size to one on the shelf on a cruise to Alaska.

An employee behind me asked if it is the same size. He came out of nowhere, and we must do that at the polls to stop the immoral folks from slipping in illegal ballots. Perhaps the Democrats need a crash course on the Bible that teaches honesty in all situations. Government is the religion of fools.

I must add a strong recommendation for Norwegian Cruise Lines if you should take a cruise. They employ great folks like Rodel from the Philippines. They work seven days a week for eight months on the seas. We need more American citizens like this man. Nancy and I have only taken two cruises, but Norwegian is the best for us. Can we swap the lazy entitled Americans for a bunch of hardworking people from the Philippines? This is the type of American that made the United States of America great.

We must stop any tax money going out that promotes sloth and promote hard work and individual responsibility. We need more God, Jesus, the Bible, and limited government now and forever. The Bible is the best guidance for a successful life and nation in my opinion. God help us!

The people in Iran are calling for the execution of the Hunter Biden of Iran. He is the rich son of the Supreme Leader Khamenei who has ruled for thirty-three long years. These Islamic terrorists, mullahs, and security forces are killing protesters by the dozen again. They murdered a twenty-two-year-old by the name of Mahsa Amini for not wearing a headscarf properly.

Obama, Biden, and other idiots ignored the good people in Iran trying to overthrow the world's greatest terrorist-supporting regime. Most Democrats love the Muslim Brotherhood terrorists. The real Hunter Biden is lucky that the Republicans are only calling for jail time for him so far.

As I write this book during August 2022, the socialist Democrats are convening grand juries and issuing subpoenas to many folks who rang the bell about many illegal ballots being counted for creepy Joe during 2020 and 2021. They issued a subpoena to Mike Jones who helped start the good Pennsylvania Economic Growth PAC that we are supporting now. They enabled the bloodbath in York County back in May, where Wendy Fink and Joe D'Orsie destroyed RINOs Stan Saylor and Keith Gillespie.

Some GOP members of the Pennsylvania house and senate gathered after the 2020 election to debate the possible seating of Trump electors for the electoral college. They knew that many illegal ballots were counted by the Wolf regime and by the Pennsylvania Supreme Court. They ultimately did not do their jobs to throw out all illegal ballots *before* certifying the rigged election. This happened in several states such as Wisconsin, Arizona, Michigan, and Georgia. It is shocking how many government idiots ignored the state and federal constitutions to count illegal ballots. They are traitors and should be hanged.

Let us remember that thirty-one members of the US House objected to the certification of Ohio's Republican electors in 2005.

Many Democrats accuse Republicans as the only ones to object to electors. The leftist imbecile from South Carolina James Clyburn objected. He rescued creepy Joe's campaign in 2020 from Bernie Sanders. Flipping Ohio would have made the climate change idiot John Kerry president. Boy, that was a close one.

The corrupt federal and state government prosecutors and judges are targeting Rudy Giuliani and Lindsay Graham too. They should target Clinton, Obama, Biden, Harris, Pelosi, Schumer, and many other corrupt Democrat fools. The US House and Senate should have never certified the 2020 election with all the illegal ballots counted. We are paying a big price for their corruption or cowardice now with the horrible Biden regime.

I am still asking Twardzik in the Pennsylvania house and Argall in the Pennsylvania senate the following. "How many illegal ballots were counted during 2020?" Here are the latest sweet emails to them. Is this too much? I wanted to sugarcoat it. Argall will not answer, and Twardzik said he does not know. Should they be in jail? Maybe it is just me.

> *David Xu* (dave224422@yahoo.com)
> *To* Senator David Argall
> Sunday, August 21 at 7:48 p.m.
>
> Hi, David,
>
> Are you dumb or rude or both? I asked you several times how many illegal ballots were counted in 2020? Why did you certify corrupt results? What about 2021 and 2022? Will you be punished or go to jail? Do your job. The US Constitution has you in charge of election rules and laws. Have you seen frankspeech.com? They provide a lot of evidence that Trump won by 494,000 votes. Is that right? Can you cut your salary from the ridiculous $92,000? Your job should be part-time. Can you cut the slots in

the house to sixty-seven from 203? We have too many idiots in the government. Cut welfare and pave the roads? Have you seen Highway 61? It looks like Somalia. Will you outlaw mail-in ballots and drop boxes today? Will you require voter ID now? What is wrong with you? Cut back government now. I am finished being nice to you because you are bad for our country.

David Xu
Army vet, thirty years, LTC, MBA,
Christian, Conservative
http://www.wethepeoplecoalcountry.com

*****

David Xu (dave224422@yahoo.com)
To Tim Twardzik, Tim Twardzik
Sunday, August 21 at 7:52 p.m.

Hi, Tim,

Are you dumb or rude or both? I asked you several times how many illegal ballots were counted in 2020? What is your number? Why did you certify corrupt results? What about 2021 and 2022? Will you be punished or go to jail? Do your job. The US Constitution has you in charge of election rules and laws. Have you seen frankspeech.com? They provide a lot of evidence that Trump won by 494,000 votes. Is that right? Can you cut your salary from the ridiculous $92,000? Your job should be part-time. Can you cut the slots in the house to sixty-seven from 203? We have too many idiots in the government. Cut welfare and pave the roads? Have you seen Highway 61? It looks like Somalia. Will you outlaw mail-in ballots and drop boxes today? Will you require voter ID now? What is wrong with you? Cut back government now. I am finished being nice to you until you prove that you are not bad for our country. I asked you to return the election cheating declaration. Where is it? Someone said that you signed it.

David Xu
Army vet, thirty years, LTC, MBA,
Christian, Conservative
http://www.wethepeoplecoalcountry.com

Even the strippers cheat with mail-in ballots. A strip club is challenging the results of a union vote in California regarding mail-in ballots. They said many are illegal. Can we please just go with only one lap dance per customer per day and only one day voting at the strip clubs without the mail-in ballots? Amber needs to focus on John, her salary, tips, and health plan. Her ballot must count.

An Obama judge in Georgia by the name of Leigh May is ignoring the US Constitution's speech and debate clause that protects representatives and senators from being questioned about their legislative efforts. RINO Graham was investigating election fraud and deciding whether or not to certify the election. He collapsed like a deck of cards after the incident on January 6, 2021. He should have stood tall and objected to all the illegal ballots from many states and forced the state employees to throw out all illegal ballots. Ted Cruz suggested this but was not supported in the swamp.

The Republicans must arrest and prosecute all the idiots who have violated our state and federal constitutions. We have far too many immoral and dumb government employees. There will always be a few, but we have allowed the fools to grow government so big and powerful. We the People will rule soon. Conservatives and Christians must unite.

I think I know how Bon Scott felt on February 18, 1980 (the day he died in London in the car alone). He worked so hard singing for AC/DC for over two hundred concerts from July 1977 until his death. I campaigned almost every day from May 2021 until March 2022 for US Senate and peaked at 1 percent in the polls.

Bon had a big problem with booze and drugs, but nonetheless I can empathize for working so hard and not having much to show for it. He died with only $31,162 in the bank and no house, wife, or known kids. He loved the ladies and partying. Jesse Fink wrote an outstanding book entitled *Bon Scott: The Last Highway*.

My brother Tom and I saw AC/DC in on August 10, 1978, in Fayetteville, North Carolina, and they were awesome. Angus lay on the floor and spun around while doing guitar solos. I remember wondering why the government idiots allowed drug dealers to openly sell disco biscuits (quaaludes) during the concert. It was like the politicians wanted their youth dumb, on drugs, and dependent on welfare.

I will always remember Bon sharing the story about their song "Whole Lotta Rosie." She was a "big, fat woman from Tasmania," he explained before performing the song. He was hilarious screaming and prancing around. Good times.

On the way home to Danville, Virginia, brother Tom started dozing off while driving our beautiful blue Oldsmobile Cutlass with chrome wheels and dual exhaust. We asked that he pull over and let someone else drive. The next thing we know we are spinning around hitting construction barrels on the side of the highway in the rain. This was late at night after the concert.

"You just bought my half of this car," I informed Tom after we stopped spinning and realized that we did not flip over. We had pooled our limited funds to buy the sexy car from our older brother Al a couple months before. I drove home with the sides of the car dented and scratched end to end. Good times.

I hope and pray that the horrible Biden years are an example of God allowing us to go through hardships so that we can be who He's called us to be. I remember the Republican Party woman on the campaign trail telling me, "We are not perfect, but the Democrats are crazy now."

We have a morality problem in America. The rednecks cannot even enjoy a cold beer and a fair Cornhole World Championship anymore. Both teams in Rock Hill, South Carolina, used illegal bags during August. They were too small. The immoral folks in leadership positions lie and cheat every day, and the children think it is okay. Leaders must preach honesty and safety, or they get ignored.

We must get back to the Bible and morality as a society. This cultural rot is taking its toll on America's success and strength. This BagGate incident only hurts the honest rednecks who love a good and fair cornhole match. The top players make up to $250,000 per year in this silly game.

The leader sets the tone for the organization. Look at all the immoral people in the Biden administration. The leader lies all the time and others follow his lead. We need Christian and conservative leaders who will always tell the truth. Communists and socialists lie, cheat, and steal to gain or maintain power and money. Look at the CCP.

It is amusing as I write this book during August 2022 that so many dimwitted folks such as the Starbucks leaders voted for socialist Democrats who have been praising criminals for years now must close many stores due to criminals hurting their employees and doing drugs in their bathrooms. Will these Democrats still vote for the cheerleaders of criminals during November 2022? These low-information voters are being punished for their ignorance. It is amusing for sure.

It would be fun to be in the DC swamp if I had won my race voting against all the corrupt bills. I watched the Senate Democrats in 2022 threatening the private equity billionaires and millionaires to take away the huge tax benefits of carried interest. Trump tried to drain the swamp of these politicians who threaten policy harm, collect campaign cash as extortion money, and then decide to spare the target at the last moment. They do this with all industries and the lobbyists on K Street every election cycle so they can get reelected over and over. Can we please have term limits?

People follow the money in any situation. That is what separates us from the animals. Do you remember when a newspaper published the salaries of all the National Hockey League (NHL) players back in 1990? The salaries were secret until that writer suddenly brought pay transparency. Most players were jealous of Lemieux and his $2 million salary.

Many players shifted from emphasizing defense to offense when they noticed that offensive players made more money. The team performance suffered due to this sudden imbalance. We must prevent former greedy government idiots from lobbying current greedy government idiots. These Democrats and RINOs love big government and the revolving door.

The projected advertising spending for my senate race here in Pennsylvania is $250 million for the 2021–2022 cycle. Wow. Perhaps it is true that most American voters do not read anymore and just watch television and listen to music. Total spending for the nation for this cycle is $9.7 billion. This proud redneck burned $4,000 and had a great time. Thank you very much.

The commies in Russia sent thousands of advisers to set up the CCP in China in the 1930s and 1940s. The commies in China have already sent thousands of advisors and spies to the great United States to try to set up a socialist group dictatorship. We must put them in or under the jail.

I am trying to have a rally near DC to demand that the politicians throw out 100 percent of illegal ballots from 2020 within ten days. They should have done this in 2020 if they were honest. Amanda Chase (state senator from Virginia) wants to speak. She is known as Trump in heels. I would love to get her involved and frighten the corrupt Democrats into outlawing drop boxes and mail-in ballots. Our friends from Ohio with Tom Zawistowski's WTP group want to come.

The geniuses in Illinois are accepting mail-in ballots from anyone now (August 2022), which is three months *before* the November election. The Democrats in Delaware County, Pennsylvania, are setting up forty drop boxes for November. This gang counted many illegal ballots during 2020. They are addicted to cheating to win elections, and most Americans are very angry and worried about it. We will destroy them in November if we rely on God and Jesus and common sense. Many WTP folks are going to watch the drop boxes to deter the cheaters. This was done to great effect during the Arizona primary during August 2022 where Kari Lake prevailed.

You have to love this story. The socialist Democrats running Starbucks said the socialist Democrats running the United States government National Labor Relations Board (NLRB) improperly handled mail-in ballots for a union vote in New York. But they love mail-in ballots for cheaters in our elections. Do the cheaters at Starbucks dislike the cheaters in the federal government? Wow. They love wasteful government programs if someone else has to pay for them.

We are making progress in taking back our country from foolish children such as Biden. Progress is always relative to what came before and after the current time. I think of the funny line from Sigmund Freud from Austria in 1933. The Nazis were burning his and many other books in Germany. This caused the following observation from the famous pervert author who happened to be Jewish. "What progress we are making. In the Middle Ages they would have burned me. Nowadays they are content with burning my books," Sigmund observed.

Even a monkey can get lucky sometimes. A monkey at a zoo in California stole a cell phone from a patron and dialed 911 this month (August 2022). He did not answer when the human operator called him back to check on the emergency. Perhaps he urgently needed Chinese takeout. I am a lucky monkey to have run for the US Senate and met so many great and kind folks.

There is one monkey tale that is not amusing. A Chinese bioresearch company just bought 1,400 acres in Florida for monkey research. Who allowed this? Perhaps they should be locked in a zoo for a long time. We could give them a choice of zoo or circus as Jerry gave George on *Seinfeld*.

There are over 100,000 monkeys locked up in China and Asia for dangerous and cruel research. We must stop this 99 percent of these projects. They are too dangerous, just like that lab of fools in Wuhan.

A truck crashed in Montour County, Pennsylvania, in January, and several monkeys escaped. A woman stopped to help and contracted conjunctivitis when a monkey bit her. We are lucky nobody died. Can you imagine if the Chinese idiots release another virus in Florida?

I must give some love to President Trump and his team for their tremendous success from 2017 until 2021. They packed as much success as Creedence Clearwater Revival (CCR) did from 1968 until 1972 with all their classic rock hits. Trump cut regulations and taxes and promoted small business, conservatives, hard workers, and Christians.

We must finish that Trump border wall. I believe that Trump would have finally cut spending if he had prevailed in 2020. All the illegal ballots and criminals stole the election for sure. There would be no encore in 2021 for Trump. This calls back to John Fogerty and his dumb refusal of no encores at shows. Americans love the encore. Perhaps we will get Trump 2.0 in 2024 and his big chance to severely cut back the government and spending. This would prove me right yet again (big surprise).

We are winning more and more. The US Supreme Court just ruled that our rights in the constitution, Second Amendment, and Bill of Rights do not vanish when we leave the house. Thank goodness Trump put three conservative Christians on the court to protect us. Commies always write vague laws to arrest the noncommies. Ginsburg should have gone to jail.

I am thinking about buying a piece of leftist memorabilia at auction. Bonhams is going to sell two dirty dandruff- and sweat-stained collars that the liberal hero wore before she expired during 2020. I guess they ran out of that crap from the Titanic. Thank goodness Trump replaced her with the conservative Christian Amy Barrett. I live for the day when they exhume Ginsburg from Arlington National Cemetery. She is not a veteran, ignored our constitution, and should not be anywhere near there.

"For my friends, everything. For my enemies, the law," explained the dictator Benavides from Peru. Now we would be in better shape if they arrest Hunter Biden for gun law violations and other crimes.

The current situation in Peru is what should happen in America. President Pedro Castillo was facing impeachment for a lot of evidence of corruption. He tried to disband Congress and the judiciary, but several cabinet members resigned, and the military arrested the would-be dictator. There is a massive amount of evidence to impeach Biden, Harris, and many others right now. Why do the folks in the US House and Senate not act on corrupt government folks? Our open border is only one example of violating their oath to our sweet constitution.

Democrat Obama, Biden, and friends supported the Muslim Brotherhood terrorist supporter President Mohamed Morsi when he was deposed in Egypt during 2013. He rightfully died in prison in 2019. The socialists and communists in Cuba, Venezuela, Nicaragua, Bolivia, Mexico, and the United States support the corrupt Castillo today as he sits in prison in Peru. How about orange jumpsuits for all his supporters? Where is the US military on all this corruption?

Miami, Florida, gives us hope to turn this US ship around. Socialist Democrats ran the city for decades, causing inflation, high crime, corruption, class warfare, burdensome regulation, and low or falling economic growth. Most voters got fed up with the dumb socialists and hired a Republican mayor during 2018. Mayor Suarez and his team reduced taxes, cut spending, cut costs for taxpayers, increased the police budget, arrested criminals, cut regulations, and promoted economic growth. This led to a doubling the tax base and an outstanding place to live. Many folks are moving there from cities and states ruined by ignorant Democrats.

"A recession is when your neighbor loses his job. A depression is when you lose yours. Recovery begins when Joe Biden loses his," Mayor Francis Suarez. We can right our ship when we hire a new sheriff.

Biden is just like Alberto Fernandez, president of Argentina. Inflation is 64 percent, and people must carry around wads of pesos to buy anything. They stuff bills in many pockets and pray that the many violent criminals do not rob and kill them.

The US will be exactly like Argentina if fools like Biden run our government. The politicians like Vice President Kirchner live like kings and queens, while the normal, common folks suffer under socialism.

We must remove all CCP idiots from America. They are pushing lies and propaganda on WeChat, TikTok, television and radio stations, in newspapers, and online. They lie about Russia's brutal war in Ukraine, racism in America, and the greatness of socialism and communism. Over 19 million people in America read this commie propaganda. They are being lied to. This must stop.

Perhaps creepy Joe is not doing anything about it because he and Hunter made millions in China for influence peddling while Joe was vice president in the corrupt Obama years. I think the best way to deal with the creepy Bidens is to flush them all down the toilet. I have a campaign video on YouTube doing exactly this. Very classy.

"Our constitution was made only for a moral and religious people. It is wholly inadequate to the government of any other," said President John Adams. Adams was a moral leader who rode his horse for days to political meetings in Philadelphia. There was no pay or benefits in those lean years. Our founders worked hard for our future. Biden, Harris, Pelosi, Schumer, and other socialist Democrat idiots will not do anything unless they are paid handsomely.

Tom Petty was awesome when he sang, "I won't back down." I will never back down when it comes to destroying socialism and communism here or abroad. We need more God, Jesus, and the Bible. Me and my family will destroy the evil folks totally. There will be a red wave in November this year, and we can celebrate. This old soldier still has some fight left. God wins!

New York City is a good example of what America will look like soon if we do not destroy the Democrat socialists in November. Only 8 percent of the registered voters bothered to vote during the August 2022 primary in Manhattan. A judge threw out a gerrymandered district plan and forced two horrible leftists to run against one another. As a reminder, only 8 percent of the Chinese population are members of the corrupt CCP. The Democrats are trying to implement the CCP model in the great United States.

Nadler beat Maloney by a wide margin in this one-party area of America. These idiots have taxed and regulated for the last thirty years so much that many business owners have left town. They are borrowing and taxing like crazy today to support the welfare idiots who still vote for them. Chavez did the same thing in Venezuela with tax money (oil money) to ruin that nation.

Trump posted mock praise for Nadler saying he is "high energy, sharp, and quick-witted." He said Maloney is "the better man and has my complete and total endorsement." Trump is the funniest politician we have ever had.

Biden and so many others should go to jail for violating our constitution and laws. Biden canceled student debt for over 40 million irresponsible college students during August 2022. This is clearly illegal and hopefully a judge will stop it. This stupidity will cost the taxpayers over $300 billion. Many of these deadbeat college graduates joined the riots during 2020 and love socialism and communism.

The judge should put Biden under the jail for this and keeping the border wide open. The list goes on and on. Most Americans still work hard and do not even go to college. They should not have to pay the bills of ignorant and lazy college graduates. Some of the dumbest people I have ever met went to college.

Life is full of misunderstandings. Democrats do not understand why limited government is best. It reminds me of the foreigner from a poor country visiting America as an exchange student. The host family is very religious and have a large painting of *The Last Supper* on the wall with Jesus and the disciples sitting on the same side of table.

The foreigner is constantly practicing his English. He is a hard worker. The family goes out to eat on his first day in America. He rushes to the podium in the lobby of the restaurant.

"Do you have a table for twenty-six?" the foreigner asks the maître d'.

"Why do you need that? Your party is only thirteen people," the puzzled maître d' asks.

"We all want to sit on the same side of the table," the sweet foreigner explains.

Our We the People of Coal Country group is trying to get conservatives to run for school board. We had great news out of Florida this month (August 2022). Twenty-five out of thirty school board members endorsed by Governor DeSantis won or advanced in their races. Let us remove all the immoral union folks from our schools. We love the 1776 PAC that helped with these victories.

We had a great time at the WTP rally in Bloomsburg on August 27, 2022. Webb and Stacey Kline and Sam Faddis put on a great event. More than 1,500 conservative Christian folks came out. Jack Maxey spoke about analyzing Hunter's laptop during October 2020. He said most journalists and politician ignored him when he sent copies to them.

These sick RINOs and Democrats gave the election to Biden even without all the cheating. Over 20 percent of voters who voted for Biden now say they would not have if they had known about all the immoral activity and crimes on the laptop from hell.

Maxey said that Louis Freeh and his team harassed a Romanian journalist to silence her coverage of the crimes. These deep-state fools give America a bad name doing crap like this. They should be shamed and arrested if they violate any laws. Freeh was a terrible FBI director back from 1993 until 2001.

Catherine Engelbrecht spoke about all the election cheating during 2020. She and her team analyzed cell phone data to track many mules who stuffed ballots in drop boxes. She and Gregg Phillips helped make the outstanding movie *2000 Mules*. We are in trouble if these fools are not arrested.

I met a WTP leader from somewhere in Pennsylvania, and she told a funny story. A group recently advertised a business expo for only black and brown business folks. This good lady could not take the racism anymore.

"I read that you are having a business expo in Scranton, and I would like to reserve a table. I own a white-only business. Please call me back," the good conservative said on the phone machine of the group promoting the event. Nobody called her back.

"You are the queen of confrontation. Good for you," I told her at the rally. The racists should be arrested for violating many local, state, and federal laws. America is the least racist nation that ever existed. Only ignorant people believe otherwise.

The corrupt FBI gang raided President Trump's house in Florida during August 2022 for no good reason. We must keep demanding that all deep-state actors like Christopher Wray be investigated and put in jail if guilty. The sick DOJ and FBI folks gave a pass to Hillary Clinton for having top secret documents at her house and deleting over thirty thousand of them.

The same fools at the FBI had Zuckerberg and friends at Twitter and other places cover up Hunter's laptop crimes and immorality of Joe Biden and his brother. Kevin Clinesmith, the immoral lawyer who falsified a FISA warrant to spy on Trump and his team, got off with probation. We must have accountability and honesty from all government employees.

I think back to Paul Revere shining lights from the Old North Church steeple in Boston to warn the other patriots that the British soldiers were coming to raid the ammunition depots near Concord and Lexington in 1775. I wanted to warn others about the socialists and communists in the great United States of America while running for senate. These dogs hate capitalism and limited government. How can you work with them? There can be no bipartisanship with these fools.

In 1775 as in 2022, many Americans believe that all is well, and the commies are not a couple of votes away in the US Senate from imposing sick socialism on all of us. Most people in our land wanted to remain in the United Kingdom and thought the patriots were exaggerating about the abuses being carried out by King George III. I could tell while campaigning that many folks nowadays think we are exaggerating about the strength of the really dumb socialists. They still think it is enough to pull the lever in the voting booth for all Republicans and be done with it. We cannot afford their political ignorance anymore. RINOs are just as bad as socialist Democrats.

I am sure that Paul Revere had a nice ride but equally sure that he would be embarrassed to put his horse up against my awesome 2013 Harley-Davidson Breakout in a race to spread the good news or bad. That is why they call me Big Daddy. To be honest, the only one who calls me Big Daddy is myself. It is so sad, but true.

A little-known fact is that many folks actually did call Paul Revere Big Daddy until he and other patriots failed miserably to reclaim Maine from the British during 1779. Dismal leadership and coordination among the Americans led to a debacle with over 474 killed, wounded, captured, or missing. Okay, I made up the Big Daddy part of this true American disaster.

Mike Lindell asked that we get the cast vote record from our county government idiots. Below is my request, and beneath that is their nonanswer. They will not provide the information. What are they hiding? For whom do they work? We need fewer government folks who are lazy, corrupt, and/or dumb for sure.

David Xu (dave224422@yahoo.com)
To Lebo, Lois
Tuesday, August 30 at 4:31 p.m.

> Thanks for nothing. You are a really helpful government employee. We must get back to limited government with fewer government lazy, union and/or dumb folks. Big corrupt government sucks.

The United States is kind of like a big ship whose alarms are going off. It will take many conservative Christians to turn this ship around. We must remove all RINOs and socialist Democrats now.

Perhaps we need to punish everyone who votes for a socialist Democrat. We could bring back spanking as the Cassville School District did in Missouri this year. I remember being spanked by the principal in Florida as a kid. He drilled holes in the paddle, which made it worse for the bad little kid. It was unpleasant, but I deserved it. The principal did alter my behavior for sure.

Perhaps we need to punish anyone who does not vote. Only about 30 percent of Americans vote during primaries and 60 percent during general elections. These lazy and ignorant people are killing us by allowing socialists and commies to run our government such as Wolf, Fetterman, and Shapiro.

We need a red wave. We need something huge like the molasses wave in Boston during 1919. A tank collapsed in a warehouse and caused a forty-foot wave that killed twenty-one people and demolished buildings. Can you imagine over two million gallons of molasses flowing at 35 mph? We need a big red wave this November for Republicans to retake our government from socialist fools.

The streets of Boston smelled like molasses for months after the disaster. Does freedom have a smell? Perhaps it is the smell of jet fuel from awesome American F-16s or diesel army trucks such as Deuce and a halves early in the morning. I remember that smell from driving slowly on dark dirt trails early in the morning at Fort Bragg on our way to shoot artillery day and night. Freedom does have a sound as explained by my biker sister Betsy in Goldsboro, North Carolina, many years ago. She lived near the Seymour Johnson Air Force base. Two Air Force F-15s flew over our heads one day during lunch, and she said the following: "Do you know what that is? That is the sound of freedom." How true that is sister. How true that is.

The real Seymour Johnson from Goldsboro died in a plane crash in Maryland during 1941. He was a test pilot and hero.

Do you ever question your sanity? I surely did while running for senate and sitting though long, boring speeches by not so bright politicians and candidates. I read that many folks are paranoid about dementia and Alzheimer's disease. But no matter how crazy you think you are, there is always someone else more unbalanced. Perhaps I am more stable than the nut who just paid over $12 million for a Mickey Mantle baseball card from 1952. I am definitely more stable than the other nut who paid $9 million for a sweaty jersey worn by some soccer player by the name of Diego Maradona.

Well, it finally happened. The US government is paying out so much welfare that over 57 million able-bodied Americans are not working at all. They are taking it easy while over 160 million Americans work. We have over 11 million job openings too. Perhaps we need to cut welfare to the bone and make the lazy folks work full time. The socialists are raiding the US piggy bank to get to communism without a shot. Let us destroy them in the November elections. Bye-bye, Chavez and Biden.

You face some odd comparisons in politics. I found out that I share one thing with the Soviet Union leader Mikhail Gorbachev. We polled at the same percentage in our races. He only pulled 1 percent of the vote during his comeback run in 1996. I rose to a respectable and lofty 1 percent during 2022 in my Senate race.

In 1996, not many Russians loved his push for restructuring and openness from 1990 that led to the dissolution of the failed socialist-communist nation. Gorbachev died at age ninety-one during August 2022. At least I am still kicking. The evil Putin came to power in 2000 and now runs the mafia nation trying to force Ukraine at gunpoint back into the fold.

Do you remember Margaret Court? She was an awesome tennis player from Australia who won twenty-four major singles titles and sixty-four total major titles, including doubles. Most of the immoral media and tennis people ignore her because she believes in God, Jesus, the Bible, and does not support same-sex marriage, LGBTQ, and other woke stuff.

Margaret was the queen of tennis from 1960 until 1977 and world number one in 1962. She dominated even after having two children and still holds many records. We honor this lady who is now a minister at age eighty. We need another tennis organization run by conservatives and Christians to punish the immoral other league that will not honor this great lady and athlete. This is what the LIV Golf tour is doing now to punish the horrible Democrats and RINOs who run Comcast, NBC, CBS, and/or the Golf Channel.

Our old RINO friend in the Pennsylvania house Tim Twardzik finally awakened to reply to our screams about Democrat election cheaters. His baby steps are outlined below. I keep telling him that the legislators and not the judges are in charge of our elections. Will someone please get a copy of our sweet constitution to brother Tim? Who wants to run in the next primary against my oldest boy?

Tim Twardzik (ttwardzik@pahousegop.com)
To David Xu
Tuesday, September 6 at 5:14 p.m.

David,

    I joined thirteen other representatives to successfully sue Gove Wolf and the state to declare ACT 77 Unconstitutional. The Pennsylvania Supreme Court eventually overturned the decision and we are taking the lawsuit to the Federal Supreme Court. We also filed additional challenges to the Act 77 because of Pennsylvania courts declaring the envelope date not valid so the entire Act 77 is invalid. I am continuing to work toward safe elections including voting to support voter ID and election audits.

Rep. Tim

    I look forward to the day when government is run without racist fools like Loretta Lynch and Eric Holder. These two socialists are busy these days shaking down big corporations like Amazon and Starbucks with exaggerated claims of racism. If you are obsessed with your skin color, perhaps America is not the country for you. Lynch should have been punished for meeting with Bill Clinton at an airport while Hillary should have been facing a grand jury for destroying top-secret documents. Lock her up!

    Holder should have gone to jail for allowing guns to be given or sold to violent idiots in Mexico. One of the guns ended up in the hands of a criminal who killed a US border agent. This was known as the Fast and Furious scandal. Holder should have been arrested for contempt of Congress also.

    Can we have three cheers for Benjamin Auslander who busted the Tredyffrin-Easttown school district leaders in 2020 with hiding the fact that they were teaching critical race theory garbage? The government idiots assured the parents that they were not teaching CRT to kids and only to teachers. Yeah right. Benjamin persisted and had to go read the documents himself because the administrators would not mail or email the incriminating documents to him. Any government idiot who lies to parents or other taxpayers must be fired.

The ever foolish and very ugly Randi Weingarten, the American Federation of Teachers president, said, "Critical race theory is not taught in elementary schools or high schools." Perhaps this liar should be fired and jailed. This idiot does not have kids but is in charge of union folks teaching our kids. She has the face that would make a bear run up a tree. We must get unions out of the government. Corrupt unions are the gateway drug to socialism and communism.

We must stop the censorship online. I noticed that the socialists running Google just allowed Parler back on the App Store during August 2022 after removing it during January 2021. The weak RINOs and corrupt Democrats have allowed the big tech folks to censor conservatives and Christians for years and years. This must stop now.

Trump's Truth Social applied to be on Google's App store but was denied during 2022. What right do these commies have to censor anyone in the digital town square? Can we please have a leader like Calvin Coolidge sometime soon? He was an awesome governor of Massachusetts from 1919–1921 who punished the Boston policemen for going on strike. This great president of the United States from 1923–1929 believed in God, Jesus, and the Bible, cut spending, and granted citizenship to all Native Americans born in the United States.

Many of the good people in the We the People groups are going to watch polling stations and drop boxes in November to deter and catch election cheaters. This paid dividends in the July primary in Arizona where Kari Lake prevailed. Many RINOs are not into this. I email a woman with the state GOP, and here is her weak and dumb reply. We will stand up for our laws and constitution even if Shapiro and other Democrat and Republican fools will not.

Rachael Vermeulen (rachaelv@pagop.org)
To David Xu
Tuesday, September 6 at 1:39 p.m.

Good afternoon, David,

Thank you for reaching out with your questions! To answer your questions about drop boxes, in 2020 the Pennsylvania Supreme Court offered an opinion that drop boxes are not polling locations, so they are not allowed to have any kind of observers at them by candidates or political parties. Then Josh Shapiro stated that he would prosecute anyone serving in a watcher role as intimidating voters. The PAGOP and the RNC are not allowed to encourage anyone or suggest that they are allowed to fill an observer role at drop boxes.

As for people being arrested, I know there are ongoing investigations both in Pennsylvania and nationwide, but our focus is on this upcoming election and making sure that we have poll watchers across the state.

Here is the link to sign up for a poll watcher training:

RNC: Pennsylvania Election Integrity Training (signupgenius.com)

We continue to hold trainings weekly and are building up the schedule of both in-person and virtual trainings. If you cannot attend the listed trainings, that is okay. We will be adding more both in person and virtually over the next few months before election day!

Best regards,
Rachael Vermeulen
Regional Election Integrity Director
(Lehigh, Northampton, Carbon, Berks, Schuylkill, and Lebanon Counties)

We love the Babylon Bee website. They kill it every week. They are comedians who have been drawn into the culture wars. I about fell out of my chair back in March when they named Rachel Levine Man of the Year. The commies at Twitter locked their account because of violating their rules about hateful conduct. Thank you, Kyle Mann and gang, for giving us a good laugh during these dark days. A man dressed as a woman is still a man.

They say never say never, but I will never run for any office again. I am quitting politics as a candidate. Call this crazy old veteran for the next war. I am a soldier through and through.

Perhaps another run for office could be possible if I were like the jellyfish they are studying in Spain that can cheat death and rebirth itself. That would be awesome to turn back our biological clock as that jellyfish does. Let us travel to the coast of Italy to learn from these amazing creatures. This sounds better than the fountain of youth sought out by Ponce de Leon in 1513 in Florida.

I do not know whether to laugh or cry about the Biden gang forgiving his 40 million overeducated and underemployed voters for their college loans. Most of these lazy and ignorant college graduates are from middle- and upper-income households.

This dumb program will cost us over $1 trillion over time and make inflation worse. The socialist Democrats are insulting every hardworking American who pays off their loans with pride. Good luck with the elections in November idiot Democrats. Tell Fetterman to take a shower and clean his hoody and get ready to interview for a private sector job.

The college debt forgiveness scam by the Biden gang pumps more tax money to the socialist-communist morons running Columbia and other universities. At least they can share their love of socialism with more students and get a pay raise. My heart is with the blue-collar hard workers in America I met on the campaign trail. They make a ton of money and now pay tax to help the arrogant college employees attend more seminars in Florida during the winter.

Well, it had to happen again. Our government is in full breakdown mode. They cannot even make Fat Leonard stay in his mansion in California. This 350-pound piece of crap from Malaysia bribed many American sailors in exchange for huge Navy ship servicing contracts in Asia. He was busted in 2015.

This criminal cut off his ankle bracelet and fled on September 4, 2022. Some dumb judge let him out of jail to stay in luxury. Perhaps the judge is an ignorant Democrat? Leonard's neighbors reported seeing several moving vans coming just before he escaped. That is top-notch police work to miss that little clue about the impending escape.

I hope weak judges do not let the Navy officers out of prison early. They were provided prostitutes, hotel rooms, meals, cigars, and more than $500,000 pocket money for giving the fat man over $35 million in overcharges on ship contracts. The Biden gang is offering $40,000 of our tax money if you see Fat Leonard on his way back to Malaysia.

Any judge who lets out a repeat offender should be fired and forced to attend the funerals of the victims. Many judges are not following our constitution and laws and should be punished. Perhaps they should go to jail. We must have honest and accountable folks in our government. Some judge let an idiot out of jail recently in Memphis who drove around killing four people and actually filmed it on Facebook. That judge should be put away for a long time.

Ezekiel Kelly was sentenced to three years in prison in 2020 for attempted murder, but the criminal judge let him out after only eleven months so he could drive around killing other people. Why would a judge do that? It would be justice to see the judge and Ezekiel share a prison cell for many years.

The hardworking Memphis police finally announced at 7:00 p.m. that this guy was armed and dangerous. That is fine, but he started the rampage at 1:00 a.m. Why did it take eighteen hours to notify the law-abiding citizens? All the cops could not have been in Dunkin' Donuts at the same time.

The Democrat gun-control commies just persuaded the woke credit card companies to track gun purchases. The CCP took guns away from Chinese citizens seventy-three years ago and have abused and killed millions of them ever since. Let us destroy socialism and communism. We better use a check or cash when buying a gun and ammo the next time. The Chinese citizens can only bring a kitchen knife to the gunfight with corrupt government folks. That sucks for them.

The hits just keep on coming. A New York state judge ordered Yeshiva University to grant official recognition to an LGBTQ club. Luckily, the US Supreme Court put this stupidity on hold during 2022. This university is the flagship institution in America for Jewish higher learning.

We must remove the government idiots such as this judge who violate our constitution and try to ram immoral stuff down our throats. Of course, the socialist Democrats will lie, cheat, and steal to win elections because government is their religion. Their religion is the religion of free stuff. We worship God and Jesus and bow to no man. These dark times will pass soon.

Ignore the climate change idiots such as Biden, Xi, Fetterman, and Shapiro. China's emissions have increased by 11 percent in the last six years as America's decreased by 6 percent. The socialist commies only want to rule and abuse people, and they will go down in flames.

The CCP has 258 coal power plants now and 174 more coal mines or expansions in the works. They are playing the Democrats for fools. John Kerry is as dumb as he is ugly and is a useful idiot for the Chinese. It could be worse. What if he did not have all that ketchup money from that woman he married? The Trump team prioritized economic growth and jobs and keeping America the sole superpower. Can we please have some smart and Christian government folks soon?

The United States gets about 30 percent of its power from natural gas. China is at 8 percent and gets 58 percent of their power from dirty coal. The CCP liars are spending a lot of yuan misleading dumb Americans about climate change. We are paying a big price for so many ignorant Americans. The CCP is terrible for the environment and human rights. Perhaps we should shut down many liberal colleges.

We need strong, conservative, and Christian leaders. We do not need woke, socialist, and weak leaders, such as Pope Francis and King Charles. This fake climate change duo are embarrassing their institutions daily now. Putin would not even meet Francis in Kazakhstan when they were there at the same time. Francis requested a meeting for some dumb reason. Now Francis does not even lift a finger after the CCP arrested Cardinal Joseph Chen in Hong Kong on political charges. You will remember that Chen flew to the Vatican to try to persuade Francis from making a sick deal with the CCP in 2020 allowing them control over who leads the Catholic church within China. Francis would not even meet with Chen at the Vatican but meets with Hollywood fools such as Leonardo DiCaprio all the time.

King Charles III said in 2008 that we only have eight years to act to avoid a "climate change disaster." He must be very poor prophet to utter something dumb like that. The year 2016 has come and gone, and Mother Earth is fine. I bet the British government folks stop him from going to the next climate summit in Egypt. His stupidity is rivaled only by AOC. Charles should hook up with AOC if things do not work out with Camila. The elephant ears on Charles would match the horse teeth of AOC.

Most Americans want and will get all criminals arrested and a sealed border if they elect conservatives and Christians. Look to Haiti if the Democrats prevail in the November elections. President Moise was assassinated during 2021, and the killers are still free. The corrupt government folks just ended over $400 million in fuel subsidies, and the lazy criminals went crazy.

Gangs are blocking the ports and looting. Inflation is running above 30 percent because of government mismanagement and corruption. Perhaps we should deport all socialists and communists to this fool's paradise. AOC could be in the legislature and cry all day long. Violent animals are kidnapping anyone with money and demanding ransom. The Clintons raised a lot of money for their charity's work in Haiti, but not much found its way to actually helping the Haitians. Hillary and Bill needed the money for some nice vacations. The criminals are torching nice beach houses.

The UN had a peacekeeping force there from 2004 until 2017 to mediate between the gangs and thugs. Some of the soldiers impregnated and raped some local women and gave them sexually transmitted diseases (STDs). That UN group is awesome. Can we finally get the diplomats vacationing in New York City to pay their overdue parking tickets?

Our dumb friends at the Federal Reserve have raised interest rates five times during 2022 after saying over and over that inflation was transitory. They also cheered the massive borrowing and spending for welfare by the Biden team. We will be lucky if the federal funds rate (rate at which banks can borrow from one another) does not hit 18 percent as it did in 1980 after the incompetent Carter regime was thrown out of the White House. We must show the door to many of the 23,000 Federal Reserve worthless employees when Republicans take over in 2023.

We always love it when states cut spending and taxes. The good news is that eleven states reduced income taxes in 2021, and ten did so during 2022. The federal government idiots have borrowed a lot and bailed out poorly run Democrat states under cover of the CCP virus.

The danger is that some Democrat states will file for bankruptcy when GOP adults take over, and the free money stops coming in from the irresponsible children running Washington, DC. They better start cutting spending and welfare in California, New York, Illinois, etc. because many hard workers moved to Florida to get away from stupid Democrat politicians and the chaos they created.

"Everything else can wait, but the search for God cannot wait," George Harrison.

CHAPTER 8

THE LAID-BACK REDNECK

SEPTEMBER 2022 THROUGH THE
NOVEMBER 8 GENERAL ELECTION

I do not want to see a repeat offender.
I want to see a dead offender.

—Ted Nugent

Bill Barr and many others should face a grand jury for lying about massive election cheating. He told Trump and the world that the cheating would not have affected the election. A FOIA request to the DOJ just came back during September 2022 with no records of investigations by the DOJ regarding election cheating during 2020. Barr said they did investigations.

It appears that he did not do any investigations and lied to his boss about it. Our buddy McSwain, who ran for Pennsylvania governor, said there was cheating in and around Philadelphia, but Barr would not let him have a press conference or investigate the crimes.

Mueller and his team lied about Roger Stone and many other folks in order to punish Donald Trump. These government idiots should be punished for abusing their positions and ignoring the facts and the law. When will Durham punish these deep state fools? Where is Durham? I think someone saw him in Maryland recently. Trump really exposed how many corrupt fools are in the government. Cut it back! We need someone like Calvin Coolidge in 2022.

The truth will come out sooner or later and the guilty must pay a heavy price for treason, election cheating, and/or sedition. The question is, "Why are so many Americans immoral, greedy, and/or dishonest?" Did they just skip ethics training class at work? Did they ignore the Bible and good works of Jesus Christ? Did their parents teach them right and wrong? Will this lead to another civil war? See *Redneck Dystopia*. What is going on in America? I am going to sleep now. Wake me up for the next war.

Where are the arrest warrants for all the Democrats who run 501 C3 nonprofit organizations? The IRS rules state that they cannot engage in voter education or registration with bias or favor one candidate over another. These criminals did this with abandon before, during, and after the 2020 election. We must have equal justice under the law now. Vote GOP forever.

We must listen to government workers who quit such as Brandon Garcia. He resigned from the Bureau of Alcohol, Tobacco, and Firearms (ATF) in 2022 and has a lot to say. "The last time moral was this low was probably 2013 to 2016. That was the last time we had an administration openly criticizing law enforcement." He said the emphasis now is for ATF agents to punish law-abiding gun owners and not real criminals. Can someone please lock up these government idiots?

I pray that we do not have a war while the foolish Democrats are in charge of our government. Biden has released over 200 million barrels of oil from the Strategic Petroleum Reserve in order to win the midterm elections in November. Adults know that this reserve is meant to be used for war or other national emergencies. It is not to be used because stupid Democrats cut our energy production in pursuit of exaggerated climate change and tanked their poll numbers before an election. Trump had the reserves topped off.

Biden sold some of our reserves to the CCP and bought from the Russians who invaded Ukraine for no good reason. Why are the folks getting elected getting dumber and dumber? Perhaps they cheat. See frankspeech.com.

It is not all bad news. Do you want some good news? They caught Fat Leonard in Venezuela. He should do hard time for bribing many greedy fools in the United States military. Perhaps we should make the corrupt military folks give him massages in prison every day. He flew there from Mexico and was heading to Russia. Fry his fat ass!

I like the prison humor. George and Jerry love it too. Here is one from *Seinfeld*: "Why do we need solitary confinement? Do we really need a prison within a prison? I thought the weightlifting and sodomy were enough punishment."

Here is some more good and funny news. Zuckerberg's net worth dropped from $126 billion to $56 billion during 2022. Perhaps his obsession with the metaverse is really stupid. He and other children love to pretend they are in the cartoons with avatars. Good job Mark. What grade are you in now? Will he get to play online from his prison cell for election cheating and censorship of conservatives and Christians? His cellmate can dress him up as a beautiful lady perhaps.

The Fifth US Circuit Court of Appeals just ruled in September to uphold Texas's anticensorship law. The court said, "We reject the idea that corporations have a freewheeling First Amendment right to censor what people say." Justice delayed is justice denied, but we count this as a big win against the fools running Facebook, Google, Amazon, and Twitter. Now can we lock them up for violating the constitution and our laws? This would be redneck justice and therefore righteous.

America's large technology companies get 58 percent of their revenue outside America. This is the highest share of the eleven groups in the S&P 500. This is one reason that big business is no longer a friend to We the People. We must force them to adhere to American biblical values, laws, and our sweet constitution. Many leaders of big tech hate a strong US dollar, which is great for the citizens and their retirement savings.

Microsoft, Alphabet, Meta Platforms, and others must be forced to pay their share of taxes and to stay out of politics. Many of them love Biden, socialism, communism, and ignore the long-term health and success of America. They view America as a business and not a great country. The monopolies must be broken up.

When the US dollar goes up in value, their sales in other countries are worth less. It is sad, but many owners and managers of big corporations are anti-America. They want illegal and legal immigrants to drive down wages. This screws normal Americans who want to work hard and buy a nice house. Immigrants are a new drain on taxpayers also with all the welfare.

Many political judges should be impeached and perhaps arrested. Kagan, Sotomayor, and Jackson on the US Supreme Court come to mind. They said that the conservative majority of the court hurt the court's credibility with some decisions like the Roe decision returning abortion to the states.

These Democrat fools want to ignore the constitution and law when making decisions. Like politicians, they blow with the wind. That is what socialists and communists do. Chief Justice Roberts said, "Simply because people disagree with an opinion is not a basis for questioning the legitimacy of the court."

The main job of the Supreme Court is to decide which laws and actions are constitutional and which ones are not. They should ignore trends and what is popular. They are not politicians. They should not be politicians in black robes. The original constitution is the law of our land.

The foolish Ketanji Jackson cannot even define what a woman is. The Senate should never confirm such morons. Thank God for our original constitution and moral, conservative, Christian judges who love America.

James Madison explained the general welfare clause in our constitution as spending for the military and a limited government. Many fools in the executive, legislative, and judicial branches have perverted or ignored this part of the constitution for decades and brought us to the point of ruin. They must be stopped now before it is too late.

Most of the laws passed by Congress violate our sacred constitution now. The Supreme Court members can rule tonight that most laws violate the general welfare clause and help balance the budget and take power from the corrupt politicians. Obamacare is the worst.

It is hard to believe that Fetterman is dumber now in September 2022 than he was before his stroke in May. It is bad to have a stroke, but this idiot was too dumb to be in government or any leadership position long before this. He said, "Now send me back to New Jersey" at a campaign rally when he really meant to send him to the District of Columbia.

Oz is having a field day pointing out that this guy is actually dumber than Joe Biden now. He wants to release murderers also. He is quite the candidate nowadays. I wonder if the union bosses are happy with their man-child. Millions of union dues have been sent to this fool.

He reminds me of the kid in my eleventh-grade class who sniffed lighter fluid in the back of the classroom to get high. I wonder if he remembers chasing the black guy with a shotgun for no good reason while he was a failing mayor in Braddock. Crime in his village went down after he left office.

Fetterman is running ads criticizing Oz for being successful and buying several nice houses. How many houses does this loser have? I bet he could only rent a tiny apartment if not for union and government money flowing into his bank account. Is he a jealous child in elementary school or a candidate for US Senate? This guy is a joke. Somebody needs a diaper and pacifier.

Biden and his team should be given the Guinness World Record for going in reverse. The organization really should take the trophy from Scot Burner tonight and hand it to creepy Joe. Burner set the record for the fastest mile driven in reverse at 48 mph in a Corvette in Kentucky. I always wanted one of those sports cars. I can dream.

Biden and other fools have reversed all the accomplishments of the Trump team. They did it in record speed and should recognized for ruining a great country and economy in under two years. It almost seems intentional, but I vote for gross incompetence. Trump had GDP growing, inflation down, crime down, the border sealed, and conservatives and Christians supported.

Conservatives and Christians must remain strong and on offense. The Democrats and nine RINOs who either lost their primaries or are retiring voted in the US House during September 2022 to have judges and not legislators interpret and decide election laws. This is clearly unconstitutional and must be terminated. The constitution states that the Congress or state legislators control elections.

This is why they are so determined to pack the Supreme Court and other courts with socialist commie fools like Ketanji Jackson. This genius cannot even define what a woman is. This is an impeachable offense according to most Americans.

These fools want to increase the number of House and Senate members it takes to object to electors for reasons like cheating. It is obvious to me that Trump won in 2020 after seeing massive evidence at frankspeech.com and other places. It only takes one House member and one senator to object now. The uniparty people want to raise this to 33 percent of each chamber in order to cheat with mail-in ballots and drop boxes and no ID.

We have traitors within the government who must be purged. They do not obey nor respect our sacred constitution and laws. Several times in our history politicians have arranged dual electors in close elections. The Biden gang is trying to criminalize this now. This is outrageous and must be stopped.

Governor DeSantis is doing a fantastic job in Florida in promoting limited government and capitalism. Flying illegal immigrants to liberal places like Martha's Vineyard was genius. Biden and other fools have allowed over two million illegal immigrants into our great country. Who is going to pay to support these criminals? This is so stupid.

Biden and the Democrats have our Southern border wide open to criminals and terrorists. There have been over five hundred bombings in Sweden in the last two years. The government idiots let in millions of migrants. Many are Islamic and want Sharia law and hate Christianity and Western values. Many are just lazy criminals who do not even speak the language. Good job, Swedes.

DeSantis talks about a Great American exodus. Tens of thousands of people are evacuating from the socialist commie cities and states of the north and heading south for economic opportunity and freedom. Let freedom ring. If you love huge and corrupt government and welfare, move North. If you love limited government and low taxes, move South. What a country. The Navy veteran DeSantis would be great for 2024 and small business.

I like business because there is usually accountability. The owners and managers demand that the employees are honest and hardworking in making and selling products and services. Somebody's money is on the line with the business investment.

The federal government idiots have borrowed over $31 trillion buying votes from dumb and lazy people. They wasted over $1 trillion on interest this year alone. Should they be waterboarded until they reduce spending and taxes? Cut the welfare. Vote for GOP conservatives and Christians and common sense!

Business is almost always less wasteful than government because you have people spending other people's money in government. They care less about burning cash. Business owners promote productivity or making more with less. Government idiots do not care about being productive. Many government teachers do not care about what the kids learn. These union folks only care about their salary and benefits.

There is little accountability or honesty in the US government now. The board, managers, and owners of Charter Communications just relearned the principle of accountability. The people running this business were acting like government employees and were punished by a court.

A Texas judge and jury just awarded $1.1 billion to the family of an old lady who was murdered by a Charter technician in her home during 2019. The jury decided that the employees and their negligence led to the murder and robbery. The jury found that Charter committed forgery by faking the victim's signature on an arbitration agreement after she was murdered.

It is all about leadership. Good leaders are honest, smart, and accountable. Creepy Joe, Fetterman, Shapiro, and Kamala are none of those things. We need jail time or execution for perpetrators of treason, sedition, and other felonies. George Washington knew this, and that is why he executed spies and traitors when fighting for the awesome United States.

Below are documents from my Right to Know (RTK) requests to the Schuylkill County government folks about election cheating. They would not give up any of the requested documentation and kept saying I was asking questions. They do not answer questions believe it or not. Are they hiding something? What are they hiding? Are they lazy, dumb, or corrupt? Is their behavior suspicious? You be the judge.

Below is the response from a Pennsylvania GOP employee about mail-in ballots and drop box stuffing. Is Shapiro breaking the law in saying he will prosecute observers? What kind of a person encourages election cheating? Doug Mastriano is our man for governor running against this socialist fool. He will stop and arrest the election cheaters.

Are many GOP folks afraid of a midget named Shapiro who loves huge and corrupt government and criminals? Has he ever had a real job? The Democrats are trying to have many drop boxes around the state as they did during the 2020 election. Perhaps they would like to cheat again? I am living in Venezuela? I do not remember moving. Did that table get lost in the move? I cannot find it anywhere.

As more and more people depend on welfare from the government, they give up more and more of their freedom to idiots like Shapiro and Biden. Count me out on this deal. I bet over 60 percent of the Democrat Party love this deal. Over 99 percent of the Democrats in the US government love this deal. Fetterman sucks! The constitution must be obeyed.

The United States is still very strong compared to other nations. The fools in DC should cut spending but could borrow another $26 trillion, and we would not be at the debt level of Japan, Italy, or Greece. China has bigger problems than the US. They do not have enough fossil fuel for all those people.

Over 60 percent of the loans for their debt diplomacy or Belt and Road Initiative are to countries in financial distress. The working age population is declining in China also. Their economy will probably never exceed ours, and it should have decades ago with triple our population. Nobody wants the control-freak commie model except a few unhinged socialist American Democrats. The groupthink in the CCP is taking its toll. Somebody needs to put obese Papa Xi to bed. The hair dye is affecting his brain function.

Fetterman is the same as many, many immoral politicians who lie to get elected. During the end of September 2022 (about one month before the general election against Oz, he removed Black Lives Matter from his website. This idiot promoted criminals just because they were black for years and years. How sick is that? He is just like Obama in trying to get people to hate one another based on race. They are evil and stupid for sure. Real Americans are colorblind.

For wisdom and hope let us turn to the CEO of Goya Foods, Bob Unanue. He said, "My mother taught me to not take candy from a stranger. The politicians are giving candy out in exchange for controlling people and making them slaves. They are ruining our purpose in life (our work) and making many people dependent on welfare. God is great." What a leader and what a company with over $1.5 billion in revenue last year.

Did you say you want more welfare? You may want to watch a court case in Mississippi against former NFL star Brett Favre and others. The state filed a civil suit against thirty folks for misusing federal tax money that was supposed to help poor people.

An audit revealed that over $77 million was misspent, stole, or wasted. Over $5 million was wasted on a volleyball stadium at Favre's alma mater the University of Southern Mississippi. The only way that this would make sense is if most homeless were huge volleyball fans. If this were the case, then we can feel good about our welfare system that the homeless are still hungry but can take in a volleyball game anytime they want on an empty stomach. Now the Democrats are making real progress on the issue.

The government idiots paid Farve $1.1 million of the welfare money for speeches that he never gave. At least he paid back that tax money but did not pay interest on it. Good job on helping the poor folks! I would love to read the speeches he planned to give. Did he write it down? Those poor people in Mississippi could sure use some motivational words. When can we expect indictments for the government idiots such as former Governor Phil Bryant? The rumor is that Farve pressured Bryant for the stadium where his daughter played volleyball.

Conservatives and Christians do not have much time to turn this ship around. The federal government idiots have wasted and borrowed so much money that the annual interest bill on our $24 trillion public debt is over $1 trillion for 2022. The inflation that Democrats caused has led to higher and higher interest rates for everyone. Let us rise up and vote out the fools now. Buckle up, Americans.

The deep-state folks can sure make us laugh. The Department of Homeland Security (DHS) put out a blog post recently about how to brush your teeth and floss. They suggest fluoride toothpaste and brushing the tongue.

Perhaps these 240,000 government idiots should focus on locking down our border and deporting illegal aliens and less on dental hygiene. But then again, the teeth in the head of Mayorkas do need immediate attention. Can someone put a rug or toupee in the headquarters budget for my oldest boy also? He looks like a turtle in a suit and tie for goodness' sake.

The IRS employees are in the running for the most corrupt government idiots. Five current and former IRS employees have been charged with stealing hundreds of thousands of tax dollars from a program to help businesses cope with CCP virus lockdowns. Prosecutors say this group bought luxury cars and trips to Las Vegas with the loot. Are they skipping the mandatory ethics training class over there at the IRS? Now Biden and other fools want to hire 87,000 more IRS agents to go after hardworking Americans.

If the leader does not preach ethics and safety, his employees will not bother promoting them either. The employees will emphasize what the leader promotes or pays attention to. It is the blind leading the blind with the Biden regime. The incompetent politicians have shoveled over $7 trillion out the door in the last two years by blaming the CCP virus. Most of the spending is waste, fraud, and abuse to get elected.

Here is another attempt at waking up Argall and Twardzik. Why will they not throw out illegal ballots and prevent cheating?

(dave224422@yahoo.com)
To Senator David Argall, Tim Twardzik, Tim Twardzik
Wednesday, October 5 at 9:03 p.m.

David and Tim,

Can you remove the illegal voters from our voter rolls now? Audit the Vote PA has over 220,000 and lookaheadamerica.org has 142,000 illegal people on our Pennsylvania voter rolls tonight. Do your job and throw out all illegal ballots from 2020? How many were counted? I have asked you many times. What is wrong with you? You are overpaid at $92,000. Earn at least some of your pay. Are you lazy or corrupt? You control elections. Get rid of the machines. Have you seen all the evidence at frankspeech.com? Require a voter ID. Get rid of all drop boxes and mail-in ballots. Why are you allowing cheaters in our elections? Should you be indicted? Most Americans do not trust our elections because of people like you.

David Xu
http://www.wethepeoplecoalcountry.com

Audit the Vote PA was founded by Toni Shuppe and Karen Taylor in 2021 to examine what happened in the 2020 election. Toni was an engineer at a power plant earlier and then started her own business. Karen worked at General Motors and then in the medical field before pushing to audit the rigged elections. These patriots have uncovered massive irregularities and cheating in our elections, but most judges and prosecutors will not lift a finger to secure our vote. Immoral Democrats control the executive and judicial branches of our state. Weak and dumb Republicans control our full-time and wasteful legislature. Things are changing now with the lazy and slow judges finally enforcing our constitutions and laws while the illegitimate Biden gang burns down America. We must arrest all socialists, communists, and election cheaters now!

Things are looking up. Conservatives and Christians have taken over governments in Sweden, Brazil, Italy, Britain, Poland, and Hungary recently. This shows that most people around the world want law and order, good schools, lower taxes, a moral or Christian culture, and/or personal freedom. The socialists, communists, and globalists have demonstrated time and time again that they and their policies are failures.

The Europeans will be lucky if they do not freeze to death this winter because the idiot socialists such as Angela Merkel depended on Russia for energy and deactivated their fossil fuel and nuclear power plants. She was one of the many who demonized Americans for enjoying fossil fuels while the VW employees were busted for cheating on diesel emissions tests for years. The Audi CEO went to prison for lying about emissions tests to please the dumb climate change politicians.

Watch the video of the German diplomats laughing at Trump at the UN while he predicted that they would suffer for depending on Putin for cheap power. The illegal and legal immigrants are expensive, and many are dangerous too in Europe today thanks to fools like Merkel.

Corrupt and stupid families such as the Bidens are all over the world. The Hunter Biden of Uganda offered one hundred cows as dowry for the new, improved prime minister of Italy Giorgia Meloni. He is quite taken by her beauty and threatened to invade Italy if his dumb offer is refused. Believe it or not, he is a general in the army and son of the corrupt dictator who has been in power for thirty-five years. I guess my awesome Grandmother Glenn Cox was right when she said, "It can always be worse." We called her Mama.

My grandparents had some classic lines as follows. "Davey, there is a snake in that bottle," explained Poppy or Albert Cox when I came in drunk one night as a teenager. He had to open the house door because I lost my key while riding my Harley-Davidson. He wore a nightgown, open-back slippers, and a pointed hat (a very cute old man). He was the only person in my life to ever call me Davey. I miss that man.

"There is nothing good outside after midnight," Mama explained the next day to her wild teenage grandson. She also said, "Perhaps we have too much freedom in the USA." She was talking about Americans doing drugs, getting drunk, and other dumb stuff and not following the Bible. My dad was a big drinker. The Bible is the best way for a successful life for sure. We need more God, Jesus, and the Bible.

Trump and his team did a great job. They tried to buy oil for $24 per barrel during 2020 but were blocked by fools such as Schumer and Pelosi. Can we please have term limits? Trump was trying to top off the Strategic Petroleum Reserve (SPR) at very low prices. Biden and his team are draining it now in a desperate attempt to lower inflation they caused before the midterm elections in November 2022.

These idiots ignore the purpose of the SPR as a buffer during wars and other national emergencies. They think it is a campaign tool paid for by hardworking taxpayers. We will be lucky to not be invaded before destroying these Democrats in the election. Perhaps we need an IQ test before anyone can be on a ballot for any office.

The Democrats have controlled the House, Senate, and White House for two years after the rigged elections and increased spending by $9 trillion. They have caused forty-year-high inflation and rampant crime. It is time for a change back to GOP policies. Biden is even begging for energy from the dictators in Venezuela and Saudi Arabia to no avail when we have plenty of energy beneath American soil. Fools such as Fetterman, Shapiro, and Austin Davis cheer them on.

I am hesitant to make predictions. We do not know what will happen one minute, one day, or one week from now, but here it goes. I predict an awesome red wave in November with over six gains in the Senate and over forty-six in the US House. Mastriano, DelRosso, and Oz will win. The GOP gained fifty-four in the House and eight in the Senate in 2014, but many of them were weak and/or dumb RINOs who fought Trump's America first agenda.

Do you want more proof that the socialist Democrats and RINOs want a group dictatorship like the CCP has in China? The corrupt FBI folks asked or told the corrupt Facebook folks to bury Hunter's laptop and crimes in 2020. This criminal behavior is inspired by the CCP's behavior since 1949.

The CCP just told bankers in China to avoid publishing politically sensitive research heading into the five-year meeting of the CCP idiots. The Twentieth National Congress meeting is scheduled for October 16, 2022. Fat boy Xi is expected to be crowned supreme leader for a third term. This is bad enough for the Chinese citizens who want democracy, but many greedy and immoral American bankers will follow the commies with censorship in and outside China.

These American banks kowtowing to the commies in China are insured by the American taxpayer also. We must arrest or deport all socialists and communists in America. Bankers and all Americans should be decoupled from China and commies anywhere. It is a matter of national security. Always remember that many Russians moved to China to set up a communist paradise in 1949 and now many Chinese have moved to America to help set up a communist paradise in our awesome constitutional Republic. They must be destroyed.

Our RINO friend Jeff Bartos is raising money and supporting the socialist Democrat Shapiro. This Bartos appeared a little too overjoyed when Parnell was arguing with his ex-wife in divorce court about spousal and child abuse. It is a bad situation, and nobody should be happy about it. The establishment fools must be thrown out of government. Thank goodness Bartos was rejected twice by the GOP primary and general voters.

I noticed that Bartos did not campaign with Shapiro before the May 2022 primary. He seems like the type of guy who lies to get elected and then betrays the voters. Many, many RINOs are out there. Perhaps this is why Bartos would not talk about all the illegal ballots counted in 2020 in Pennsylvania and elsewhere. This is opinion.

The greatest compliment for me as a candidate for US Senate was, "He is the real deal." I heard and read that from only a few good people and loved it. Governor Ron DeSantis is the real deal to me. He loves limited government, low taxes, and freedom. The state has issued more than 1.5 million new business licenses from 2020 until 2022, the most of any state.

He would be a great choice for US President if Trump would abstain from running in 2024. Floridians dodged a bullet in 2018 with the immoral, socialist, and dumb Andrew Gillum. The police found this loser in a hotel with drugs and gay men. DeSantis barely beat the union idiot 49.6 percent to 49.2 percent back then.

Gillum was indicted on twenty-one felony counts, including wire fraud and making false statements regarding his campaign operations. This fool hangs out with male escorts and crystal meth and came out as bisexual in 2020. Can we please keep this moron out of government or any position of authority?

Real heroes are hard to find. Jesus is my hero. Laura Morgan is a hero for standing up to the racists in Texas. She worked for Baylor Scott and White Health and was fired for refusing to take implicit bias training. This crap encourages preferential treatment for non-whites. Why are these people so stupid to promote racism in the ultimate land of equal opportunity America? She helped the sick and injured for thirty-nine years without regard to race and should have been lauded and promoted.

Many fools running states, medical schools, and other organizations are requiring woke training that requires racism to combat nonexistent racism. They should be fired and prosecuted for racism. "Treating patients, coworkers, family members, and my superiors in a fair and respectful manner is the practice I have subscribed to during my entire thirty-nine-year nursing career," Laura explained to the idiots in leadership positions before they fired her.

The times are getting more and more dangerous with the illegitimate Biden regime. They do not understand national security at all. Their tiny brains can only obsess about fantasies such as climate change. The Democrats have cut off some benefits and will not allow over 62,000 army reservists to drill in 2022.

Why did Biden and other corrupt fools rescind Trump's order to ban TikTok unless it was put under US ownership? It should be banned ASAP for helping the sick CCP folks spy on Americans. Many people are wasting a lot of time on this platform when they should be working to support themselves, family, and retirement.

Whomever owns and controls ByteDance and TikTok should be banned from the United States. They are corrupting our youth. We need strong and Christian young citizens for the military. This is a national security issue. Republicans will destroy this threat when we take back our government and nation from socialist fools.

Perhaps creepy Joe is protecting the commies because Hunter went around the world like a vacuum cleaner, sucking up millions of dollars peddling influence and favors. Hunter, James, and Joe received millions from the Chinese, Russians, and others for many years. Will someone arrest those creepy Bidens and Obamas? You may want to look at all those stock buys from Pelosi's drunken husband too. Our national security is at risk. Biden's whole team is weak and ignorant on national security.

"Take a look at the national security apparatus of the Biden administration, and you will be struck by one thing. There is not a man or woman among Joe's appointees who has ever been in a fight. Joe himself spent his life as a politician and a shill for the credit card industry. His appointees are all academics, Democratic Party hacks, and Chinese Communist Party puppets," Sam Faddis, retired CIA.

When will the Biden gang be punished? They are selling liquefied natural gas to the Chinese who are selling it to the Europeans, Japanese, and Koreans. The CCP is making hundreds of millions of dollars on these deals in 2022. Biden and other traitors must go to jail for supporting the Chinese and making Americans pay more for energy.

The Chinese government idiots want to destroy America and freedom. Tell me why Biden, Blinken, Harris, and others should be spared. This is sick stuff. Can we please get Trump back or bring in DeSantis? I was the best qualified candidate for US Senate in

Pennsylvania to help save our country. I hope Oz is on our team and not Oprah's team.

He should consider that she gained back all that weight he helped her lose way back when. She ignored his advice. That was a real battle against a huge wave of fat and meat. He was lucky to make it to the other side without her eating him. I think about Fat Bastard in the Austin Powers movie. I heard Oz had to buy a cow scale for his office at that time. The limit was six hundred pounds and very nice with a digital readout for Oprah. This is opinion and fact.

I think about my competitors in the US Senate race from time to time. They pop up in the news sometimes. I love it when President Trump talks about Pocahontas (the fake one from Massachusetts and not the real one from Virginia). Elizabeth Warren tried to celebrate Indigenous People's Day this month, and it did not go well. Everyone remembers that she lied about being an American Indian to get jobs.

"You honored them by stealing jobs, money, and opportunities from them. No American alive today has taken more from Native peoples. For at least this one day, you should hide your pale face in shame," Gerry Callahan responded. Pocahontas is front and center in the White House in my fictional book *Redneck Dystopia*. It is hard to believe that these morons get elected. Her buddy Richard Blumenthal lied about being in Vietnam. He had a little case of stolen valor and should be prosecuted.

Today's holiday is really Columbus Day to honor Christopher Columbus. He was a great explorer and serious Christian. Ignorant people do not care to read history, which explains that slavery was all over the place, and he did not bring it to America. Evil folks still have slaves now in China, Africa, Mexico, the Middle East, and other lands. There would be no America (the greatest nation to ever exist) without Christopher Columbus.

Nancy and I love to walk around New York City, but it is getting hard to do with so many criminals preying on people. And it does not help when Governor Hochul is acting like Chairman Mao and taking the guns away. I usually do not carry my pistol for fear of being arrested by the socialists running the government.

Governor Hochul and friends legalized recreational use of marijuana in 2021 for equity reasons. Now they are rewarding convicted criminals by putting them first in line for licenses for these dumb businesses. How many people will become addicted to drugs because of these stupid Democrats buying votes?

Hundreds of millions of tax money will be wasted helping purchase and renovate drug dealer storefronts. What a country we have now. How many illegal ballots were counted in 2022 in Hochul versus Zeldin? He would have expanded educational opportunities for poor kids while she refuses to do that and helps them get high on drugs.

Mao would be proud of the American communists trying to take our guns away. He took all the guns away from the Chinese people back in 1949. That is what the socialist Democrats are trying here, and make no mistake, we will stop them. The constitution is crystal clear that the Second Amendment is absolute. A few judges and lawyers decided over the years to limit our Second Amendment. They should be punished severely.

Thank goodness a federal judge just halted a really dumb new New York law that made it a felony to carry a gun in restaurants, trains, buses, bars, and in Times Square. Why are they protecting horrible criminals? Is this some ill-conceived, "get out the vote" program for violent folks? These fools want to spit on the constitution. The judge also said the law's requirement to show good moral character was too burdensome. There can be no justice with criminals running the government such as Hochul, Harris, and Biden.

Arrest all the criminals now. Jean McGuire, a ninety-one-year-old civil rights activist, was just stabbed in a Boston park during October 2022. She was walking her dog when some fool attacked her. The police are still looking for the fool. Why were the police not roaming the park? Were they at the doughnut shop? Why is Democrat Mayor Michelle Wu weak on criminals? Jean was the first black person to serve on the Boston School Committee. She is expected to recover.

Our original thirty-page constitution will be enforced soon. Governor Hochul looks and acts like a communist monster on the order of Chairman Mao who killed over 40 million Chinese. She has the crazy eyes and should be deported to China tonight. It may be better to let her stay here and take away her government bodyguards, salary, and benefits. A new, improved Governor Lee Zeldin will take over soon.

The Biden gang begged the Saudis during 2022 to delay an oil production cut until after the US midterm elections. Is that illegal collusion? Is that a tad bit worse than Trump asking Ukraine to see if the Bidens were engaging in criminal activity while creepy Joe was vice president?

The weak, corrupt, communist, and dumb Democrats and RINOs such as Joe Biden and Lindsey Graham are financing both sides of a war by sending billions of our tax money to corrupt Ukraine and jacking up the price of oil for Russia. Biden and friends are begging the evil Iranians for another dangerous nuclear deal while Iranian soldiers are in Crimea training Russians how to use drones to kill Ukrainians. Can we please decertify the election and bring back President Trump?

Vote GOP to stop the stupidity! It is a crying shame that David Xu did not make it onto the ballot for November 2022.

The Marxist Democrats in the House impeached Trump for a legitimate phone call to Ukraine. Biden and other morons cut US energy production, increased taxes during a recession they caused, triggered massive inflation, and then tried to beg dictators for more oil to limp through another rigged election.

The reports out of Russia say that the government folks are grabbing homeless men off the street and shipping them to the combat zone in Ukraine. This actually may be worse than the Democrats here waking up homeless folks in 2020, filling out their ballots, and mailing them in to select creepy Joe. The American homeless were taken advantage of, but at least the Democrats did not ship them off to war. Maybe next time.

Putin is now hiring gangs to snatch men and send them to the front lines in Ukraine after ten days of training. On a recent raid on a business center in Moscow, gang members grabbed musicians who were trying to practice, a delivery man in the wrong place at the wrong time, and a very drunk disabled man in his fifties, according to the *Wall Street Journal*. Boy, I am glad we do not live in Russia.

The voters are sick of big, corrupt socialist government and the uniparty fools. I am confident that many state and local conservatives and Christians will take office also. God and Jesus always win! That is what we know for sure.

We have been worried about our favorite candidate for US Senate John Fetterman. What a shame it would be to be deprived of more dumb comments and insights from him. The Babylon Bee reported, "Asked if he has cognitive ability to be a senator, Fetterman blinks twice for yes." If ever anyone is in danger of losing any more brainpower, it is this guy. He could not count to ten before his stroke.

Millions and millions of Americans have been censored by our socialist-communist friends online. I submitted a right to know request to the government idiots to see if they were involved. As you can see below, they divulged nothing. Many government employees hide behind vague and complicated laws and rules. Do you think I should have sugarcoated my request?

These people do not seem to realize that they work for We the People. They do not work for the Democrat political party. We must fire and prosecute all lazy, immoral, or incompetent government idiots to make America great again. Trump is right on this one.

Fire all the lazy and immoral union teachers and socialist Democrats now! The average score on the ACT college admissions test is the lowest in thirty years. The government idiots are ruining the next generation. Vote GOP!

The Democrat lockdowns, strikes, masks, vaccines, and other dumb policies have damaged many children mentally and physically. Lazy teachers go on strike and ignore our precious children. Many teachers love money over kids. When will we get corrupt unions out of government? The Dems and RINOs are to blame.

Did you say you want more unions in the United States? May I refer you to France where leftist union idiots are on strike again. They work at oil refineries and the strikes have left over 30 percent of French gas stations low on supply. The temperatures are dropping amid this unnecessary energy crisis brought on by left-wing nuts wanting more pay and benefits. Fuel prices have risen a lot, but these socialist people only focus on their own greed.

The corrupt and/or lazy French government people such as President Macron have more than half their fifty-six nuclear reactors offline now too. They let corrosion form on pipes that cool the reactor cores. That is kind of important in preventing a meltdown. They have plenty of money for welfare though. We should fire any union employee who refuses to work hard. Vicarious learning is important (learning from the mistakes of others).

Well, well, the Democrats keep saying that our elections are safe and secure. True the Vote revealed that the employees at Konnech were storing American election information within China. Some of their contractors were also within China with super administration access to the systems.

Why are the socialists and communists not in jail tonight? The *New York Times* writers called this a conspiracy theory and then retracted their ignorant statement. We really need to identify and punish all socialists, communists, and others who hate America tonight.

These people work on election systems in our country. Konnech also did work for the fools running the Pentagon. Where are the FBI, DIA, and CIA employees on this? Are they too busy harassing conservative Christians at school board meetings and antiabortion preachers?

The Democrats are planning to cheat during the 2022 elections again as they did in 2020. The Pennsylvania legislature and the US Supreme Court ruled that undated mail-in ballots cannot be counted. Democrat Leigh Chapman, acting secretary of state, is telling the county elections officers to count them anyway.

These criminals must be imprisoned. She and other fools are breaking the law and spitting on the ultimate law (the constitution). Where is the prosecutor for this moron?

"Pennsylvania Democrats' consistent disregard for the election rules set by the legislature has resulted in Pennsylvania being a national election administration laughingstock," explains the Republican National Committee (RNC) during October 2022.

Many MAGA Republicans are fighting back and will stop election cheating. We have been enjoying Zoom meetings about poll watching. Heather Honey with Pennsylvania Fair Elections and Andrea Raffle with the Pennsylvania GOP are very motivated and knowledgeable about how the lawless Democrats cheated in 2020.

The GOP leaders have been incompetent or corrupt on election cheating for decades, and we have paid a heavy price with the Biden and Wolf gangs. They only had 500 poll watchers in 2020 for the entire state. We will have between 15,000 and 20,000 this year to identify and correct mistakes and crimes on and around election day November 8.

Cleta Mitchell spoke at one of our meetings and described the lawlessness of the Democrats in counting illegal ballots. She helped prepare a lawsuit in Georgia after the 2020 steal, but the fools in charge never assigned a judge to hear the case and massive evidence. Why would the government folks and judges do that? Perhaps they are lazy, dumb, and/or corrupt.

We have 9,155 polling stations in Pennsylvania. This is way too many and lends itself to cheating. The Democrats cheat in many ways. If a voter submits incorrect or missing information on their request for a mail-in ballot (MIB), the ballot should not be counted until the person shows an ID or corrects the mistakes. This is how illegal ballots were counted before. The judge of elections at each polling station is the only person we can address issues to on election day. Most of them are good, but some are corrupt. The slow judges would not act to throw out many illegal ballots before, so we must step up and secure our elections.

I have no doubt that conservatives and Christians will have a great day in November. Good Americans volunteer to make this a better place and put the criminals in jail. Most Americans are sick of high inflation, illegal aliens, and criminals hurting and killing people caused by stupid Democrat policies.

Republicans are pointing out illegal activity now *before* the election. The GOP is suing Pennsylvania for illegal guidance for counting ballots and other things. Patriot Toni Shuppe and Audit the Vote

PA are helping to remove many people from our voter rolls to prevent or reduce fraud.

The Democrats will not clean up the voter rolls. They keep dead people and others who moved on the rolls. Criminals submit ballots for these people. Why are most Democrats immoral? Did they skip ethics or morality classes at home and in high school?

Lying is bad. Telling the truth is good. Get with it people! Have you read the Bible? It is full of great advice for a successful life. Mike Lindell has a lot of evidence of election cheating. He is a great American for burning a lot of his money and securing our elections. We donate to his very effective legal fund.

Linda Sheckler and many others are making progress in removing ineligible people from the voter rolls. She is strong and identified over four hundred Penn State students who do not live in a closed dormitory and requested that the county take them off the voter rolls. Poll watchers should report any issues at pennsylvania.protect-thevote.com.

The Pennsylvania GOP will have over seventy lawyers on duty on election day to handle any issues. This was not done in 2020, and the cheaters took advantage. The Pennsylvania Supreme Court halted an investigation in 2020 of voting machines. Why would they do that? These same Democrat judges allowed the counting of ballots for up to three days after election day. This is clearly illegal in Pennsylvania.

A GOP group just filed a complaint about government idiots sharing unregistered voter lists with left-wing groups. There is a lot of evidence at Frank Speech about Democrats inflating voter rolls using these names for illegal ballots.

"Why are election officials in Delaware County, Pennsylvania, illegally mailing out ballots for the 2022 midterms before the logic and accuracy tests have started?" asked Sidney Powell and Emerald Robinson. These ladies work hard to tell the truth about corrupt government folks. Leah Hoopes reported in our Zoom meeting that they are violating ballot and machine testing procedures in Delaware county again. She did a great job in exposing how horrible and corrupt Josh Shapiro is. Many illegal ballots were counted over there in 2020 for creepy Joe and the Ho.

The money pouring into the Senate races like mine is a testament to the ignorance of many American voters and citizens. The politicians buy TV ads because so many people do not read anymore. Most Americans are good at their jobs, but they should keep up with civics, government, candidates, and politicians more. From September 5 to October 14, candidates and their allies for my Senate race (Oz and Fetterman) burned over $62 million on broadcast, cable, satellite TV, digital, and radio advertisements, according to the FEC, Adimpact, and the *WSJ*. The socialist idiot Warnock, conservative Christian Hershel Walker, and friends have wasted over $74 million on that Senate race in Georgia. Do the voters even know that Warnock's crying wife said on a police camera that he ran over her foot with his car? Do the voters know that he votes with crying Chuck Schumer and against limited government over 98 percent of the time? Do the voters know that over 70 percent of the laws passed by Congress are unconstitutional?

Can we please get good teachers to make children read and write more and watch less TV? Our nation's survival depends on educated and hardworking citizens. We cannot take any more dolts such as Stacey Abrams. She spends her days grazing and chewing cud (food that returns to the mouth from the stomach to be chewed for the second time), sucking up union dues, and saying dumb stuff.

I spoke to a very nice old high school friend, Joe Moore, recently. He is sixty years old and was going to retire soon but cannot now with the massive inflation caused by all the borrowing, welfare, and spending by the socialist Democrats. Joe and his brother Monty were great baseball players from Dan River High School near Danville, Virginia. We battled it out on the gridiron as kids. He and other Virginians destroyed the immoral and incompetent Democrats in their elections in 2021.

Abrams sure looks pregnant but does not mention it and lectures the rest of us to abort our babies so we can withstand the abusive inflation caused by her Democrat Party friends. I wonder how much her food budget is now. It has be huge. Why does she eat so much? Perhaps Oprah and Oz can help by telling her what not to do.

Does she have four stomachs or compartments like a cow? That would be awesome. She would be great Michelin woman, but she cannot define what a woman is now. She reminds me of that Rodney Dangerfield joke. "Two men could make love to her at the same time and never see each other."

I hope and pray that Republicans can fire and punish woke military fools for trying to radicalize and weaken our military. Mark Milley, chairman of the Joint Chiefs of Staff, should be the first to go for telling communists in China that he would warn them before an American attack. The death penalty is very good for traitors such as him. What about this other idiot in uniform Michael Gilday, Chief of Naval Operations? He refused to say whether or not he thinks capitalism is racist in front of a Senate hearing.

China, Russia, Iran, North Korea, and other nations are threatening the US-led world order. The weak socialist Democrats are playing with fire and could cause chaos if our soldiers and military are not strong and awesome.

We will be lucky to retake our nation from fools before they cause another world war. The bloated Lloyd Austin, secretary of defense, seems retarded and wears a mask and shield together when meeting foreign military leaders. He should be severely punished for embarrassing us on the world stage. How did he ever get promoted to four-star general?

He is the perfect walking argument against affirmative action. The Biden gang hires people based on race and other irrelevant traits and not on merit and ability. This leads to bankruptcy in the business world and death and destruction in the military world.

We are going to help Deborah Jordan over in Luzerne County. She is battling horrible Democrats who want to put out many drop boxes for illegal ballots again. The American people are awake now, and the Democrats cannot win unless they cheat.

I love the way Deb does a lot of research before ever opening her mouth. This good American and her We the People team will defeat the socialists soon. The socialists pose as their friends but want you and I to pay to support all the illegal immigrants in Pennsylvania and across this great nation. The criminals should be deported.

Dennis Smith called the other day. We went to high school together in Danville, Virginia, many moons ago. He works for an energy company and cannot believe that Biden and his climate change buddies have restricted energy production in America. Dennis is a wonderful man, husband, and father who sent his kids to Liberty University.

We are surprised Biden did not have a sex scandal like Jerry Falwell Jr. with the pool boy and his wife. The wife and pool boy had a great time on the hotel bed in Miami while the weird husband watched and giggled. I guess Biden was too ugly to have a sex scandal or paid off the others.

We need a good look at the Biden files at the University of Delaware. The government idiots running the school are protecting this piece of crap (creepy Joe) by hiding his Senate records. We believe Tara Reade's accusation that Joe sexually assaulted her in 1993. Where are the Me Too movement leaders when you need them?

How about these Democrats taking it easy on the criminals and communists? Now we have *antifa* thugs smashing coffee shops in Portland, Oregon, during October 2022 just because the police were having a Coffee with a Cop event. What is wrong these morons?

I sure hope they elect Christine Drazan to lock up the criminals before it is not too late. Maybe next time the barista could throw hot coffee on the criminals. That would be awesome. We love the cops… and coffee!

We the People are going to take back our country with the November elections. We can do great things if we stick together like the good people in Tennessee. Matt Walsh led many people to demand that Vanderbilt University Medical Center stop castrating young boys and performing double mastectomies on young girls.

The monsters at that medical system are mutilating children and making a lot of money doing it. Why are they still walking around free? These are monsters in lab coats and business suits. Where are the prosecutors? The transgender pushers are worse than the drug pushers. You can quit drugs, but your genitals and breasts cannot be reattached.

Children should focus on reading, writing, math, science, and the Bible and not on changing their gender. This stupidity must end. Adults should work hard, support their families, and prepare for retirement and not waste time changing their gender. This is one of the dumbest things I have ever heard about.

The United States was founded by Christians and based on biblical values. We better get back to the Bible and common sense soon. The atheists, communists, and other fools are trying to destroy God, Jesus, the Bible, the constitution, and the great United States of America. Let us take back our government and nation now!

There is a breakdown in government. Nancy and I drove to the DMV on a Thursday recently. The government idiots under the leadership of Wolf, Fetterman, and Shapiro only work on Tuesday, Wednesday, and Saturday. Why are these lazy union folks getting paid for full-time work? They were rude and incompetent before, but at least they were at work Monday through Saturday.

Doug Mastriano will clean this crap up in January. Why are the RINOs David Argall and Tim Twardzik doing nothing? Are they worth the $94,000 per year we pay them? Perhaps I will rattle their cages and wake them up. I guess they are busy with shredding events. They love to have these all the time. What are they shredding? Why do you need to shred documents all the time? They keep expanding the Pennsylvania government and welfare, and that is fantastic because we need more unemployed, opioid addicts walking around day and night bothering the hard workers and stealing from them.

David Xu (dave224422@yahoo.com)
To Senator David Argall, Tim Twardzik, Tim Twardzik
Thursday, October 20 at 5:50 p.m.

Hi, David and Tim,

You are doing such a good job. We love the deep and wide potholes on Highway 61. It is fun to try to miss them all. You are so helpful in letting the Democrats cheat in our elections. The way you stopped the 2020 audit was genius. Hardly anyone noticed. How many illegal ballots were counted in 2020? Did you really certify that election? The DMV is only open three days a week and following your example of hard work. Perhaps you are worth half your $92,000 salary. Can we claw back your taxpayer funded pension? It is great that you are allowing the union lazy government teachers push CRT and transgender stuff. You must love our conservative and Christian kids. You really showed your fiscal conservatism by passing the 2023 budget with $300 million more than the little dictator Wolf requested. That was so sweet to expand government again. You are the best RINOs money can buy. Keep up the good work. Do you need anything like campaign donations? They sell pocket constitutions at Hillsdale College if you need one. I think it says we should have limited government and not full-time or long-term politicians. Have you heard of Mastriano, DelRosso, and Oz? We are supporting them. Are you supporting Shapiro, Davis, and Fetterman? Have a blessed day now.

David Xu
Army Vet, thirty years, LTC, MBA, author
of *Redneck Dystopia*, concerned citizen
http://www.wethepeoplecoalcountry.com

Pennsylvania is in the top ten of states with outbound migration. About 40,000 people moved out of Pennsylvania from July 2021 until July 2022. The big, corrupt, expensive, incompetent uniparty government supported by Twardzik, Argall, Shapiro, Wolf, Fetterman, and other fools is a major reason why many of these people left Pennsylvania. When will they cut spending and get back to the limited government mandated by the state and federal constitutions?

Obama and Biden have given billions to the terrorists running Iran. Why did they do this? Are they dumb or corrupt or both? They are funding both sides of the war in Ukraine. The Russians are buying and using drones from Iran to bomb the heck out of the Ukrainians. Why are the Democrats so tight with the evil mullahs and so standoffish with the Iranian protesters in the streets trying to topple the brutal regime?

The Russians have more money because Biden has restricted American energy production and caused high inflation. Biden and other fools are wasting billions of our tax money to defend the weak and corrupt Ukrainians. They should be forced to negotiate a peace deal and stop the war.

Perhaps the Ukrainians should not have paid Hunter $83,000 per month for nothing and bought military gear. I thought Obama and Biden were foreign policy experts. We need American first GOP folks in the House and Senate asap to defeat the uniparty.

Perhaps the Democrats can learn from our friends in Israel. They have moved away from socialism and communism and toward capitalism in the last thirty years. They know that diplomacy is only effective after you have economic and military strength. Biden and other fools do not understand this truth.

The American socialist Democrats are weakening our military and economic power and trying to force diplomacy on other nations who are ignoring and laughing at them. The Saudis just cut production after Biden begged them not to until after our midterm elections. Should he be impeached for that? We need to drill, baby, drill as Trump did to get back to energy independence.

Biden had foolish insults for the Saudis after they took out Khashoggi who supported the terrorist Muslim Brotherhood network. Putin ignored Biden and invaded Ukraine. Foreigners the world over are laughing at the United States with an illegitimate idiot as president.

While the Democrats live in a fantasy world with taxpayer-funded security, the rest of us are forgotten and must fight off or kill criminals who attack us all the time. They will not protect us from stupid criminals, but the socialist Democrats running the Social Security program just began to allow confused folks to select their gender.

There are only two genders according to good, intelligent, conservative, or Christian people. The Republicans will stop this insanity and remove the folks who hate America and the Bible.

The RINOs should learn vicariously from the Conservative Party in Britain. Liz Truss only lasted forty-four days as prime minister during October 2022. She tried to cut taxes to spur economic growth, but her party members wanted to keep making the same mistakes they have been making for twelve years in power.

In some ways, the parliamentary system is better. You can dump the really bad leaders like Boris Johnson quickly, but it does not take many good or bad folks to do that. The Brits dumped Truss and elevated the globalist Sunak with only 357 party votes in parliament. The other 172,000 Conservative Party members, and the 48 million citizens could not vote either way on this matter.

Shawn and Devin Hartman with the Mastriano campaign led a group of us door knocking a few times during October. Doug is lucky to have these patriots volunteering for his campaign. We met many good Americans, and 90 percent want the same things. They want criminals arrested, low inflation, plenty of jobs, less welfare for lazy people, more limited government, term limits, and a sealed border. Most of the voters are not thrilled about Oz but will hold their nose and vote for him. He is better than RINO Toomey and much better than commie Fetterman.

The American RINOs and Tories love massive welfare, Green New Deal crap, higher taxes, huge and wasteful government, and a socialist Federal Reserve bank that monetizes the debt by printing money like crazy. We must purge the GOP of RINOs who are helping the Democrats destroy America with huge, abusive, expensive, and corrupt government.

Earmark lover Mitch McConnell and his wife, Elaine Chao, who makes a lot of money in China, would fit right in with that United Kingdom bunch. He is fighting against America-first candidates Don Bolduc in New Hampshire and Kelly Tshibaka in Alaska. The establishment politicians who hate limited government suck!

The good British people finally forced the Tories and Labor Party fools to get out of the European Union. That was smart. This horrible climate change EU gang is another layer of expensive and unnecessary government for the hardworking Europeans.

The poor taxpayers must not only fund their huge and incompetent government but also another one in Brussels. These are the geniuses who turned off nuclear and coal power plants and now do not have enough power for businesses and households. They love the community organizer idiot and failed politician Obama.

The funny part of the Liz Truss story comes from the *Daily Star* paper. They bought a head of lettuce and livestreamed it to see if it could remain fresh longer than Liz could hang onto the prime minister position. The head of lettuce won. The sad part of the story is that the socialists in Parliament selected a World Economic Forum CCP-loving fool to be prime minister.

Speaking of CCP-loving folks, the Democrats running Morgan Stanley, Blackstone, Citigroup, Goldman Sachs, BlackRock, and JPMorgan Chase are flying to Hong Kong to hang out with the new city dictator, John Lee. These dumb Americans like to speak about social justice, fake racism, and exaggerated climate change but ignore Lee and other CCP fools for coercing, arresting, detaining, and imprisoning people in Hong Kong and throughout China for politics and criticizing the government people.

The Republicans should force the bankers to get out of politics and stop supporting socialists and communists here and abroad. The government insures their deposits, and we must promote honesty and other biblical values. America is a Christian nation for good in the world. Immoral business leaders must be removed and punished. How much pollution are the causing by flying jets to hang with the communist government idiots?

We all have dreams. Some would say odd, crazy, impossible, or even dumb dreams. I think of Jessi Combs who set the speed record for a four-wheel jet-powered car in Oregon at 522 mph in 2019. She died that day at thirty-nine years old in a crash caused by a front wheel failure after reaching the record speed. The Guinness World Records confirmed her success in 2020.

"That is the sound of freedom," my sister Betsy explained after two F-16s flew over our heads in Goldsboro, North Carolina. Both Jessi and Betsy are hard-charging women who succeed at anything they attempt. We need more women like them.

The Democrat lockdowns were really dumb. Governor DeSantis was right to ignore the lazy union teacher crap coming from Anthony Fauci and the corrupt unions. He and many others should be punished for hurting so many children.

"We also knew that younger and at-risk students would be the most impacted if schools were closed, and the results speak for themselves. In Florida our fourth-grade students rank number 3 in reading and number 4 in math, achieving top four in both English and math for the first time in state history, while lockdown California and New York aren't even in the top thirty," Governor Ron DeSantis.

The Catholic schools and homeschoolers did much better educating our youth during COVID than the government union folks with their lockdowns. The children work on morality based on the Bible in Christian schools also. That will help them succeed in any field. We need more vouchers and charter schools. We need fewer lazy and immoral teachers.

The federal government fools like Fauci have wasted over 82 million doses of vaccine for the CCP virus from 2020 until May 2022. These doses expired or were destroyed. The Democrats and RINOs have wasted tens of billions or our tax money for a vaccine that most Americans do not want. When will these idiots be punished?

Fetterman is just like Tim Ryan and Conor Lamb and Josh Shapiro who will say anything to get elected. Lamb won a US House seat in 2018 saying he would be anti-Pelosi and then voted with her 100 percent of the time while in the DC swamp. Oz is a weak candidate, but I hope he smokes the ultimate dimwit Fetterman.

Most Americans are not falling for the "moderate Democrat" lie anymore. Radical leftists like Barnes in Wisconsin want to defund the police even now after criminals have injured and killed thousands in the last two years. These liars set a terrible example for the kids that lying is okay.

Shapiro threatened to arrest great Americans in Pennsylvania who volunteer to watch drop boxes as they did in Arizona in this year's primary. Many of us are planning on monitoring the drop boxes anyway in November. Have you see *2000 Mules*? That movie is a gift to honest prosecutors who want to fry election cheaters. True the Vote said that watching drop boxes is not a crime and to call 855-585-2022 24/7 for help if you see any election cheaters.

We watched the debate last night (October 25, 2022) between Oz and Fetterman, and it was obvious that Fetterman is too immoral, dumb, and impaired to be a senator. He opened with, "Hi, good night, everybody." The corrupt Biden regime and Democrats just want someone who lies and is stupid to rubber-stamp their communist agenda that spits on our sacred constitution.

The rumor is that if Shapiro wins for governor, he can replace Fetterman with his illegal alien wife when he quits. These Democrats are sick and must be removed. They delayed this debate for months to allow for many mail-in ballots to come before seeing this fool speak.

Over 635,000 ballots (over 48 percent of those requested) came into the corrupt government idiots before this devastating debate for Fetterman. The voters can change their vote, but most will not take the time. He hid in his basement for months just like his corrupt friend creepy Joe. These sick Democrats do not spend time with many voters answering questions and just run TV ads all the time with union money for one-way communication. This is communism paid for by hardworking capitalists.

Oz resembles a conman but wiped the floor with Fetterman last night. He is very polished on TV from years with his successful TV show. He called out Fetterman's support for releasing criminals, banning fracking, extreme abortion stance, continuous lies, and out-of-control spending.

Oz would be a great barker at a carnival trying to get customers to see the bearded lady or the headless man in the dirty trailer with lights all over it. We need more politicians who already made their money and secured their retirement such as David Xu and Oz. The loser Fetterman is obviously jealous because he keeps talking about Oz's ten houses.

Fetterman exposed himself as a nasty, dumb, and immoral person after about 10 percent of the voters mailed in ballots. He is just like Biden and Harris. Communists do not care about the citizens. They only care about gaining and maintaining power. Look at Papa Xi punishing former allies so he can rule the 92 percent of the Chinese people not in the CCP another five years. Only 8 percent of the Chinese are in the CCP. Americans and Chinese are screwed if strong and moral folks do not take back political power from sick fools.

We have many dishonest people in our government, and they must be purged. Biden and other fools tried to get the Saudis to increase oil production to combat inflation that they caused to help them get elected or reelected during November 2022. The deal was secret but came out that the Saudis were angry that Biden insulted them several times in the last couple of years. They prefer to deal with good and strong leaders like Trump.

The jerk Jeff Bartos was spotted at a Shapiro fundraiser with his wife, Sheryl, during September 2022. Do you remember when this RINO appeared to be gleeful when Parnell was accused of spousal abuse? It seemed like this establishment fool thought the GOP nomination was his for sure.

We dodged a bullet with this chameleon in 2018 for lieutenant governor and this year for US senator. Does he really support the socialist and corrupt Democrat Josh Shapiro over our Christian and conservative veteran Doug Mastriano? We have way too many fake Republicans like Bartos. We need a lieutenant governor like Mark Robinson of my old state North Carolina. He is a patriot for sure.

Biden has released over 165 million barrels of oil from our Strategic Petroleum Reserve to get more corrupt folks elected in 2022. This energy is to protect the American way of life during wars and other emergencies. It is not for dumb politicians to hide their communist climate change policies. Can we please have some honest people in our government? Is that too much to ask?

Some good news came out of China. The one hundred richest people there saw their net worth decrease by $573 billion in the last year. That is great because these folks are tight with the evil CCP clowns. The less money they have to try to dominate other nations, the better. They are locking down their citizens to prevent uprisings. This authoritarianism is bad for business. We must keep the communism out of America to keep us great.

Fetterman will vote for any bad treaty between the United States and other nations as long as he keeps his power and money. The climate change fools will not understand or admit that it creates more pollution to import oil from dictatorships than to produce it ourselves. They are only obsessed with political power and money, and most Americans do not trust them as far as they can throw them. I felt this when meeting many voters on the campaign trail.

Never forget that the communists in the local, state, and national media lied and said Fetterman is fine for months now. These fools lie to the good Americans to get socialists, commies, and other sick people elected. See Fetterman, Wolf, Biden, Obama, Clinton, Pelosi, Schumer, Shapiro, etc. Vote GOP to get back to the constitution.

"Fifteen Republican state representatives sent a letter to Acting Secretary of the Commonwealth Leigh Chapman after they discovered that over 240,000 illicit ballots were sent out in the state prior to the 2022 midterm elections. Deputy Secretary Jonathan Marks testified in September before the Pennsylvania House that counties are responsible to verify the voter ID when a completed ballot arrive to the county. The counties argued that this was nonsense. The ID must be verified before a ballot is even sent out," according to Jim Hoft of the Gateway Pundit on October 26, 2022. These ballots must not be counted, according to state law, until a voter produces an ID. The Democrats did this same crap back in 2020 and cheated Trump. I did not see our boy Twardzik's signature on the letter. Argall and Twardzik must be removed and punished for not standing up for honest conservatives and Christians.

We must get back to one day voting with paper ballots to stop all the Democrat cheating. Arrest all election cheaters to make America great again. We watched the debate and thanked God that we were at home enjoying the awesome American dream down on our farm in Ashland. We will leave the running for office to others now.

Shapiro, Fetterman, Wolf, Krasner, and other government idiots are supposed to throw criminals in or under the jail. Instead, over one thousand people in Philadelphia have been killed since January 2021. About 1,938 have been shot just in 2022. Vote GOP for common sense and law and order!

We must demand politicians and government employees who are America first. The US diplomats let the Huawei CFO stay in a $12 million mansion in Canada under house arrest while the US government tried to extradite her for violating laws in helping the evil Iranian regime. Meanwhile, two Canadians were arrested in China as retaliation and spent their time in filthy, crowded, cold prisons.

Why are American taxpayers paying to fly Canadian prisoners from China to Canada on American jets? The communists running Canada should provide planes and pay for this. Why was the Chinese CCP-loved princess criminal Meng allowed to live in luxury while the Canadians were in harsh jails?

The folks in our government are weak and should be removed. Most American politicians are imbeciles and worthless. They waste extreme amounts of tax money without punishment. Who is that awesome former US Senate candidate with the Chinese name? Oh, that is right, David Xu is the man who would treat your tax dollars like his own. That cat is all right.

The fools at Biden's State Department are paying drag queen theater performances in Ecuador now. They should be promoting Christian American values as has been done since America's founding. Foreigners are laughing at the immoral and sick Americans trying to push this stupidity on other nations. I pray to God that we can stop these fools soon. The Chinese are funding copper mines in Ecuador, while America is funding immoral crap.

We had some bad news during October 2022. The corrupt DOJ employees arrested our friends Catherine Engelbrecht and Gregg Phillips for not revealing their source in the Konnech scandal. They helped prosecutors with evidence of Eugene Yu allegedly transmitting information on American election workers to CCP folks in

China. Catherine and Gregg did a fantastic job accumulating massive evidence of election cheating from 2020 until today. There is no way Biden and Harris won. Unfortunately, most judges and prosecutors will not look at it and/or indict the election cheaters. She gave a good talk at the Bloomsburg We the People rally we attended in August. It would be justice to see the judge who locked up Catherine and Gregg behind bars. That would really be the thing.

We are in a cold war with China. The CCP fools are allowing their chemical companies to make more ingredients for fentanyl than ever. The Mexican cartel folks buy this crap and ship into America through our wide-open border thanks to Biden. Overdoses are skyrocketing while the CCP and American useful government idiots are having a great time and living their best life. One really dumb government teacher in New Jersey overdosed on fentanyl during class with students watching.

We had more good news for freedom-loving Americans out of Everett, Washington. The hardworking employees of "Hillbilly Hotties" sued the city over its dress code law that made it illegal for them to wear bikinis while serving coffee.

Thank goodness for judges who actually enforce the awesome original constitution and know the difference between a man and a woman. A federal judge ruled the law unconstitutional for these fine ladies. Perhaps we need some more good judges who will throw out unconstitutional moves by Democrat Party executive and judicial branch folks (think Wolf, Shapiro, and Pennsylvania Supreme Court) who change election laws in order to cheat.

Judge Ricardo Martinez (a normal man?) got to the bottom of the case by spending a lot of time at Hillbilly Hotties doing research. He was seen getting coffee at least ten times per day to see everything relevant to the case. He is trying to see all the bare evidence.

Perhaps the truth can be reported on Twitter now that Elon Musk has taken over. Pelosi's drunken husband, Paul, was beaten by a homeless drug addict in their house in San Francisco. David DePape is an illegal alien from Canada. Why is he here?

The lying socialist establishment media say he is a right-wing nut. DePape's neighbors say he supports BLM. I do not know any right-wing folks who support the BLM violent folks. I will go with what the neighbors say. Perhaps now the Democrats will close our borders. There are reports that Paul goes to gay bars and has a good time while his stupid and manly wife is gone vacuuming up money across the globe.

I say let the truth shine on all sick and lazy politicians and their family and friends. The prosecutors let Paul off without jail time for some reason for a DUI earlier in 2022. He could have killed someone driving like that. This cat better slow down and get a real woman to teach him right from wrong. Open up a Bible for goodness's sake.

We understand why Paul is looking for love in all the wrong places. How would you like to come home to Nancy? It would be like being married to a beaver or a horrible witch with toothpicks in her eye sockets. The police and prosecutors in California just cannot seem to apply the law to the rich or famous people as they do with common folks like us.

Pelosi's husband was beaten by an illegal alien. Perhaps now she and her socialist friends will finish the border wall and deport these criminals. Maybe she knows how so many others feel after being attacked by violent animals she has helped keep out of jail.

Tiger Woods should have done some jail time for crossing the oncoming traffic lane while going about 87 mph in a 45 mph zone and crashing while possibly on drugs or alcohol. He could have killed someone on a motorcycle or in a car. He could have killed a walker or jogger. The investigators did not seek a warrant for blood tests. Why did they do this? Would they do you and I the same favor?

This Pelosi incident reminds many of the time Andrew Gillum was found naked in the Mondrian Hotel in South Beach, Florida with a gay escort, another man, and meth in 2020. One fool in the room was treated for an overdose. This idiot Gillum almost beat DeSantis in 2018 for governor. Gillum's drug friend in the hotel posts porn movies online. The former mayor of Tallahassee is married to a woman with three kids. Is she a beard? "Not that there is anything wrong with that," as Jerry and George used to say. Gillum was hit with a twenty-one-count federal indictment in 2022 for fraudulent fundraising and other crimes. Prosecutors allege that he conspired with his mentor Sharon Hicks to use campaign contributions for personal use.

Gillum leads us to Eric Adams. He is the creepy mayor of NYC who likes to party all night and wear fancy clothes with an earring. The media better keep an eye on this fake idiot. A scandal is surely coming soon. He sounded drunk or high asking a guy about his earring over and over, while the guy was asking Adams a serious question a few days ago. DeBlasio was the worst type of communist, but Adams may actually be more delusional and worse for the good people of New York City.

It is one week before the November 2022 election, and over 21 million ballots have already been cast. It should be impossible to cheat in our elections. Our elections can never be secure with all the mail-in ballots and machines that can be connected to the internet. We need one-day elections with paper ballots to restore trust in American elections, and we need it now before it is too late. "War is an extension of politics," Karl von Clausewitz. This will get bloody if the Democrats keep playing with fire. They will get burned.

We need to go back to our policy back in 1950 and put all socialists and communists in or under the jail in America. The Google YouTube folks announced that they will remove any posts that point out election cheating in Brazil. President Bolsonaro just got cheated out of reelection by the communist criminal Lula da Silva, and the American communists are helping out all they can. They are so sweet.

Papa Xi and the other CCP fools were quick to congratulate their communist comrade in Brazil for stealing another election. The Supreme Court of Brazil let the convicted felon out of jail on a technicality so he could run for office again. I wonder if those judges are communist folks. Biden and other Democrat fools were quick to congratulate Lula. I wonder how many illegal ballots were counted. Sound familiar?

This stupidity must stop, and we must crush the commies once and for all. They are a threat to the American way of life. The Facebook and Twitter employees had secret portals to collude with government idiots to censor great Americans for the last few years.

The Google and YouTube people did the same thing in 2020 to help Biden steal the election from Trump. They hid all the crimes on Hunter's laptop and many other things from the voters. Can we decertify that one tonight?

More good news came on November 1. The Pennsylvania Supreme Court ruled that undated or misdated absentee and mail-in ballots cannot be counted. Hopefully, the majority Democrat court will follow through with this because it follows our laws. The court said that it is evenly divided on the issue and that the counties should segregate these ballots. That is a dumb thing for a group of judges to say, and they could still count them.

Hopefully, they will do the right thing unlike in 2020 when they let the Democrats cheat like crazy. The current court has four Democrats and two Republicans with one vacancy. The seventy-four-year-old Democrat Max Baer died during October 2022.

The US Supreme Court should have stepped in during 2020 but abstained, and here we are with the socialist-communist Biden and Wolf gangs. We pray that someone stops the ever-immoral Leigh Chapman, acting secretary of state, from ignoring the US Supreme Court and cheating to help the corrupt Democrats like Shapiro.

Good leaders are hard to find, but can we please just have honest folks in leadership positions? Elon Musk has already improved Twitter by fact-checking Biden as follows. "Seniors are getting the biggest increase in their social security checks in ten years through President Biden's leadership," the Biden idiots tweeted in November 2022.

The diverse and very unqualified White House employees failed to mention that the increase is due to Democrats causing massive inflation with reckless government borrowing and spending, massive welfare for people not to work, and restricting energy production for no reason.

The US and Pennsylvania Supreme Courts ruled that undated or incorrect mail-in ballots cannot be counted in the 2022 general election. They should have done this in 2020, and Trump would have continued to be a great president. These criminals should be punished for allowing corrupt Biden to try to ruin America.

It is November 2, 2022, and somebody found classified documents at Penn Biden Center. The corrupt DOJ and FBI folks hid this crime until January 2023. This helped Democrat fools such as Fetterman and Shapiro get elected. Can we please arrest all corrupt people in our government?

Brain-dead Biden never had declassification authority as Trump did. The criminals raided Trump's house back in August with no good reason. When will they raid Biden's houses? By the way, how did he pay for these houses? Hunter claimed that he owns one of the houses in Delaware, where classified documents were found. How did this drug addict buy a mansion? Why did the Chinese, Russians, and Ukrainians give so much money to the Bidens? Is that legal? Why is that legal? Why did the media and big tech folks cover this up before the 2020 election? They screwed the American voters.

Biden's fake victory claimed an 81,660 margin in Pennsylvania. Peter Navarro found 992,467 possible illegal votes. The WEF candidate David McCormick wanted to count undated and illegal ballots in the primary against Oz. The Pennsylvania Supreme Court fools finally allowed the illegal ballots to be counted in June 2022, but McCormick had already conceded. Shall we waterboard the cheaters and their enablers? We could break the record KSM has for being waterboarded 183 times. Just kidding, I do not approve of the technique.

> (dave224422@yahoo.com)
> *To* Senator David Argall, Tim Twardzik, Tim Twardzik
> Thursday, November 3 at 2:24 p.m.
>
> David and Tim,
>
> Are you going to decertify 2020? Have you seen the evidence at frankspeech.com, peternavarro.com, and many other places? Why are you silent? Are you stupid or corrupt?

The US and Pennsylvania Supreme Courts ruled that undated or incorrect mail-in ballots cannot be counted in the 2022 general election. They should have done this in 2020 and Trump would have continued to be a great President. These criminals should be punished for allowing corrupt Biden to try to ruin America.

Biden's fake victory claimed an 81,660 margin in Pennsylvania. Peter Navarro found 992,467 possible illegal votes. The WEF candidate David McCormick wanted to count undated and illegal ballots in the primary against Oz. The Pennsylvania Supreme Court fools finally allowed the illegal ballots to be counted in June 2022, but McCormick had already conceded. Shall we waterboard the cheaters and their enablers? We could break the record KSM has for being waterboarded 183 times. Just kidding, I do not approve of the technique.

David Xu

I watch the Senate races in other states now. The one in New Hampshire with Don Bolduc against Maggie Hassan is interesting. The Democrats wasted over $3 million attacking Bolduc's main RINO opponent Chuck Morse in the primary because they thought Bolduc would crumble in politics against her. The uniparty is alive and well in their desperate attempt to keep the establishment criminal network going.

Bolduc put his life on the line for over thirty years in the Army, while Hassan has been in government many years in different positions and refuses to have any open meetings with voters or journalists. She is the typical communist operator who does not care what the voters think or want. It is all narrative to this CCP-like fool. It looks like Bolduc is going to smoke this socialist Democrat in November. The country will be much better off with her out of government.

I spent about $600 on TV ads trying to win the primary here in Pennsylvania. Bolduc is my hero because he did not spend anything on TV advertisements to win his primary. The lazy Biden-loving Hassan refused to debate my man Bolduc even one time. She is not good enough to represent hardworking citizens in the Senate.

Do you want more good news? The market value of Facebook or Meta is down by $800 billion in the last year. The decline is over $1 trillion if you include Amazon and Alphabet or Google. It is always great when socialists and communists and other fools go down in flames. Where is that grand jury for Zuckerberg and/or the election cheating operation? How many illegal ballots were counted in 2020 and in other elections?

The Democrat leaders are a national security threat. Many good citizens will not join a woke military run by fools like Biden, Harris, Austin, and Milley. The Navy just had to raise its maximum enlistment age to forty-one from thirty-nine. The Army's is still thirty-five, Air Force forty, and Marine Corps twenty-eight. I bet they will have to raise those ages too.

Most people will not volunteer to be led by idiots during war or peacetime. Did you see that freak Austin visiting the Philippines? Senator Marco Rubio was right when he said this was "embarrassing COVID theater." You have to be a damn fool to wear a mask plus a face shield outdoors.

It is November 4. Thank You, God and Jesus, for family and friends and the Bible! Let us take up the cause of freedom and enforce the awesome constitution and be fine. Many folks are worried about America. We shall overcome the socialists and commies in four days.

It is November 5. Life is great when you learn something every day. Ted Nugent and Hunt the Vote sent an email today to help take back our country from fools. Only 50 percent of hunters vote. That is bad because most of them are great constitution-loving animal killers. I hope more get the word and vote in three days.

It is November 6. I thank God that I sucked as a candidate and get to enjoy our success and money at home and not driving around to see voters. I enjoyed the Trump rally last night from Latrobe, Pennsylvania. He irritated a few folks when he called Ron

DeSantis Ron Desanctimonious for endorsing the RINO Joe O'Dea in Colorado running for the US Senate and possibly other offenses. Oz and Mastriano are lucky to have Trump supporting them. Trump called O'Dea stupid one time.

Trump called out some politicians in the audience and pointed to one and said, "I do not like that guy." He mentioned Dan Meuser, and I wonder if Trump knows that this RINO flew to the World Economic Forum idiot convention in the spring. I wonder who it was.

Trump is so funny, like a good stand-up comedian. His insults are priceless. He said Arnold Palmer made fun of him for his short drives one time while they were playing golf. Palmer was a great golfer with four green jackets and many tournament wins. We used to love seeing him at Augusta National at the Masters in April.

Arnold would not like the socialism-communism crap being promoted by the Democrats nowadays. Nancy and I just missed meeting Palmer at the Bay Hill Golf Club one time at the clubhouse. I remember seeing Palmer tell the story of playing around with Ben Hogan at the Masters. The young Palmer struggled that day with his game. Palmer overheard Hogan say, "How the hell did that Palmer kid get into the tournament anyway?" at a separate table. He would not let Palmer sit at the same table for the lunch break. Now that was brutal even for Hogan. Palmer went on to win four green jackets after this bad day in Augusta, Georgia.

Trump said a protester has a "serious weight problem" back in 2019 at a rally. He speaks the truth about Democrats cheating in elections and many other things. The Democrat Party leaders are immoral, so most of the party members are immoral. It is all about leadership or lack thereof. Let us flush the Democrats down the toilet in two days.

It is November 7. Our big election is tomorrow. We need a huge red wave for sure. I noticed that the Schuylkill County GOP Chairman Howard Merrick has not informed me of the next meeting to address election cheating or dumping pathetic RINOs. If the GOP folks were doing their job, there would not be We the People groups popping up all across the nation, such as WTP of

Coal Country in Ashland. Conservatives and Christians have been screwed by the GOP functionaries. The trust has been broken with fake Republicans growing corrupt government every year. At least Howard likes golf. We will always have that.

Perhaps this is a situation where it is a gift to not belong to a group of weak, immoral, dumb, and/or evil people? Many lazy GOP committee members do not answer emails or calls very often. Howard said I was on the committee but has not oriented me on the situation or position. I feel unwelcome. Perhaps weak RINOs rule the county GOP operation and do not want constitutional conservatives and Christians like us.

The country and county need America-first people running the show immediately before this gets bloody. I put out Mastriano signs today. The friendly GOP volunteer Jennifer in Pottsville had a smile and many signs to get out. She gave me a poll watcher certificate for tomorrow in Saint Clair. I will hold my nose and vote for Oz, Twardzik, and other folks tomorrow.

CHAPTER 9

SHOCKED REDNECK

> Socialists cry "Power to the people" and raise
> the clenched fist. We all know that they mean
> power over people and power to the state.
> —Prime Minister Margaret Thatcher

I am shocked at what the Democrats are doing these days. Government is too powerful and abusive and elections mean more now. We spend or waste too much on elections. Democrats spent $30 million, and Republicans spent $12 million this election on their candidates. Also, $82 million was spent against Democrats and $70 million against Republicans. This outside spending data comes from OpenSecrets—a Washington, DC, nonprofit—and Fox News. Total outside spending in Pennsylvania was $194 million. This would be a lot less if we outlawed unions representing government employees. Let us do it and downsize government. Cut the fat.

"A court in Pennsylvania ruled on November 7 against the GOP when it decided that election officials can continue to notify voters whose mail-in ballots include errors, such as incorrect or missing dates, and help voters fix those problems before Election Day. Republicans in Monroe County argued that actions by the county amounted to an illegal precanvass of mail ballots, which are supposed to be kept in secure locations before being counted Election Day starting at 7:00 a.m.," according to Tyler Olson at Fox News. These judges should be punished for violating Pennsylvania and federal law and creating chaos in our elections. Some counties are doing this crap, and others are not. You cannot treat voters differently depending on where they live. This is stupid and happening right now.

David Xu (dave224422@yahoo.com)
To Senator David Argall, Tim Twardzik, Tim Twardzik
Monday, November 7 at 6:07 p.m.

David and Tim,

Are you lazy, stupid, and/or corrupt? We cannot tell. Do your job. You have had two years since all those illegal ballots were counted in 2020 to clean up our elections? How many were counted? Do you know? Why did you certify that election? Where is our full audit? Why did you stop it? Will you decertify it? Why are you silent on election cheating? Do you like it? Are you aware that some counties are doing illegal precanvassing or curing ballots and some are not? See the article on Fox News. You cannot have a fair election where voters are treated differently depending on where they live? Wake up, guys. The federal and state constitutions have the legislature in charge of election rules and not judicial or executive branch idiots. Are you mice or men? Why are you so weak? You would be dead if you acted like this in war or training for war. I have been to war and do not want to have another one because of fools like you. Are you fools? How are your shredding events going? Why are you shredding so much? Please be manly.

Pennsylvania court rejects GOP push to stop fixing mail-in ballots with incorrect dates—Fox News

David Xu
Army vet, author years, author
of *Redneck Dystopia*
http://www.wethepeoplecoalcountry.com

The King of the Idiots Fetterman filed a suit in federal court to count undated mail-in ballots on November 7. This is illegal under Pennsylvania law, but the immoral Democrats do not care. We stand with the law and constitution. Communists always have vague laws to abuse and lie to gain and maintain power. WEF King McCormick tried the same crap in the GOP primary against Oz. Oz is a piece of crap, but he is our piece of crap.

I like the move from Fetterman and gang because it shows their desperation. Most Americans believe that the Democrats have broken their covenant with them to run the government and protect them. They are supporting Republicans in all fifty states this year. The Democrats are pushing abortion and welfare while the voters want safe streets, a growing economy, quality schools, and low inflation. We love God, family, and friends. God always wins!

Over 43 million Americans have voted early. It is a mess when we have election month. How many illegal ballots have been counted? The machines must go to secure our elections. The early voters miss last minute bad news about candidates. Many voted for Fetterman before seeing him stumble in the debate with Oz.

It is finally election day 2022! Thank goodness November 8 is here. I volunteered as a poll watcher in Saint Clair this afternoon. The staff members were professional and friendly. One guy came in to vote but did not live there and had not registered to vote. The judge of elections told him to register and vote next time. He seemed to take it well. Some folks become irate when told they cannot vote.

There was WiFi inside the voting room, and that bothered me. What would Mike Lindell say? I reported it to Protect the Vote PA to be safe. It would not surprise me at all if cheaters connected via modems.

One guy had a bad day in Wisconsin after he brandished a knife and demanded that they stop the voting. Wow, and I thought I was unstable sometimes. I hope he takes half the dosage of his drugs next time.

I volunteered as a poll greeter in Ashland after the poll watching. I met many nice folks at Zion's Reformed Church. Most said they were upset about the dumb people running our government and would be voting for Republicans. That was music to my ears.

It is November 9 (the day after), and the big news is that our elections are still damaged by many cheaters. How many illegal ballots were counted? That is the main question. I do not care if one or 10,000 were counted. The answer should be zero illegal ballots counted. A small group of Americans will not secure our elections and should be punished severely.

The Democrats sold fear, abortion, and bought ballots with welfare. We are still in dangerous territory with most Americans not trusting the ballot count. The RINOs at Fox News will only call the US House 206 to 180 for the GOP and the US Senate forty-nine to forty-eight for the GOP. Why are they still counting ballots the day *after* election day? The cheaters need to pick up the pace because forty-nine house seats, and three senate seats are still too close to call. The suspense is killing me.

The mail-in ballots really helped the brain-dead Fetterman. Seventy percent of the Democrats voted early, and most missed his very weak debate performance. He could not even function without a computer. Only 20 percent of the Republicans voted by mail. The sick Democrats used the CCP virus to abuse the mail-in ballots and our election procedures.

The Democrat-controlled executive branch folks say that brain-dead Fetterman and corrupt Shapiro won. I do not believe that so many people would vote for more crime, chaos, CRT, inflation, laziness, welfare, and immorality. The Gateway Pundit reports that they have video evidence of idiots in Detroit collecting thousands of ballots after the legal deadline yesterday.

"What does this vote-rigging look like? All the corporate media outlets in America get their real-time vote counts from Edison Research—and obvious vote-rigging patterns emerge when you chart the vote-dumping in real time," Emerald Robinson. This happened in many states.

They ran out of paper in Luzerne County. They lost V-drives and did not test legally in Delaware county again. Why are so many folks immoral? This election mirrors the rigged 2020 election. Leah Hoopes is looking into the return and proof sheets for crimes. I pray that judges throw out illegal ballots this time. They ignored all the evidence from 2020 and helped install communists in the White House and Congress.

A lot of people are mad at Trump for backing RINOs like Mehmet Oz, Dan Mueuser, and J. D. Vance. Many Democrats and Independents will never support Trump or anyone he endorses, and that is a problem. Many Republicans cannot stand Trump. Trump did a great job, but we think it would be easier for someone else to win the White House in 2024.

Ron DeSantis or Kristi Noem come to mind. Tom Zawistowski, from We the People Convention, tried to deter Trump from supporting Vance in Ohio, to no avail. Our friend Dave Brown, the Shield of Truth Network, could not believe that Trump endorsed Oz.

Money corrupts. Both parties wasted over $240 million just for one US Senate seat in Georgia. God help us. We did recover from the racist communist Woodrow Wilson 101 years ago. We also shook off the lying rich kid FDR seventy-seven years ago. We can recover from the communist Democrats now only with God's help. We must somehow take back power from billionaires and their corrupt politicians who do not care about us rednecks and normal folks.

RINOs stick together. The RINO slayer Trump helped the RINO Oz win the primary in May. Then RINO leader Mitch McConnell and the Senate Leadership Fund, a Super PAC, burned over $56 million to help Oz triumph over the peanut brain Fetterman. I think this means that Oz would have voted like a RINO.

Trump should have backed Kathy Barnette as most WTP folks did here in Pennsylvania. The RINO McConnell Fund also wasted over $32 million to help the RINO Vance triumph over the 24/7 liar Tim Ryan. Trump should have backed a WTP candidate in Ohio instead of Vance. I was shocked that he backed Vance because he criticized Trump before the race, and Trump rarely forgives something like that.

It is sad that only about 4.4 million people voted for US Senate in Pennsylvania out of over 8 million registered voters. What has happened to America and intelligent, informed citizens? Are we doomed by ignorant and lazy people seeking welfare? We must keep trying to restore America to greatness, but this election was a letdown. It looks like we will take the US House and Senate. They are still counting the illegal ballots.

Voters in Pennsylvania actually reelected Democrat Anthony DeLuca, eighty-five years old, to the Pennsylvania house. Congratulations, Anthony! There is one tiny problem. He died in October. Why are so many people so dumb? In their defense, many folks used mail-in ballots before my boy died. This is another reason mail-in ballots are terrible for America.

The good people in Florida counted over 7 million votes (99 percent) by 9:00 p.m. on election night. Arizona has counted only 1.7 million votes (63 percent) on this day after the election. Why are we allowing cheaters to cheat? Somebody better go to jail.

Our We the People of Coal Country group now turns to our Schuylkill County commissioner race next year. Barron Hetherington is our man. He is a local farmer and runs government like his farm or business. He has been a commissioner for two years after being appointed by five judges after Frank Staudenmeier died suddenly in office. We need to find two other good candidates to support for this race, school boards, and other contests. It is hard to find good, successful, and smart candidates to run for anything.

Another guy running for county commissioner is George Halcovage. He is a current commissioner and accused by several women of sexual harassment and should quit. The Pennsylvania house is trying to decide whether or not to impeach him.

Who passed the Georgia law for a runoff on December 6? How long have they been punishing the hardworking citizens? The good people are sick of political attack ads from Walker and Warnock, but now they have yet another election next month. Who would demand two senate elections in two months? Only a government idiot could love this. The government idiots need to protect the citizens and repeal this law. We sure hope Hershel Walker destroys the communist Warnock.

The immoral Democrats spent more than $40 million of their donors' money meddling in six GOP primaries. The union folks love all those unnecessary government jobs. Why are they hiding their agenda and bashing America-first Republicans? Most Democrats want immoral, lazy, socialist, or communist candidates and do not care about the long-term success of America. They voted for lying vegetable Fetterman, creepy Joe, and other fools. They will do anything for power and money. Our Founding Fathers warned us about these sick people.

The Democrats voted for taking more money from hard workers and giving out more welfare to lazy folks. Shapiro, the liar, spent over $840,000 on ads to help our man Mastriano win the GOP primary in May. Most Democrats love criminals, illegal aliens, racism, and drugs. Republicans love God, Jesus, capitalism, the Bible, family, friends, and a great and successful United States of America.

It is November 10. The useful idiots are still counting ballots in several states two days after the election. France counts the ballots in one day. Leah Hoopes gives us hope. She reported that Delaware county cannot certify the election. They have over thirty-six drop boxes that cheaters love.

Delaware county had about 207,000 Democrats, 119,000 Republicans, and four thousand third-party voters in the 2020 presidential election. Gregory Stenstrom and Leah have uncovered many illegal ballots in the last few years, but the government idiots will not stop it. Their book *Parallel Election* is great. Shapiro is a piece of crap Attorney General. Many wars have been started by many people viewing their government as illegitimate. It is sad that Americans were much better off with limited government out of their lives for most of our great history. If government was not so big, we could work hard and play hard and ignore the stupid politicians like Obama and

Clinton. It is hard to do now that government is so huge, abusive, corrupt, and costly.

Several counties in New York had identical percentages for Lee Zeldin for governor. How does that happen? That is almost impossible. Did he concede too early? Mike Lindell has been reporting things like this for years, and the government fools will not stop the cheating.

Big batches of ballots come in for the Democrat, and then they stay ahead of the Republican for the rest of the election. How long have the Democrats been doing this? We pray to God for clean elections and moral people in government. Is that too much to ask? The Fox RINOs have it at 208 to 185 in the house and forty-nine to forty-eight in the Senate for the GOP. Rupert Murdoch and gang helped install Biden and cannot be trusted. Can someone please make Murdoch sell the *Wall Street Journal*? It is going downhill.

The weak Oz conceded to feeble Fetterman with only a 28,150 deficit. Why is he weak like a little girl? Mastriano has not conceded with a 476,725 deficit, according to Skook News. I bet both Republicans won. Mike Lindell said his evidence shows that Mastriano won by 6 percent, and Oz won too.

Leah Hoopes is looking for county leaders to join her fight for election integrity before the counties certify the results. Mastriano will not join the fight. I suggested Albert Gricoski with Schuylkill County. He seems good, and we have no drop boxes. County Commissioner Barron Hetherington is good with election security too.

Susanna DeJeet is a hard worker for reliable elections. She sees disturbing things coming out of Westmoreland County. Vicki and Ken Shoape from Franklin County are fighting like crazy for America and limited government. They love the black seed to fight against the CCP virus. Do not get them started if you are in a hurry.

Shane Benjamin from our WTP of Coal Country is spreading the word about our corrupt government and the need for honest people to step up. He is thinking about running for office, and I hope he does. He would improve any government operation with hard work and common sense. Boyer's grocery store is lucky to have this young man.

The North Schuylkill County school board folks are getting into the absurd woke stuff. Shane is going to the school board meeting to straighten things out. The United States was created under God in the Declaration of Independence on July 4, 1776. Why are the North Schuylkill County school board folks asking kids if they are "male, female, or not listed?" Is there another gender outside of science and the Bible?

Now it is time for the TikTok connection to this election. Most unmarried young women voted for Democrats, and many of them want to keep abortion and welfare everywhere. The CCP controls this platform and loves helping young Americans remain ignorant, immoral, communist, and/or lazy. Trump tried to outlaw TikTok for these reasons, but of course, the Democrats stopped him.

Joanne Stehr (a member of our WTP of Coal Country at www. wethepeoplecoalcountry.com) won her November 8, 2022, election big time for the Pennsylvania house. It was not even close at 17,720 for her and only a pitiful 5,820 ballots for Democrat Ryan Mock. She is a great fighter for election integrity and limited government.

We are sure she will help cut government spending and taxes in Harrisburg. We need to get her secrets on money management because she only spent about $21,000 on the race. It usually takes much more to win a Pennsylvania house race.

We need more hard workers from the private sector like Joanne in government. She was a nurse for thirty years, NRA member with a pistol in her purse, and food bank volunteer. She believes in limited government and will fight to stop all the election cheating by the Democrats and RINOs.

Here is a fun fact. Bozo Beto O'Rourke has wasted over $172 million of donors' money on three failed campaigns in Texas. About 50 percent of the money came from outside of Texas. I guess it is true that fools support fools. How did this guy graduate from Columbia? I guess the professors only require competence in communism to graduate.

Beto was a computer hacker as a teenager in the group Cult of the Dead Cow. He was arrested for DWI in 1998 after hitting another vehicle. Boy, the Democrats can pick some great candidates. He reminds me of Ted Kennedy.

Trump did a good job, but I hope he does not run again now. Many conservatives disagree, but I think it will be easy to smoke any Democrat in 2024 with another candidate. DeSantis and Noem come to mind. The day after the election www.electionbettingodds. com had Trump and DeSantis both at about 38 percent chance of getting the 2024 GOP nomination.

The Trump mistakes and baggage are a drag on GOP and MAGA success. Nonetheless, I think Trump would do a fantastic job as president again. I bet he learned a lot about what to do and what not to do. I hope he cuts spending this time if it happens. I bet he only hires MAGA folks for the cabinet.

It is November 11, and the fools are still counting ballots for the fourth day. Fox News has the house at 211 to 196 and forty-nine to forty-eight for the senate for the GOP. Why are they still counting? How many illegal ballots were counted? We need 218 to control the US House.

The mostly Democrat media fools will not call thirty-one races today. This is embarrassing for this American. I did not pledge my life to the constitution in the Army or go to war for this. Are government employees counting illegal ballots again? All election cheaters must be put in or under the jail.

Most Democrats and RINOs lie to get elected. This is what we know. A federal judge stopped Biden's illegal college loan forgiveness program three days after the election. It would have cost the taxpayers over $400 billion. Thank goodness for this victory by a Trump judge. Biden and other idiots will promise anything for a vote (see Fetterman and Conor Lamb).

Why are so many college students and graduates so stupid and lazy? Noncollege graduates should never be forced to pay for college for irresponsible people. Pay back your own loans and leave us out of it!

Ballotpedia has Fetterman at 2,637,598 and Oz at 2,460,602 and a difference of 176,996. I do not trust this information. Most voters do not trust these numbers. Wolf, Shapiro, Chapman, and other idiots should be severely punished for elections that cannot be certified three days after election day.

I hope Mastriano demands a good count before conceding. That would be manly. Oz conceded to the brain-dead guy and ran back to New Jersey like a frightened little girl. I bet he is in Turkey eating turkey by Thanksgiving. He is a Turkish citizen and US citizen. That should be illegal. I still cannot believe that he won the primary. That Xu guy was the bomb.

It does not make sense that Republicans earned 6 million more votes than Democrats in this election for US House candidates. Why did the huge red wave not come? Perhaps it is cheating with mail-in ballots and election machines. The state legislators should get rid of them, and they have that power in the US Constitution. The illegal gerrymandering should be terminated.

"A Michigan judge has released the bombshell report on the audit of Dominion Voting Systems, revealing that the machines and their software were 'designed' to 'create systemic fraud,'" Jay Greenberg reported in The Standard on January 27, 2021. What has been done about this? Why is the cheating allowed in the greatest nation to every grace the face of the earth?

Fools like Shapiro and state judges do not have that power. Read the constitution. Will the GOP legislators stop being weak and dumb and secure our elections and stand up for conservative Christians? RINOs suck.

The Democrats are still counting and cheating with ballots in Nevada and Arizona four days after the election (November 12). They are trying to make Blake Masters and Kari Lake lose. The Democrats are ruining the nation by manipulating the ballots days after the election. The US Constitution requires that election be only one day. Clarence Thomas would agree.

Many media idiots have called the Mastriano and many other elections without even being in the counting rooms. How can this happen again? We saw this movie in 2020. The fools in Alaska are still counting ballots with their stupid rank choice voting system.

We have about 240 million voters, and only about 112 million voted this time. Why did 128 million people not vote? That is 47 percent of eligible voters. This was much higher in 2020. Are they living under rocks and not noticing inflation, the open border, corrupt politicians such as Biden, woke crap in schools, and criminals running around? This does not make sense unless you consider cheating.

On January 6, 2021, Pence and the other RINOs and Democrats in Congress should have debated and probably asked the states to ensure that only legal ballots were counted. They were weak and failed to uphold our constitution and have fair elections. Trump is right that the 2020 election is still today uncertifiable.

Over sixty Republicans in the house cosponsored an objection to the election results from Arizona. Any fool should have known about all the illegal ballots counted in many different states by the corrupt Democrats. They failed to uphold our constitution, and now we suffer. The Biden gang is illegitimate and destroying America. They must be stopped!

The lying socialist media folks are proclaiming Hobbs as governor over Kari Lake in Arizona. There is no way this loser won this race. The government idiots in Arizona and Pennsylvania have not secured our elections since their debacle in 2020. The honest folks are calling for a redo election in December, and I hope they have one.

The Democrats in Massachusetts are making the same mistake as they did in Maryland and other states. The MA citizens just voted to raise the taxes on millionaires by $2 billion per year. They did this crap in Maryland a while back, and the millionaires moved out of state to their other houses. Tax revenue went down from this group of successful people. The dumb politicians had less money to waste on dumb programs. The communist teachers' unions in MA spent over $23 million to support this dumb tax hike amendment to the state constitution. It puts a 4 percent surcharge on income over $1 million per year. When will the socialists and communists learn that capitalism is much better with low taxes and hard workers? They do not care about the long-term success of our nation. The lazy and immoral union teachers will now get a raise, and our children will continue to be indoctrinated and not educated. What a deal.

The Democrats said on November 12 that Masto kept her seat in the US Senate from Nevada when over 75 percent of the voters say the country is headed in the wrong direction. This redneck does not believe it for a minute. She votes with Biden and company on everything. They cheated and found ballots to get her over the top after election day. God help us.

I would bet a good sum that Laxalt won this race if I were a gambler, but I think gambling is dumb. They are playing with fire and violence because most Americans do not trust the idiots running our elections.

This selection gives the Democrats fifty seats and with the childish Harris control of the US Senate. The seat in Georgia will be decided in December with the unnecessary runoff. Fox News has the Senate at forty-nine to fifty and the House 211 to 202 Republican to Democrat. The cheaters are still trying to win twenty-one more seats in the Congress by collecting ballots from anywhere after election day. Communists do not care about laws or what the citizens want. They will be lucky to avoid severe punishment.

Someone said they found a noose at the construction site of the Obama library in Chicago. The police offered a reward of $100,000 for whomever left it. Is this another race hoax? I wonder why they did not offer a reward for the killers of 22,900 Americans in 2021 or the perpetrators of 1,313,200 violent crimes that year.

The union construction employees were so traumatized that they took the day off from work with high union pay. Now they are deciding who will plant the noose each day of the week next week so they can go on another paid vacation. One employee said that he could make a cardboard cutout Klansman and bring that on Monday.

Perhaps they were inspired by the NASCAR idiot Bubba Wallace who was so afraid of a rope hanging in the garage in Alabama. The FBI said it was not a hate crime and just a knot. This loser should take the entire season off due to his poor performance as a driver.

This little baby better stay away from the Boy Scouts. They can tie all kinds of scary knots.

Wallace could focus more on his exaggerated racism crap and continue celebrating criminals if he quit driving cars around a track. He has a bright future in the legacy media obsessing about his skin color, like Al Sharpton. I bet there are more racists on the left than on the right. We ignore race and go with learning and hard work. That is the American way. Cut the welfare and affirmative action to make America great again.

Could it be that the Democrats do not care about all the victims of the criminals they have let run free? Could it be that they do not care about the environment? Biden and four hundred other climate change fools flew in jets to Egypt for a climate summit this month. How much pollution did these idiots cause? If they were serious, they would have the meeting on Zoom.

We had some good news from the 2022 elections. Republicans now have twenty-eight governors with the win in Nevada by Joe Lombardo. My brother Al in Las Vegas is very happy about the win by Sheriff Lombardo. Democrats only have twenty-two governors now. The bad news is that we are stuck with the corrupt Shapiro in Pennsylvania. It is shocking that more voters chose this fool over Mastriano. I believe that many illegal ballots were counted. We will push to remove all RINOs in the Pennsylvania house and senate now and replace them with MAGA folks who will enforce the state and federal constitutions.

They say money rules. DeSantis has about $150 million in a federal PAC, and Trump has about $60 million. I hope they help us elect MAGA people in local, state, and federal elections now. Many people are criticizing Trump for not giving more of his cash to our candidates this year.

The corrupt Democrats have plenty of money from lazy union government employees. They love the neck lump with the gross brain-dead Fetterman attached. We must downsize government and get back to our sacred constitution. Shapiro loves criminals and CRT and definitely sucks!

The reporters cannot get Fetterman to answer questions in DC now. Perhaps they should use big cue cards like they do at the airport when picking up passengers. We are doomed if so many selfish and ignorant voters elect folks who cannot speak or think clearly, such as Biden and Fetterman.

The CCP members are laughing at us for giving political power to fools. I think they should just sit Fetterman down in the corner of the Senate chamber with a dunce cap on. He certainly cannot contribute to making America great again. At least he can be a source of amusement or wonder. Everyone stares at the dead snake in the middle of the road. His wife and friends should be ashamed to allow him to embarrass himself and waste everyone's time.

The Pennsylvania government idiots allowed for fifty days of voting, counting, and cheating for this election. The US Constitution has one election day. The mail-in ballots are stupid, but I guess we need to rock and roll with them next year if the communists will not eliminate them. They say all is fair in love and war. Well, this is war or the extension of politics, and we must win for the sake of our great country. We have to take back political power from folks who hate our awesome nation.

Do you wonder why the Democrats love Ukraine so much and give so much US tax money to the corrupt and weak country? It is over $80 billion of our money so far. The Gateway Pundit's Jim Hoft just reported that the crypto currency firm FTX was sending money from customers to Ukraine and then returning the money to many Democrats for politics and a good time. Fried and gang gave about $70 million to Democrats in the last two years. Where were the Democrats running the White House and SEC while the Democrats running FTX stole customer money?

Democrat Gary Gensler and the SEC gang fined Kim Kardashian $1.3 million for promoting digital tokens without disclosing her remuneration for the endorsements in October 2022. She did not admit or deny the findings. How did her butt get so big?

Why do government idiots allow people settle without proving guilt? Why do they charge companies and not the criminals running the companies? Democrats love a mere slap on the wrist for no-talent Democrats with money. The corrupt and dumb Democrats love to hang out with the immoral Democrats. How is Hillary's buddy Harvey Weinstein doing in prison? Why have the Democrats not announced or prosecuted all the frisky folks who enjoyed Epstein's island? The evidence seems clear that crimes were committed.

A PAC with RINO Mitch McConnell vacuumed up some money from FTX also to help elect more fake Republicans. The dimwitted man-child owner of FTX Sam Bankman-Fried donated to six RINOs who voted to impeach Trump for nothing. Beware of politicians who get most of their money from rich fools.

FTX just filed for bankruptcy, and up to $8 billion dollars may be lost. Hunter Biden made a boatload of cash in Ukraine over the years. Perhaps a grand jury can look into this corruption now. What took you so long? Trump was right again on this. The foolish CEO Sam Fried in under investigation in the Bahamas and other places. The Democrat Party is a very rotten group these days.

"To be clear, Mr. Bankman-Fried funded his lavish donations to the Democratic Party through rampant fraud," Senator Hawley continued. "The net result was that billions of dollars were stolen from investors and handed over to Democrats and left-wing organizations," according to The Gateway Pundit. Why did the government idiots hide this scam until after our elections?

Mastriano conceded five days after election day on November 13. Leah Hoopes and other patriots were irritated because they are still finding a lot of illegal ballots in Delaware county. "Difficult to accept as the results are, there is no right course but to concede, which I do, and I look to the challenges ahead," Mastriano said in a statement on Twitter.

He will remain in the Pennsylvania senate. I guess many voters believed the immoral Democrats and their $40 million in smear TV ads. We are paying a big price for ignorant and complacent voters. We will continue to try to wake them up and take back our country.

Dodie Fetterolf-Weller is a great patriot, member of our WTP of Coal Country, and leader of the Mastriano campaign for Schuylkill County. He won 32,884 to 21,083 in our county. We did our part, but the mail-in ballot cheating in the big cities could not be overcome this time.

The fifty days of cheating with mail-in ballots worked for the Democrats and Shapiro with one million of them overwhelming only 187,437 for Mastriano. The government idiots counted 960,000 MIBs for the brain-dead Fetterman while counting only 234,400 for RINO Oz. These numbers are from Penn Live. How many illegal ballots were counted? That is the question. We must embrace the MIBs if the judges will not do their job and outlaw them.

Mastriano smoked the terrible Shapiro on election day 1,935,054 to 1,675,534 (by 259,520 votes). Our state and federal constitutions call for one election day. If the government idiots had run a legal election, Mastriano would be governor. Our state would be in much better hands with the Christian and conservative Doug Mastriano. He said after the election that we must employ mail-in ballots if the unethical Democrats use them. These numbers are from Ballotpedia.

Over 22 million people work for the federal, state, and local government now. This is 14 percent of the counted votes in 2020 and way too many people for us to support. We need to cut it back now. Many of these folks just sit around a lot of the time. There were about 158 million votes counted in 2020. Many illegal ballots were counted, and many people should be investigated.

These elections are a battle between overpaid union government employees and most Americans who want limited government as required by the state and federal constitutions. It is hard to remove communists and lazy people in the government. All commies should be arrested.

Central banks outside America bought over five hundred tons of gold this year. This is partly because they do not trust the US and its dollar as much as they used to. The uniparty fools are borrowing and spending too much so foreigners are cutting back on US dollars and putting gold into their foreign-exchange reserves. This puts downward pressure on the US dollar and our retirement funds. Good job, Democrats and RINOs.

It is November 14. The RINOs at Fox News will still not call nineteen US House seats six days after the election. Are they cheating or just stupid? Did you notice that their Democrat friends running Facebook, Amazon, and others delayed their layoff announcements until after the election to cover up the damage the Democrats have done to our economy? Is this collusion?

According to Tucker Carlson, 77 percent of delayed election results have gone to Democrats. Is that normal? Do you believe that? This redneck smells something fishy. Over 70 percent of voters think the country is headed in the wrong direction. Did these folks really vote to keep the Democrats in charge?

They did not want voters knowing about these big layoffs before the election. Their tax, borrow, and spend policies are wreaking havoc on all of us. Just the layoffs at Facebook will be over 11,000. I sure hope they are not snowflakes. Strong, conservative, and Christian hard workers are what we need now.

Elon Musk just stopped the free meals at Twitter headquarters. He is demanding that the workers come into the office too. He cut some fat too by laying off over three thousand workers. Wow, it looks like actual work will be required now. This is capitalism, where the business owner and managers make the decisions regarding their investment and responsibilities. Wow, what a concept. Perhaps we should teach this in high school instead of fifty-four pronoun options.

I hope Musk can stop the censorship at Twitter and get the FBI idiots out of the censorship business and into orange jumpsuits for violating our constitution and laws. Mary Grace does a good job covering the communists. She graduated from my old school James Madison University (JMU) and must be good.

"Just in case it's still not clear what is so egregious about the FBI in its current form. Their job is to INVESTIGATE crimes already committed. NOT to frame and entrap innocent people. NOT to police speech and thought for the possibility of a crime. NOT to stalk people and violate their constitutional rights. The FBI IS THE ENEMY OF THE PEOPLE," Mary Grace wrote on Truth Social.

May we see the emails between the government idiots and these company owners conspiring to influence American elections? I hope

Tom Fitton and the good folks at Judicial Watch can dig up the dirt on these socialists soon. They do a great job exposing government corruption.

The gateway drug to communism is found in the unions. Over 48,000 union imbeciles went on strike at the University of California. Why do they have 48,000 government employees? Isn't it funny how they did this one week after the election? The Marxists did not want to turn off the Republicans and Independent hardworking taxpayers before they voted.

Many lazy college students and graduates were fooled by Biden and the promise of reducing their debt by $10,000. Thank goodness a judge ruled that illegal. Did the judge postpone his decision until after the election to get deadbeats to vote for Democrats based on an illegal promise?

Trump gathered many hard workers into the GOP, and that is great. DeSantis has less baggage, is thirty-two years younger, served in the Navy, and made fewer mistakes than Trump and the corrupt media has not been lying about him for six years. I think they are both MAGA and would do a good job.

Most of the media folks called the US House for the Republicans today (November 15) with at least 218 seats. That is fantastic! What took so long? It only took a week. Do we really have to depend on socialists and communists in journalism for this? The Democrats are at 203 now.

Let us destroy socialism and communism in the USA now. Can we force the journalists read a history book about the horrors of communism? Can we deport them to North Korea or China for a semester abroad program?

We do miss having a strong president in Trump. Do you remember when the Russians got too close to Americans in Syria? Trump launched missiles that killed over three hundred Russians. The Biden stooges at the Pentagon just came out with a defense plan that mentioned climate change sixty-seven times. God help us! We need adult leadership and soon.

The dolts at Fox News still have the US House at 217 and waited until the last minute to show Trump's 2024 campaign kickoff announcement tonight (November 15). They are keeping hope alive that the MAGA patriots will not destroy the communist Democrats and lying media complex soon. We will try not to watch Fox anymore.

Trump and his team did a great job for four years. Let us now continue the MAGA movement with Trump and/or other folks. We have no choice but to stop the radical Democrats from leading America down the road to ruin.

The great enemy we face is from within. We can get back to energy independence and the biggest and strongest economy in the world. Economic security is national security. Biden and other ignorant children do not understand this. Two years ago, the Trump policies had this country roaring.

The RINOs make me sick the way they fight good conservatives like Trump and Mastriano so they can be the loyal opposition and keep their sweet government jobs and money. Trump exposed these anti-American fools like Mitch McConnell and Mitt Romney. Did Twardzik and Argall help Mastriano? I do not think so.

We had many victories last week. Nancy Pelosi was dumped. The US House votes went 53 million for the GOP to 48 million for the corrupt Democrats. We lost by 7 million votes in the US House in 2020, according to Dick Morris. That is a 12 million vote gain in only two years. Our folks in the US House can indict the sick and criminal Democrats and stop some of the reckless spending now.

We do not need unions anymore. There are plenty of laws that protect workers in and outside of government. The employees at the Service Employees International Union (SEIU) went on strike this month, demanding more wages and benefits. These are union members working for the union headquarters in California. It is fun to watch these Fetterman-like fools eat their own. I feel sorry for the business owners and taxpayers overpaying for employees.

Did you see communist John Kerry shaking hands with communist Nicholas Maduro from Venezuela? These fools flew over to Egypt this month for the climate summit. How much pollution did they cause on this trip?

Maduro wants money from successful capitalistic nations to pay for the horrible environmental damage he and the Chavez gang have caused. The Biden gang is trying to buy oil from Maduro instead of harvesting American oil. Can we impeach Biden and so many others?

Many folks are a little touchy if you say anything good about DeSantis. They love Trump. One woman online said I am weak-minded. Another guy said, "Watch out what you say." I am a little sensitive because I am sad that so many people voted for Fetterman. Another woman said that "God sent Trump to help us."

I wanted to tell her, "Boy, I did not know that Trump came down from heaven. That makes all the difference in the world in this GOP primary. I will never say anything good about DeSantis again. Thank you for the enlightenment."

I should tell these people that I promise for all our We the People meetings only We the Weak-Minded People are allowed. We cannot have any strong-minded people here. That would be too much trouble. We can give an IQ or history test at the door. Anyone who passes the test will be denied entry.

I am suffering. I heard Gilbert O'Sullivan on the radio singing his 1972 smash hit "Alone Again." I wanted to tell him, "Hey, suffer on your own time. Do not suffer on my time. Can I please hear something upbeat after the selection of the idiot Fetterman? He cannot even carry on a conversation. Can't you see that I am suffering? I bet Oz won that race anyway."

Gilbert avoided dating at the peak of his career to focus on his songwriting. Now that is dedication to his craft. Did he go to brothels or just get a grip on it himself? I hope he got a handle on it.

In thirty-four of thirty-five US Senate races this year, the voters reelected the incumbent or someone in the same party. In the US Senate race I was in, we are told that the communist fool Fetterman beat Oz. Do you believe that? I believe that many illegal ballots were counted again by the communists. Arrest all the cheaters!

Government is too big, abusive, and unconstitutional with over 22 million employees. This is a battle between Democrats and RINOs in unnecessary union and other jobs versus the 318 million citizens paying for the government. Cut back government to make America great!

Our friends in the Pennsylvania house finally impeached Larry Krasner, the Philadelphia district attorney, in a vote of 107 to 85. These lazy politicians are seven years too late, but they finally are trying to fire this idiot who loves criminals.

I think they should lock him up for the record 562 homicides last year and many other things. This is a baby step toward restoring law and order. Now can they finally tell us how many illegal ballots were counted by the Wolf gang in 2020 and 2022? That would be nice.

It is November 16, and I am trying to make sense of the election eight days ago. According to Gallup, 33 percent of American voters are Republican, 29 percent Democrat, and 35 percent independent. Of the independents, 49 percent voted Democrat and 47 percent Republican.

The big government loving folks at Fox News finally called the US House for the GOP at 218 to 209 today after many others already called it. I miss the days when the Fox people came at the news from the right. The weaklings now will not even talk about illegal ballots.

Of the independents in Pennsylvania, 58 percent voted for the brain dead Fetterman and only 38 percent for New Jersey Oprah buddy Turkish citizen Muslim Mehmet Oz. DeSantis gathered 53 percent of the independents in Florida and smoked Charlie Crist, the corpse, by 19 percentage points. I wonder how many illegal ballots were counted nationwide. Let us consult Mike Lindell. This research comes from the *Wall Street Journal.*

The government idiots are still counting ballots in Bucks County, Pennsylvania. The Democrats voted to count ballots harvested from nursing homes. One GOP guy opposed this illegal activity. These ballots could decide the winner of the 142 district in the Pennsylvania house. This seat could decide whether or not control of the entire Pennsylvania house is lost for Republicans.

Two weeks ago, Democrat Bob Harvie, a county commissioner, said, "You can go to a nursing home and get one hundred ballots as long as you have one hundred agent forms." This is immoral and illegal in Pennsylvania. This account is from the Gateway Pundit.

Why are Wolf and other fools allowing this abuse of our elders and election cheating?

Leah Hoopes, Gregory Stenstrom, Nicole Missino, and other WTP Patriots filed suit in Delaware county to prove in court that the fools counting ballots took ballots and V-drives into a building without watchers for six hours before going to the counting center in Chester. God bless these patriots and stop the steal!

The corrupt Attorney General Shapiro should have investigated this crap in 2020 and only cared about harassing Leah and Greg. Will he investigate and/or arrest the cheaters now? This is why most Americans do not trust our elections. We are on a razor's edge between peace and a cold or hot civil war. We must stop the election cheating to save our constitutional republic. The government idiots should be investigating and/or punishing election cheaters. It is not Leah's job, but we are so glad that she and others are doing it. There would be no WTP movement if the GOP leaders would find and support America-first candidates. We have a break down in governance because so many fools are not doing their jobs.

Leah says that the county employees deleted at least 2,778 records of requests for mail-in ballots. Is that legal? How can you certify an election like this? The Gateway Pundit and Jim Hoft are all over this story. The idiots in the Pennsylvania house and senate better wake up. Are Twardzik and Argall on the case?

To Senator David Argall, Tim Twardzik, Tim
Twardzik
Thursday, November 17 at 9:52 a.m.

David and Tim,

Are you aware of this lawsuit? What are you doing to exclude illegal ballots and arrest the stupid criminals? Leah Hoopes and other WTP Patriots filed suit in Delaware county to prove in court that the fools counting ballots took ballots and V-drives into a building without watchers for six hours before going to the counting center in Chester. Did this happen? God bless these patriots and stop the steal! How many illegal ballots were counted in 2020 and this year? How many times have I asked you that? Are you asleep? Can you refund your absurd salary of $92,000 per year? What are you doing to hold Wolf, Shapiro, Chapman, and others accountable? Most Americans do not trust our elections. You are playing with fire and a civil war. Are you a man or a child? Be manly for goodness's sake.

David Xu
Author of *Redneck Dystopia*
http://www.wethepeoplecoalcountry.com

Benny Johnson has an idea about how communist fools resembling Fetterman and Shapiro "won" their elections this year. "FTX was a money laundering scam for Democrats. They spent $50 million on electing Dems this cycle." I guess we need another investigation and/or trial for some immoral and greedy Democrats.

Bob Bishop says, "Sam Bankman-Fried admits that FTX is a crypto laundromat for the Ukrainian government." This Democrat hero Fried is in the Bahamas living the dream and playing bigshot. Bill Clinton and Tony Blair used to hang with this moron. Is this why the uniparty fools in DC are sending so much of our tax money to Ukraine?

At least we took back the US House. Representative James Comer said that whistle blowers assert that the Biden family flourished and became millionaires by simply offering access to the family. Will someone please arrest the creepy Bidens and all socialists and communists to make America great again?

Where is Tony Bobulinski? Get him on the set. He is a credible witness for sure. The media and big tech folks buried his story just before the 2020 election. I bet Trump would have won if this dirt had been presented to Democrats and Independents on the Bidens before they voted. So many of them hate Trump, and perhaps they would have just stayed home. We suffer now because of the commie fools in the media and big tech.

I am glad that we do not live in Michigan because the socialist Democrats cheated and took control of the legislature in 2022. They are ramming through a law that forces many employees to join a union. Over 95 percent of the union campaign donations go to Democrats. Michigan was a right to work state from 2012 until 2022 thanks to Republicans. Get ready for fewer employers, lower investment, and fewer jobs in Michigan thanks to commie idiots in government. Perhaps the FBI folks can try again and finally kidnap Governor Gretchen Whitmer and get someone else to veto the dumb prounion law. I would hate to see that shiny face in a dark alley. Did she have a bad plastic surgeon from the bottom of the medical school class? Did I see her in that bar in *Star Wars* hanging with Chewbacca?

Do you need another reason to avoid Democrats? China controls more than 80 percent of the supply chain for solar panels. The Democrats are lying about climate change and promoting solar panels from China. It shows again that our communists are not as smart as the Chinese communists.

I hope more voters wake up, read real news, and vote the rats out of office before we lose our great and free America forever. The Democrats are trying to follow the path of the ignorant Europeans by turning off coal and nuclear plants too soon with devastating consequences.

We love fossil fuels and energy independence. Will someone please lock John Kerry in his house to cook for his rich wife and discuss fake climate change 24/7? Why does she eat so much? I think I saw some fat-free Heinz products on the market shelf from her family's company. Perhaps she is depressed for marrying such a dumb person. He is too ugly, lazy, and dumb to interact with society. Thank goodness he is no longer in the Senate. He reminds me of Mitt Romney for some reason.

"After a bruising campaign and a protracted process of tabulating results, a local man's wife has gained control of the house in a slim but decisive majority of one vote per wife and one vote per husband," the Babylon Bee reported. "The wife announced that in order to reduce bottlenecks, new rules can be enacted with a quorum of one wife present." Now that is democracy at work in many American households.

Here is another feather in the DeSantis cap. He pushed news district maps in Florida earlier this year. This helped Florida gain four US House seats in the 2022 midterms. This enabled us to take the house from the immoral Democrats and fire the drunken Nancy Pelosi for good.

Some WTP folks are wondering if we can contest the election for Pennsylvania governor. Ken Layng from Centre County has studied a little nugget in the state constitution. The state constitution allows for a committee from both houses of the legislature to settle a contested election. We could present evidence of election cheating and illegal ballots and hopefully make a difference. There appears to be plenty of evidence to elect Mastriano, Oz, etc.

The chief justice of the Pennsylvania Supreme Court would preside. That is Debra Todd, a Democrat, who took over in October 2022 after Max Baer died in office. She is probably not into throwing out illegal ballots. We are just frustrated that our elected folks will not throw out any illegal ballots and/or arrest any cheaters.

Ken sent out a request for signatures and/or money to support the venture to ensure election security. He and his wife Megan have the cutest little dog that dances and spins around on her back two feet. Now that is a good show. They try to stop the woke fools running Penn State University from obsessing over pronouns and other dumb things.

Our friend Timothy Henning is thinking about running for the Pennsylvania senate in the GOP primary in May 2024 or as an independent in the November 2024 general election. He did a great job in the US Army for many years and in our We the People group. I suggested he run in the primary because he could drain conservative votes from RINO David Argall in the general election and help a Democrat gain power if he ran as an independent. Argall is ripe for picking after over thirty-seven long years in government supporting big and wasteful government. Why are RINOs so dumb?

It would be great to start another party and leave the RINOs behind. Perhaps that is the path we should take. These fools in the Pennsylvania house just elected a Democrat who changed his title to Independent to be speaker of the house. This does not make sense because the GOP has 101, and the Democrats only have 98 in the house. Why are the Republicans so weak and incompetent? It is getting hard to take these fools.

Argall is part of the problem due to being in the Pennsylvania house and senate for the last thirty-seven years. Government spending has gone up most years this joker has been in the legislature. RINOs are fiddling while Rome burns.

I hope Tim runs and runs hard to cut back government and adhere to our glorious Pennsylvania and US constitutions. We need more honest and courageous military veterans in government. The uniparty is alive and well at the local, state, and federal levels and slow walking us to socialism or communism. Some of the Schuylkill County GOP committee leaders rarely answer my calls and emails and should be replaced by patriots who will enforce our constitution and restore limited government.

We really need to cut the fat in government or clear out the dead wood like Argall. He reminds me of the following joke. Question: what is the difference between the long-term, lazy politician and a catfish? Answer: one is a scum-sucking bottom feeder, and the other is a fish. Look at the crumbling roads with trash on the sides in Argall's district and tell me how much he cares about Pennsylvania and the hardworking folks. Perhaps he has too much fat inside his skull to think critically. Is that real hair or a rug? Foolish state politicians passed over 24,000 bills or laws in 2022. How many stupid laws did Argall and team pass? Why is government getting bigger and bigger? Why are lazy and rude government workers not fired? Why are so many people getting welfare? Ask Mr. Argall and his buddy Tim Twardzik with their $92,000 salaries. Why were so many illegal ballots counted in our elections for Democrats?

The federal government has its turtle (Mitch McConnell) and Pennsylvania has its catfish (David Argall). RINOs are just slightly better than Democrats. Both groups suck when they ignore our constitution and buy votes with welfare. Do we have limited government that is mandated by our constitution? What size orange jumpsuit does the corrupt politician wear?

"Society in every state is a blessing, but government, even in its best state, is but a necessary evil, in its worst state an intolerable one," Thomas Paine wrote in Common Sense during 1776. The British government in his day was corrupt and unaccountable just as our government is today 247 years later.

Why is it so hard to lock up the criminals? There were over 126,000 major crimes in New York City in 2022. That is up 22 percent from 2021. Mayor Eric Adams and other idiots should be removed and punished for allowing so many people to be victimized by these thugs. There is no excuse for these weak and dumb folks in leadership positions.

We are in a bad situation with the corrupt uniparty, but we have hope that the US Supreme Court will help us out. They will decide whether or not to hear a case on January 6, 2023, that could outlaw massive mail-in voting and a lot of cheating. Timothy Bonner and his team will show that Pennsylvania and other states violate article 1, section 4 of the US Constitution by failing to specify a place for someone to vote and the accountability that involves.

Reminder: the Pennsylvania Supreme Court changed election laws in 2020, illegally throwing our elections into chaos with massive cheating. These foolish judges and Wolf administration folks who violated our state and federal constitutions deserve to be severely punished.

There is no way to stop cheating with mail-in voting by the Democrats and some Republicans. People around the world realize this, but the uniparty fools continue the corruption. Act 77 in Pennsylvania during 2019 allows for fifty days of cheating, while the Pennsylvania constitution mandates one day in November for voting.

How is that legal? Should Wolf, Leigh Chapman, and others go to jail for enabling at least two years of illegal elections. We surely think so. The US Supreme Court folks should have resolved these issues before the 2020 election. They failed to do their jobs and caused stupid politicians such as Biden to degrade and embarrass America.

"States and cities governed by leftist politicians have seen crime skyrocket. They've seen their taxpayers abused, they've seen medical authoritarianism imposed, and they've seen American principles discarded. The woke agenda has caused millions of Americans to leave these jurisdictions for greener pastures, Florida Governor Ron DeSantis. Can we please get rid of the failed politicians such as Wolf and Shapiro? Shapiro took money from the criminals at FTX for his leftist campaign in 2022. When will they be investigated, arrested, and/or go to jail for corruption?

Our RINOs in the Pennsylvania house just elected a Democrat who called himself an independent speaker of the house. You do not need enemies with friends like that. Sixteen of the 101 Republicans voted for this Democrat Mark Rozzi. The Democrats only have 98 members in the house. What is going on? Rozzi's title should be speaker of the uniparty fools for growing government every year at our expense. Benjamin Franklin must be mortified.

Our friends in the Berks County Patriots group are appealing a court order that denied a manual recount of ballots from the November 2022 election. Sam Brancadora, his wife, and gang do a fantastic job of representing conservatives and Christians in Berks County. Some fools on his county elections board said that they would not verify signatures on mail-in ballots for the election. How is that for a free and fair election? Did Mastriano and Oz win?

The United States Constitution, through the Fifteenth Amendment adopted over 150 years ago, states, "The right of Citizens of the United States to vote shall not be denied or abridged by the United States or any State." Furthermore, the Pennsylvania constitution guarantees citizens the right to vote and for the "free, fair, and correct computation and canvass of the votes cast," Sam explained during January 2023. God help us.

Our election cheating champion Josh Shapiro was told in 2021 about Biden making about $911,000 at UPenn from 2017 to 2019 for a no-show job by the group Take Back Our Republic. Attorney General Shapiro and gang did nothing about this corruption. Also, why did Amy Gutmann make about $4 million as president of this low-quality school or get appointed by Biden to be the US ambassador to Germany? Her salary was a lot higher than other college presidents. She used to email with Hunter Biden about setting up a think tank. This is from USSA News and Nick Givas. The CCP and Chinese folks gave more than $50 billion to this ridiculous woke college. This is where they let a man swim against women in tournaments. This is opinion.

Do you want more Democrat rule? I encourage you to see California. Their natural gas prices are five times the national average due to the stupidity of the government folks out there. They do not allow enough storage of this great fossil fuel. Remember this if the greaseball Gavin Newsom runs for president. If we are forced to use mail-in ballots, give me a lot. Vote GOP to make America great again!

I suggest you contact your 401(k) administrator and tell them that you do not want your money invested in ESG funds. The corrupt and communist Biden gang passed a rule by the Labor Department that empowers retirement fund managers to invest in these political funds that often have a lower return on investment than good funds.

The 1974 ERISA law requires that retirement plan sponsors act solely in the interest of participants and beneficiaries. The government idiots should be fired and punished for encouraging the violation of federal law. They just want money from conservative hard workers to fund stupid, leftist, immoral programs and organizations. These jerks never sleep when it comes to moving America to the left and to ruin.

Corrupt Biden and the socialist Canadian Prime Minister Trudeau flew down to Mexico during January 2023 on a great free trip to celebrate and enjoy delicious free meals with AMLO. AMLO is the communist President Obrador who has centralized power in the Mexican government and racing toward dictatorship.

Biden, Trudeau, and many others would love to do this in our free nations and must be stopped now. Did you see the pictures of Trudeau in blackface at a party? He should be removed from office for this and harassing the patriotic truck drivers who protested his dumb policies.

The Mexicans are allowing millions of illegal immigrants to transit through his country and enter the United States illegally. This crap must stop. I hope and pray that the US House under the Republicans can stop these criminals from coming here. The sick Democrats know that over 80 percent of these criminals would vote for them in a heartbeat for the long-term welfare.

It is so bad that the NYC imbecile Mayor Adams flew to the border on his free trip this month to beg for billions of tax money to pay for these criminals. He is letting them stay in luxury hotels in NYC for free and the working people are getting angry at seeing all the free loaders. I bet the millions on welfare are worried about being cut because of all the welfare to foreigners.

New York spends more Medicaid (free health care) on home health care each year than the other forty-nine states combined. The Democrats love the welfare for Americans, but it is getting too expensive for the foreigners in their peanut brains.

They will not make the lazy folks work and several cities and states are headed for bankruptcy soon unless they cut spending or raise taxes on the hard workers. I bet Adams sees a weak and stupid Biden and is just trying to run for the presidency. How much money does he spend on clothes? I bet he looks at himself in the mirror all day instead of running the city.

How do so many fools get elected? Do tens of millions of Americans really love welfare and government money so much that they ignore our country's long-term success? Is it too late to save America? I was more confident that we could save our great meritocracy in 2021 than I am now in 2023. We can save America, but it may be too late with the massive election cheating on top of the abundance of welfare. So many Americans are not thinking about our future in a socialist or communist nation. The Fetterman win really shocked me. The Senate should expel that pro-union man-child tonight. Why is he so dumb?

Imagine if all fifty states were like Illinois. Our nation would be a bankrupt mess run by an obese fool. Now imagine that every state is like conservative Wyoming. The Republicans out there are trying to pass a bill that outlaws electric vehicles until 2035 to protect their oil and gas business. That just sounds right.

On the other hand, the morons in California just voted to ban gas-powered cars by 2035 even though they are having rolling blackouts now due to their horrible leadership. They have neglected their power grid and wasted a boatload of tax money on wind and solar projects that do not work many days and nights.

Shapiro selected our RINO friend Pat Browne as the secretary of revenue for Pennsylvania on January 12, 2023. This fool had at least three DUI arrests and was in the Pennsylvania legislature for twenty-eight long years.

Thank goodness Jarrett Coleman beat him in the May 2022 primary by only 24 votes and won against the Democrat in November. Our friend Sam Faddis wrote a good article about Browne the swamp rat on Substack at *and* expert analysis and commentary. Many so-called Republicans do not represent us at all, and it is great the good folks in Lehigh County took this dude out. Let us take out Argall now.

I thought Elon Musk was going to stop the censorship on Twitter. They locked my account on December 10, 2022, and it was still locked on January 18, 2023, despite my appeal. What is the offensive tweet from me? I sent the following, "@TomFitton @ elonmusk @ggreenwald @Twitter Did the commies censor the first official (see FEC) redneck candidate for US Senate David Xu?"

Why did they lock me out for this question about censoring my Senate campaign? The Twitter employees approved one of my tweets for advertising while my account was suspended. I hope Musk fires more of the dumb people employed there.

I believe that Trump did a good job as president and would do a better job as president if he wins in 2024. We would support him for sure. He is hilarious and this Truth Social post below made me laugh today (January 19, 2023).

Making a big political speech today at Trump Doral, in Miami. The Fake News says

I am not campaigning very hard. I say they are stupid and corrupt, with the Election still a long time away. But do not fear, MANY GIANT RALLIES and other events coming up soon. It will all be wild and exciting. We will save our country from DOOM and MAKE AMERICA GREAT AGAIN!

I would have pushed for tax cuts, regulation cuts, and government spending cuts in the US Senate. These actions would lead to lower inflation and interest rates and higher confidence in the US economy. These policies could have led to more home sales and a roaring economy. Instead of this direction with patriots like me, existing home sales declined in 2022 thanks to stupid Democrats and their socialist-communist welfare policies. It was the slowest year for home sales since 2014 when Obama, Biden, and other idiots ran the government and the economy into a ditch. When will people learn not to vote for fools?

Here is more good news during January 2023. The fools running Alphabet Google are laying off over 12,000 employees, and the dumb people running Microsoft are firing over 10,000 folks. Do you think most are Democrats voting for bigger and bigger government and more welfare? Perhaps this will take money from the horrible Democrats who are ruining our sweet nation. I wonder if the executives waited until after the 2022 midterms so as to help idiots like Fetterman get elected.

Why have the Democrats sent over $120 billion to the corrupt country of Ukraine? If I were in the Senate, I would not approve it. We should have forced them to make peace with Russia before a war broke out. Trump and his team would have mastered this. We need adults to run the government. Where has all this US tax money gone? Hunter was paid millions from Ukrainians.

Sometimes I wish I were in the Senate. Some Democrats in Congress are pushing the Biden gang to control apartment rents nationwide. You cannot make up these tales about fools. Let us review. The Federal Reserve folks held interest rates at zero or near zero for so long that house prices went through the roof. Many people rented places instead of buying places. Demand increased faster than supply and prices went up for apartments and rental houses. The socialists and communists do not study basic economics. The unnecessary lockdowns hurt many hard workers.

Also, the CDC idiots told landlords not to evict any deadbeats. The government judges refused to declare this crap illegal. The landlords jacked up rent since the pandemic to recoup their losses and protect themselves. Rent controls always lead to fewer apartments. Smart investors will avoid dumb politicians if they can. Most problems are caused by government idiots. Any questions? When are some of them going to jail for spitting on our constitution and our rights? We can dream. When are they going to throw out all those illegal ballots from 2020?

"Despite Congress's failure to act, Pennsylvania could well go down as the worst case of election theft in our country's history. When election officials halted the count on election night, President Trump was ahead by 700,000 votes. But three days later, they declared that Joe Biden had won. President Trump was winning by the greatest margin on election night, that I believe Democrats were convinced they couldn't catch him. So Democrats stopped the counting, blocked Republicans from even entering the building, and then somehow counted an alleged 1.4 additional million ballots without oversight. That gave the race to Biden three days later on November 7. Pennsylvania voters wanted an explanation for how Joe Biden made up a 700,000-vote deficit with no oversight, and then won the state by 80,555 votes. So where did the votes come from? Traditional Democrat areas like Philadelphia didn't have enough of a margin to make up nearly three quarters of a million votes. Philadelphia only had about 700,000 votes cast total, so they needed to make up the difference in other counties," stated Christina Bobb in her book *Stealing Your Vote*.

Will our RINO guys Twardzik and Argall do anything about all those illegal ballots counted during the last few years? Will they prevent future elections from being stolen? Will they keep their heads in the sand? Are they just boat anchors? How far can I take the silly nautical theme? Shall we throw them overboard if they remain weak and dumb? Socialists and commies run right over weak Republicans. The truth shall set you free.

We must destroy the leftist media in America before we become communist like China. The liberals at AT&T threw OAN and Newsmax off their DirectTV network recently affecting over 13 million people. The Republicans in government must stop all the censorship of Christians and conservatives before it is too late. The fools are turning America into Venezuela.

TPG Capital and AT&T own DirectTV and love Democrats and big government. According to the FEC, the political donations from the TPG folks have gone 90 percent to Democrats since 1993. Many rural citizens have DirectTV because there is no cable in their neighborhoods. I emailed Dan Meuser in the US House to stop the censorship. All Americans must be informed and engaged to return us to the limited government required by our constitution. The commies want ignorant voters to sleepwalk into socialism or communism.

Now here is something new. The Chinese communists flew a surveillance balloon over the United States during February 2023. Biden and other weak fools refused to shoot it down. This would be a great way for the commies to deliver an electromagnetic pulse device (EMP) that could destroy our power grid and most electronics.

I guess the Chinese commies flew the balloon over our country to prove they are stronger than when the Westerners subjugated them during the Opium Wars from the 1830s until the 1860s. The greedy British and French businessmen made a ton of money selling opium to dumb and weak Chinese citizens back then. The invaders forced the Chinese to sign unfair treaties and took over Hong Kong for many decades until 1997.

Some Chinese person had a funny comment on the spy balloon online. He said that they lost control of a weather balloon because they could not get chips from the Americans. The CCP folks are saying it is a weather craft and not a spy craft. I guess they think everyone is as dumb as they are.

Perhaps the commie militants in China are worried and acting out because many people outside China are realizing that communists can kill many folks if the capitalists are weak. The United

States, Japan, and the Netherlands just agreed to restrict advanced computer chip manufacturing equipment going to China. The CCP folks are weak in developing this technology and are dependent on smarter westerners to make chips. Semiconductors are important to any nation these days.

We are at a very dangerous time now with childish people in important government positions. Are most Americans aware of the humiliation the Chinese suffered because they were weak and stupid? Most Chinese know this history well. The same thing could happen to any weak nation. I bet most Chinese citizens are not into the reckless behavior of the CCP fools. Most of them only have one or two kids and do not want them sacrificed in an unnecessary war started by crazy and paranoid communists.

Perhaps the Chinese commies just want more attention on their spy operations to distract from their virus killing millions of people in China and abroad, dumb lockdowns, human rights abuses, aging population, huge government debt, no women in the Politburo, and one-child policy disasters. They remind me of the joke about the old couple going to counseling. The enormous wife wanted more quality time and affection from the redneck husband.

The wife listed her many complaints about her husband, such as working all the time, and then the attractive, young male therapist stood up and asked her to stand up. He kissed and hugged her for a long time and then addressed the bored husband. "Your wife needs this at least three times per week. Can you do that for her?" the therapist asked the redneck husband.

"Well, I can drop her off here on Mondays and Wednesdays, but I have golf on Fridays," the husband explained. Our good Harley-riding veteran friend Linda Swinehart found this joke online.

Biden and many others deserve to be in shackles or worse for letting over six million illegal immigrants come through our Southern border from 2021 until 2023 and for now letting a Chinese spy balloon fly across America. The immoral Democrats in charge do not or cannot protect Americans anymore. Joe and Hunter were flying around on Air Force One while the communist Chinese were gathering information about us with this balloon. God help us.

We will be invaded if we are too weak. Keep your gun handy. Trump and his team made America stronger. Conservatives and Christians must stand up and keep America strong and great. Woke babies must be ignored at US colleges and throughout the nation.

We protested in Hershey at Tom Mehaffie's office on February 1. He is a super RINO who voted for a Democrat speaker of the Pennsylvania house, and now he refuses to vote with the other one hundred Republicans to open the people's house for business. Because of this GOP fool and all the Democrats, we are paying two hundred politicians $94,000 per year to do nothing. They should be outlawing mail-in ballots and preventing cheating in our elections.

I was surprised that a huge Teamsters union tractor trailer was parked in front of Mehaffie's office when I arrived on Chocolate Avenue for the protest. Several union thugs called our ladies sluts and prostitutes. They are very rude. We must remove all unions from our government because over 90 percent of their political donations go to Democrats who grow government bigger and bigger and take our freedoms. This is how the ultimate union fool Fetterman was elected. Most union workers are okay, but most of the union leaders love huge and wasteful government.

Gwyn Fowler filmed the protest in Hershey. She is a great patriot and a wonderful filmmaker who captures the protesters in action. Her Rumble channel gwynny7 is full of inspiring videos, and I highly recommend it. Gwyn's exceptional political knowledge helps her document important grassroots events featuring conservatives and Christians fighting for our golden constitution and the limited government it mandates.

We will be lucky to avoid disaster with so many dumb and weak people like Biden running governments across the world. General Richard Barrons in the United Kingdom just said that his country would run out of ammo in one day if they had a hot war with Russia or any country. Biden and friends are depleting our ammo depots and shipping it to the corrupt Ukrainian government folks. The Chinese are building up their ammo supplies.

This, too, shall pass. More and more Americans are waking up to the dangers of socialism and communism. Many people in the media and big tech are trying hard to keep Americans in the dark on the reckless behavior of the Democrats. Americans have been protecting socialist Europeans for decades. The weak and ignorant Europeans will not or cannot protect us if we are invaded. God always wins. Our faith is in God.

From David Xu
To Senator David Argall, Tim Twardzik, Tim Twardzik
Monday, February 6, 2023

David and Tim,

Can you cut government spending now? You are violating our state and federal constitutions with all your dumb government programs and massive welfare for lazy folks. The constitution mandates limited government. Do we have limited government now?

David Xu
Army vet; books: *The First Official Redneck for US Senate, Easy Riders, Redneck Dystopia, Orphans in the Barn*

We must get unions out of government. The fools in the Pennsylvania house and senate pay employees too much and now the state pension fund has only $71 billion in assets and a whopping $115 billion in liabilities. Wolf, Shapiro, Fetterman, and many others love huge government and hire too many government employees. If they were smart and responsible, there would be enough assets to cover all liabilities. No government employee should be allowed to join a union. Unions should not be allowed to promote or buy stupid politicians.

If there were a gold medal for stupidity for government employees, Karen Decker from the US Mission to Afghanistan would surely win it. She tweeted and promoted black history month, Beyoncé, and Lizzo to the poor and starving Afghan women during February 2023. The Biden gang allowed thirteen of our soldiers to be killed during their outrageous surrender during 2021, and now they are promoting Lizzo. What are they thinking?

I have a better idea. How about we clear out two or three seats on a Delta flight for Lizzo's fat ass and leave her in Afghanistan on a six-month diet program? That would certainly help her more than a Jenny Craig plan or Doctor Oz. He helped Oprah lose weight, but it did not take.

Lizzo can enjoy a small bowl of rice daily in her mud dwelling instead of huge gourmet meals at hotels here in the awesome and capitalistic United States of America. Why on earth does she eat so much? Someone please get this person a mirror and a huge Burka that covers the entire large body and all fat with the net screen face cover with tiny eye holes. That would be awesome.

We could chip in for some sugar-free gum since she loves to chew so much. This would stop some of that awful singing too. I miss the days when MTV played great music and videos and not *Sixteen and Pregnant* replays and no-talent musicians 24/7.

Let us get a quote from a local tarp business for poor Lizzo. She looks kind of like a Western black-legged tick. They are found mostly in California by the way and spread Lyme disease. That is another reason to avoid that redneck dystopia on our West Coast. Sorry for the plug for my 2020 book *Redneck Dystopia*.

"This is so cringe we are going to have to apologize to the Taliban," Communications Director for US Representative Rich McCormick explained. Fox News covered Karen Decker's fifteen minutes of fame for dumbness.

California lost over 508,000 people from April 2020 until July 2022 due mostly to government by fools. New York state lost over 524,000 over the same period. It turns out that most hard workers avoid stupid Democrats and huge government. Can you imagine that?

I do have to give credit to Lizzo's manager. How on earth did she sell so many bad songs? Tom Waits credits his wife for his success. I love his song "Make It Rain."

"She rescued me. I'd be playing in a steakhouse right now if it weren't for her. I wouldn't even be playing. I would be cooking in the steakhouse," Tom Waits explained in Paul Maher's book.

I attended a meeting set up by Sam Faddis with Judge Patricia McCullough and was very impressed with her. She is running for the Pennsylvania Supreme Court and deserves our support. She was the rare judge who ruled that our ballots must follow the law and have valid signatures and dates. The Pennsylvania Supreme Court disagreed back in 2020 and allowed the Democrats to count many illegal ballots for creepy Joe and Willie Brown's girlfriend. Joshua Prince was at the meeting and impressive as well. He is running for the Commonwealth Court of Pennsylvania. He helped defeat some of Governor Wolf's illegal and immoral lockdown restrictions. Wolf kept his family business open during the pandemic but shut down many other businesses for no good reason. This was clearly unconstitutional, but the judges allowed it. We need conservative and Christian judges asap to stop immoral and dumb politicians.

AG Josh Shapiro appealed her righteous ruling and helped Wolf appoint the wrong twenty electors. US Representative Mike Kelly and others filed a lawsuit to challenge about 2.5 million mail-in ballots. The Pennsylvania Supreme Court Democrats rejected several suits and thereby rejected our state and federal constitutions and laws. So many judges make law instead of doing their job of enforcing our constitution and laws.

We pray for the Brunson brothers and their appeal to the US Supreme Court to throw out all illegal ballots from the 2020 election and remove all illegitimate office holders.

"The oath of office requires that aid and comfort cannot be given to those levying war through a rigged election as a presidential rigged election is a threat to the Constitution when members of Congress become aware of such allegations an investigation into these allegations is required or they become violators of their oath of office," Raland Brunson explains.

"If a person who takes the oath of office owes allegiance to the United States," Brunson continues, "and the United States code regarding treason states that whoever owing such allegiance violates this allegiance shall be incapable of holding office, then wouldn't it be fitting that they shall be removed from office as well?"

Lock them up. How many illegal ballots were counted in 2020? They should have answered that question during 2020. We are in 2023 now. Many people in government have violated our constitution and laws.

The hardworking people of Pennsylvania have been hurt by the partisans who voted for Fetterman over their state and country. He is in the hospital for the second time in the first month of being in the US Senate. He said that he is depressed. Walter Reed hospital is supposed to be for military people and not politicians. I was treated there while working at the Pentagon.

Many fools in the Democrat Party knew that he could not function as a normal human being after the stroke. He should have dropped out of the race to recover. This sick group used the Biden basement strategy and hid his weak condition from the voters instead. They are terrible for America.

Fetterman and his dumb voters made a mockery of our democracy. How many illegal ballots were counted? Why did the corrupt media, politicians, and big tech people put their Democrat Party ahead of our nation? Why did his wife, family, and friends allow this? George Washington warned us about idiots putting their party ahead of our great country. The Walter Reed employees helped me while I was on Army active duty. The hospital is for soldiers and not lying, lazy, corrupt, and/or dumb politicians who lived off their parents until they were forty-nine years old. Fire Fetterman. Good job, Democrats. That odd Xu candidate sure looks great now.

Some good news. Over 67 percent of likely voters believe that capitalism is a better system than socialism in a Rasmussen poll during February 2023. We need more God, Jesus, the Bible, and limited government ASAP! We need to cut many government programs that violate our limited government constitution. Violating that document is a felony. It is the law of the land.

Fire all the bad teachers and get the parents involved in their schools! No kids can do math at grade level in 53 Illinois schools and for reading it is thirty schools. What are the union idiots doing with the billions of tax money they get annually? The big fat Governor Pritzker may run for US president. Good luck, big boy. Can he read and do math?

I had a dream (Nancy jokingly called it a dumb dream) to be the first official redneck to run for US Senate. The Federal Election Commission (FEC) folks confirmed my success on their website in 2021. My hero Andrew Jackson will always hold the title of first redneck to run for president. He was awesome with the open houses at the White House until the drunks had a big fight there in 1830. We toured his house, museum, and farm near Nashville, Tennessee, in 2021. He was a great American and we need him today. He deserves to be on that $20 bill forever.

I accomplished my dream and so thrilled about it. It was a dangerous dream, but at least nobody died. We ate a lot of bad food and listened to many boring campaign speeches from idiots and RINOs. A few speeches were actually not that bad. One guy spoke of his childhood with fondness. He was so proud of learning to tie his shoes at age twelve.

The risk of alienating Democrat neighbors and friends was rated as high. The Democrats working at McDonald's could have spit in the french fries. The risks were real. The fear was real, but we overcame it. We did not crumble or cry like AOC on January 6. We paid the cost and received the benefit.

I think about Frank Sinatra's hit "My Way." He sings about letting the record show that I took the blows and did it my way. I ran this senate campaign my way. A flawed candidate I was to refuse to ask every Tom, Dick, and Harry for money. I was brutally honest with the voters. I am content with my one and only political campaign experience.

We consumed a lot of institutional and mediocre cake, pie, and coffee at GOP events. Sometimes the bathrooms were far away, filthy, and crowded. I think I saw a snake in the porta-potty one time at a county fair. It could have been a chewed-up Slim Jim. We will never know, but it was gross. I took a lot of crap from angry and rude voters who treated me like a used car salesman and was glad to do it. Thank you very much!

As I finish writing this book, it dawns on me that the main reason I ran for the United States Senate in the first place was as follows. This simple redneck from the South needed some new material for another book. I had writer's block. So here it is. I do it for the love. Let's go, Brandon!

I thought getting two thousand signatures and paying the $200 state filing fee to get on the GOP primary ballot would be easy. How hard can that be? I was wrong.

I do feel lucky to not be a candidate anymore, but not as lucky as a group of boys in Britain. A Hooters restaurant sponsored a boys' soccer team, according to the *New York Post*. Now they are living the dream. I guess the ladies should cover up a little more for the young men.

We loved Hooters as teenagers and young men. I wanted to try the Hooters airline, but it was not around very long. The stewardess outfit was priceless. It operated out of my mother's hometown Myrtle Beach, South Carolina, for about three years until 2006. Larry the Cable Guy said that he booked an aisle seat and prayed for turbulence.

Please slap me if I ever mention running for office again. Nancy would love that role. Once is enough for a lifetime. But you should try it for sure, and we will stand behind you. You can take the bullets for the team next time. We need more God, Jesus, the Bible, and limited government mandated by our glorious constitution. God bless you and your family!

"Let perseverance finish its work so that you may be mature and complete, not lacking anything," says James 1:4. I thank God for letting me run for the United States Senate and meeting so many great patriots. They were the wind beneath my wings. Nancy and I tried to buy and move on to forty-six acres in the Poconos. We love the mountains, but our land deal fell through, so we bought a condo on Hilton Head Island. The Lord works in mysterious ways.

We love the hard workers. I am exhausted from writing this book. Somebody please give me some eggnog. I think I saw it in the store again for the fall. I want some without the liquor. I am addicted. My sweet grandparents Glenn and Albert Cox loved that crap, but it goes right to my ankles and thighs.

We pray to God and Jesus to help us stop this disaster caused by evil and ignorant folks running our government. We love good and hate evil. God will lift us up. We cannot give up. This, too, shall pass.

I better take it easy with the eggnog. I never want to look like Fat Leonard. Did they catch that fat bastard after his escape in California? Our dumb, corrupt, and lazy DOJ folks are trying to extradite him from Venezuela, but it is hard when his butt is dragging on the floor at 360 pounds. Whatever happened to all those corrupt US military folks who took bribes from Fat Leonard?

Rednecks are not perfect, but we try. Duct tape is great to fix anything. Where is Andrew Jackson when you need him? Thank You, God and Jesus, for a wonderful and full life in the land of milk and honey.

I am rolling down Highway 81 at eighty mph going from Frackville to Gordon on my 2013 Harley-Davidson Breakout and thinking about nothing. The roar of the engine and wind are all I need. It is a balmy sixty-four degrees in November, which is unusual for Ashland, Pennsylvania. I think about riding my Hog with friends back in the summer of 1984 and smile. Life is good when government is limited and out of mind. I realize that I am thirty-eight years older and thirty mph slower. It sucks getting old.

This American dream is still awesome in 2022. Nancy and I are living the dream. We just need to get the stupid politicians out of our pockets and off TV. I feel sorry for the folks in Georgia. They have another unnecessary runoff election in December that Hershel Walker will win. Big government sucks!

We are headed to Las Vegas now to see my older brother Al over Thanksgiving. He is always good for a laugh with opinion stated as fact. It never gets old. God bless our free, Christian, conservative, capitalistic, and great United States of America!

REDNECK FOR US SENATE

Website Frozen on March 14, 2022

> I am not here for a long time. I
> am here for a good time.
> —The awesome Bon Scott,
> lead singer of AC/DC

March 14 update

I did not make it. I have decided today to suspend my campaign for US Senate from Pennsylvania. Nancy and I have been at this about a year and met so many great, kind, generous, and Christian folks. This was always a guerrilla redneck campaign self-funded with about $4,000 and duct tape for an old soldier with some health issues. We used to call each other rednecks all the time in the South. Us rednecks love capitalism, limited government, and the freedom to work hard and play hard. We despise full-time and long-term fake politicians in suits and ties. I have never begged anyone for anything and did not want to start now by begging for campaign contributions or even signatures to get on the GOP primary ballot. I wanted to see how far my platform and ideas would go and promote capitalism and our great American meritocracy along the way. We had a lot of fun with great people across the state. I learned a lot about myself. No, just kidding, I learned nothing about myself. I hate myself. Let us destroy socialism, communism, and tribalism now to save America from the radical leftists. Let us cut welfare and government spending before they bankrupt America. Let us remove all corrupt, lazy, and immoral Democrats and RINOs (the establishment or uniparty) from our government now. They only care about ruling over others and making a lot of money. We love God, Jesus, the Bible, and the original constitution. We need normal, common folks in DC with accountability and honesty. We need union, lazy folks out of government. Thank you volunteers for all your help. Thank you voters for all your cruel observations and very creative insults. I will carry that pain and good humor with honor for all my days. Sometimes silence is louder than thunder, and perhaps you gave me the highest compliment in saying that I do not belong in the group of corrupt politicians in DC. Better days are ahead. The constitution will be enforced soon. America is the greatest nation ever to exist. Let's go, Brandon! Thank you to everyone who helped me try to get on the GOP primary ballot for US Senate from Pennsylvania. We must remove the corrupt politicians now. Let us get back to the Bible and Constitution to save America!

We get signature forms this week!

My GOP opponents have wasted over $30 million trying to buy this US Senate seat from Pennsylvania. I have spent about $3,000. I want to get back to the limited government mandated by our sacred constitution. (www.davidxuforsenate.com)

Please help me in getting signatures this week to get on the GOP primary ballot for US Senate. Please email dave224422@yahoo.com if you can get some signatures, and I will get the form to you. I need two thousand signatures from registered Republicans from February 25 until March 13. Let us take back our country from socialist and communist fools! Thank you and God bless!

The Platform

- Dave Xu for US Senate from Pennsylvania.
- Conservatism in the GOP.

- First-time candidate.
- Government is too big, abusive, and expensive.
- Obey our sacred Constitution to get back to the required limited government to make America great again and prevent socialism and communism. The Second Amendment is absolute.
- Cut federal spending by at least 10 percent now.
- Break up big tech, big business, and big media and enforce our Constitution coast to coast.
- Term limits for house of representatives, senators, and Supreme Court members and remove anyone who violates our constitution and laws.
- Pass a Balanced Budget Amendment to get government out of our lives.
- Ensure that the Supreme Court remains with nine members.
- Promote a convention of the states to restrain the federal government. Sign the petition at www.conventionofstates.com.
- Reduce the power and political, racist actions of the Federal Reserve bank.
- Ensure that all voters must show ID and that no illegal ballots are counted.
- Arrest all criminals and fund more police.
- Primary May 17, 2022, general election November 8.
- I need registered Republicans in Pennsylvania to help get two thousand signatures between February 15 and March 7 in order to get on the GOP US Senate primary ballot on May 17. Please email me to help. Thanks! Email us at dave224422@yahoo.com. February 15, 4:00 to 8:00 p.m. at the American Legion in Frackville for petition signing to get on the ballot.

David Xu for Senate

Values you believe in. We must get back to the limited government mandated by our thirty-page sacred constitution. You need a representative that will support your ideas, fight for the needs of your community and earn your respect. For someone who truly cares for our great country, look no further. Socialism, communism, and racism suck.

Serving the community. Dave Xu helped defend our constitution for thirty years in the US Army (Active and Reserve). He works tirelessly to make America a better place through volunteer work, hard work, and charity. Dave grew up in Virginia and Florida and loves dog-eat-dog capitalism. MBA, LTC, Artillery, Airborne, Pentagon duty, author, small business owner, college program head and instructor, Christian, husband of Nancy, father of Sammy, conservatism is the stuff, Dave Xu for Senate.

Priorities for the Senate. Obey our constitution for limited government. Cut spending and taxes. Reduce regulations. Break up big business, tech, and media. Pass term limits. Pass a balanced budget amendment. Ensure the Supreme Court has only nine members. Promote a convention of the states. Reduce the power of the Federal Reserve. Ensure all voters show ID and only legal ballots count. Finish the border wall. Continue with the Trump agenda to keep America great. Dave Xu for Senate.

United by a common goal. Your candidate knows the value of being connected. We must take our government back now. The socialist Democrats and RINOs have brought America to the brink of ruin. God, Jesus, and the Bible are great. Nobody should be forced to get a vaccine. Vote for GOP outsiders and Xu for Senate.

Get involved. Your candidate can't win this race without your help. Flyering, word of mouth, and donating are all ways of helping us achieve our goals together. Please follow Dave at gettr, gab, clouthub, mewe, or FB. Mail checks to PO Box 322 Ashland, Pennsylvania, 17921. Contributions are not tax-deductible for federal income taxes and limited to $2,900 for the primary, plus $2,900 for the general election. Thank you and let us make some noise…like ACDC!

Your donation is an opportunity to be part of something bigger. Show your candidate that you have their back. Support this first-time candidate take back DC from the deep state and corrupt politicians. Give today! Contributions are not tax-deductible for federal income taxes and limited to $2,900 for the primary, plus $2,900 for the general election. Paid for by David Xu. First official redneck Candidate for US Senate in America's history. See fec.gov.

Corrupt fools control TV debates. I tried to get into the debate on TV this month, but the organizer required that we beg voters or spend over $100,000 on our campaign. The corrupt Democrat and RINO fools are hurting normal, hardworking voters by denying normal, conservative candidates like me to represent them and speak on TV. Nancy and I do not want to give our hard-earned $100,000 to some greedy and corrupt media owner so they can keep true patriots out of Congress. The Dems and RINOs have a uniparty going on, and we will destroy it soon.

I need two thousand signatures before March 14 to get on the GOP ballot. The state politicians had months to settle the districts. They did not do their jobs again. Vote for me for US Senate, and we will drain the swamp! Email dave224422@yahoo.com to help. I do not want your money, but I need your signature and vote. Thank you and we need more God, Jesus, and the Bible! (https://www.pghcity-paper.com/pittsburgh/david-xu-debuts-visionary-redneck-art-film/ Content?oid=21267247)

Delayed signature petitions. Some slow judges have delayed the period we can get signatures to get on the US Senate GOP primary ballot. We cannot start on February 15 as planned, and I will post the new dates soon. Thank you for your support! Email me if you can help at dave224422@yahoo.com.

The government folks are incompetent and corrupt. The government folks who forced lockdowns, vaccines, and mandates on us are incompetent and corrupt and must be removed from government and in many cases punished. They spit on our constitution and laws to gain or increase their power over the common man and woman. This is the first time in history that politicians have shut down economies for a virus. The lockdowns will cost many more lives and over $16 trillion from 2020 until 2025. The lockdown kings also killed or hurt many hard workers by coddling criminals in the name of fake racism. Racism is not tolerated in any county in America. The lazy union teachers must be fired for refusing to put our kids above their pocketbooks. American capitalism is the best way with limited government.

Can you help me get two thousand signatures? I need registered Republicans in Pennsylvania to help get two thousand signatures between February 15 and March 7 in order to get on the GOP US Senate primary ballot on May 17. Please email me at dave224422@ yahoo.com to help. Thank you!

Three cheers for Senator Manchin. What great news that Joe Manchin killed the BBB bill from the socialist, corrupt Democrats. This would have cost the taxpayers over $5 trillion and discouraged many folks to not work and collect welfare. Biden and other liars said it was free. Let us cut back government as per our awesome constitution. Socialism and communism are in a few countries, but we cannot have that crap here. We need to balance the budget and argue about ideas…like it used to be. We need more God, Jesus, and the Bible!

This is the end of the redneck for US Senate campaign website for David Xu.

REDNECK DAVE XU'S TOP TEN CAMPAIGN RULES

1. Focus on normal, hardworking, taxpaying citizens and their needs and wants. Look them in the eye and give them respect. Ask for their vote. Do not ask them for their money. Try to ignore socialists, communists, nontaxpayers, ignorant people, media, the haters, evil people, illegal aliens, criminals, racist fools, and lazy folks.
2. Avoid Democrats and RINOs (the uniparty). They have grown government way beyond the limits of the constitution and must be punished. Help remove them from government and indict them if appropriate. They have taken freedom and a lot of money from the good and successful citizens. Take the campaign straight to the people and bypass the corrupt establishment characters.
3. Blame everything on big, corrupt, wasteful, incompetent, abusive government (for example wars, hatred, envy, racism, ignorance, sloth, immorality, inflation, uncertainty, joblessness, hopelessness, distrust in government institutions, criminals hurting and killing good people, reducing investments in companies that hire good folks).
4. Expose the incumbent's bad decisions, laws, corruption, laziness, lies, misplaced priorities, hypocrisy, and policies.
5. Promote and obey the Bible, America's greatness, and sacred original United States Constitution. They are the primary doc-

uments for a successful life and campaign. Always trust in God and Jesus.

6. Stay out of the abortion debate as a man or politician. I will never promote this or tell a woman she cannot do this. It is a bad situation left to the woman. It should be legal.

7. Tell the voters what you will cut. The constitution mandates limited government. Many laws and programs are unconstitutional. Include rock and roll references whenever possible.

8. Use humor as much as possible. Make fun of yourself. Admit mistakes. Voters seem to like it.

9. Educate voters on the issues. Many people only watch TV and do not read much. Know the facts and share your opinions based on the facts. Share that people with money will not invest and hire people if they are taxed too much. We must treat capital with respect, or it will go elsewhere (other states or other countries).

10. Get Democrats and Independents to join the Grand Old Party or Republican Party.

ABOUT THE AUTHOR

David Xu was born in Danville, Virginia, and has lived in Florida, Virginia, North Carolina, and Pennsylvania. He is Christian and conservative. He was in the United States Army (active and reserve) for thirty years, LTC, Airborne, Artillery, Combat, and Pentagon duty, taught community college business courses, and was self-employed in IT. He earned an MBA from James Madison University. He and his wife, Nancy, enjoy family, friends, Harley-Davidson motorcycles, walking, RVs, reading, bicycles, ducks, geese, and traveling. Their favorite TV show is *Seinfeld* and saw him live in August 2019 in Reading (great show). David loves rock and roll music, concerts, and documentaries. Lynyrd Skynyrd is his favorite band of rednecks from Jacksonville.

David Xu, LTC, MBA, Combat, Field Artillery, Airborne, retired after thirty years in the United States Army and three years at the Pentagon. He owned a small business and taught business courses at community colleges for many years and was a program head. His recent work includes three *Easy Eddie* books, *Redneck Dystopia*, *Easy Riders*, and *Orphans in the Barn*. He started We the People of Coal Country to defeat socialism and communism. He spends time in Ashland, Pennsylvania, and Hilton Head Island with his charming wife, Nancy. Their son, Sammy, graduated from NYU and lives on Long Island.

Printed in the USA
CPSIA information can be obtained
at www.ICGtesting.com
LVHW040858300923
759464LV00051B/633